500 FAMILY
DAYS OUT

Produced by AA Publishing

Editorial: lifestyleguides@theAA.com

Front Cover Photos: (top) AA/Neil Setchfield; (middle)
AA/Kenya Doran; (bottom) AA/John Wood

All other photographs: 1 AA/Jamie Blandford;
3 AA/Douglas Corrance

Printed in China by Leo Paper Products

Directory compiled by AA Lifestyle Guides Department
and managed in the Librios Information Management
System and generated from the AA establishment
database system.

theAA.com/shop

Published by AA Publishing, a trading name of AA
Media Limited whose registered office is
Fanum House, Basing View, Basingstoke,
Hampshire, RG21 4EA
Registered number 06112600.

A CIP catalogue record for this book is available from
the British Library

ISBN 978-0-7495-6459-9

A04301

Welcome to the Guide

This mini guide is aimed at families with children looking for things to do and places to visit. We have included useful information about museums, art galleries, theme parks, national parks, visitor centres, stately homes and other attractions across Britain and Ireland. Entries include contact details, along with a short description and details of opening times, prices and special facilities. We hope this guide will help you and your family get the most out of your visit.

Contents

❶ WILDEN

Wild Britain

65A Renhold Rd MK44 2PX

❷ ☎ 01234 772770 📠 01234 772773
e-mail: enquiries@wild-britain.co.uk
web: www.wild-britain.co.uk

❸ dir: From A421 take Gt Barford slip road. Follow brown signs

Join the Adventures of Urchin the hedgehog as he explores the countryside. Meet British animals in the presentation shows. Visit the steamy tropical butterfly house to experience what the future could hold for Britain. Children's arts and craft activities every day.

❹ ❺ Times Open Etr-Oct, 10-5. Fees £6 (ch16 £4.95, under 2's free, concessions £5.50).* Facilities
❻ 🅿 ▭ ♿ toilets for disabled shop ⊗

---

❶ The directory is arranged in countries, counties, and in alphabetical location order within each county.

❷ Telephone Numbers have the STD code shown before the telephone number. (If dialling Northern Ireland from England use the STD code, but for the Republic you need to prefix the number with 00353, and drop the first zero from the Irish area code).

❸ Directions may be given after the address of each attraction and where shown have been provided by the attractions themselves.

❹ Opening Times quoted in the guide are inclusive - for instance, where you see Apr-Oct, that place will be open from the beginning of April to the end of October.

❺ Fees quoted for the majority of entries are current. If no price is quoted, you should check with the attraction concerned before you visit. Places which are open 'at all reasonable times' are usually free, and many places which do not charge admission at all may ask for a voluntary donation. Remember that prices can go up, and those provided to us by the attractions are provisional.

∗Admission prices followed by a star relate to 2009. It should be noted that in some entries the opening dates and times may also have been supplied as 2009. Please check with the establishment before making your journey.

Free Entry **FREE**

These attractions do not charge a fee for entry, although they may charge for use of audio equipment, for example. We have not included attractions that expect a donation in this category.

6 Facilities This section includes parking, dogs allowed, refreshments etc. See page 6 for a key to Symbols and Abbreviations used in this guide.

Visitors with Mobility Disabilities should look for the wheelchair symbol showing where all or most of the establishment is accessible to the wheelchair-bound visitor. We strongly recommend that you telephone in advance of your visit to check the exact details, particularly regarding access to toilets and refreshment facilities. Assistance dogs are usually accepted where the attractions show the 'No Dogs' symbol ⊗ unless stated otherwise. For the hard of hearing induction loops are indicated by a symbol at the attraction itself.

Credit & Charge cards are taken by a large number of attractions for admission charges. To indicate which do not accept credit cards we have used this symbol at the end of the entry. ⊜

Photography is restricted in some places and there are many where it is only allowed in specific areas. Visitors are advised to check with places of interest on the rules for taking photographs and the use of video cameras.

Special events are held at many of these attractions, and although we have listed a few in individual entries, we cannot hope to give details of them all, so please ring the attractions for details of exhibitions, themed days, talks, guided walks and more.

Attractions with *italic* headings. These are entries that were unable to provide the relevant information in time for publication.

...and finally Opening times and admission prices can be subject to change. Please check with the attraction before making your journey.

Symbols & Abbreviations

☎ Telephone number

♿ Suitable for visitors in wheelchairs

🅟 Parking at Establishment

Ⓟ Parking nearby

🍺 Refreshments

🏛 Picnic Area

🍽 Restaurant

⊗ No Dogs

🚌 No Coaches

✳ Admission prices relate to 2009

⛲ Cadw (Welsh Monuments)

♯ English Heritage

🌿 National Trust

🌿 The National Trust
    for Scotland

🏴 Historic Scotland

Abbreviations

BH Bank Hoildays

PH Public Holidays

Etr Easter

ex except

ch Children

Pen Senior Citizens

Concessions (Students, unemployed etc)

SANDY

RSPB The Lodge Nature Reserve

The Lodge SG19 2DL
☎ 01767 680541 🖹 01767 683508
e-mail: thelodgereserve@rspb.org.uk
web: www.rspb.org.uk
dir: 1m E of Sandy, on B1042 Potton road

The headquarters of the Royal Society for the Protection of Birds. Explore peaceful woodlands, colourful gardens and the Iron Age hill fort on Galley Hill. The house and buildings are not open to the public, but there are waymarked paths and formal gardens, and two species of woodpecker, nuthatches and woodland birds may be seen, as may rare breed sheep. Various events through the year include Shakespearean plays and Feed the Birds day.

Times Open all year, Nature Reserve: dawn to dusk. Shop: Mon-Fri 9-5, Sat, Sun & BHs 10-5. Closed 25-26 Dec. Fees Reserve, Gardens & parking: £4 per motor vehicle (RSPB members free). Facilities ❷ ㅠ (outdoor) ♿ (partly accessible) (gardens some steps, nature trails vary some steep sections) toilets for disabled shop ⊗

WHIPSNADE

Whipsnade Wild Animal Park

LU6 2LF
☎ 01582 872171 🖹 01582 872649
e-mail: marketing@zsl.org
web: www.whipsnade.co.uk
dir: signed from M1 junct 9 & 12

Located in beautiful Bedfordshire countryside, Whipsnade is home to more than 2,500 rare and exotic animals and is one of the largest conservation centres in Europe. Hop aboard the Jumbo Express, a fantastic steam train experience, and see elephants, rhino, yaks, camels and deer, along with wild horses, and learn about their lives in the wilds of Asia and Africa. Other highlights include the Lions of the Serengeti, the sealion pool, and Birds of the World. The Discover Centre is home to tamarins, turtles, big snakes and sea horses among others. Visitors can also enjoy the picnic areas, keeper talks and animal shows.

Times Open all year, daily. (Closed 25 Dec). Closing times vary.* Facilities ❷ ㅁ ㅠ (outdoor) toilets for disabled shop ⊗

WILDEN

Wild Britain

65A Renhold Rd MK44 2PX
☎ 01234 772770 📄 01234 772773
e-mail: enquiries@wild-britain.co.uk
web: www.wild-britain.co.uk
dir: From A421 take Gt Barford slip road. Follow brown signs

Join the Adventures of Urchin the hedgehog as he explores the countryside. Meet British animals in the presentation shows. Visit the steamy tropical butterfly house to experience what the future could hold for Britain. Children's arts and craft activities every day.

Times Open Etr-Oct, 10-5. Fees £6 (ch16 £4.95, under 2's free, concessions £5.50).* Facilities
🅿 ⛽ ♿ toilets for disabled shop ⊗

WOBURN

Woburn Abbey

MK17 9WA
☎ 01525 290333 📄 01525 290271
e-mail: admissions@woburnabbey.co.uk
web: www.woburn.co.uk
dir: Just off M1 junct 12/13

Set in a 3,000 acre deer park, Woburn Abbey has been home to the Dukes of Bedford for over 300 years and is currently occupied by the 15th Duke and family. The Abbey houses an important private art collection including paintings by Canaletto, Gainsborough, Reynolds, Van Dyck and Cuyp and collections of silver, gold and porcelain. An audio tour is available (charged), guided tours on request. There are extensive informal gardens, pottery and a fine antiques centre. Events include Plays in the Park between June and August.

Times Open 15 Mar-3 Apr & 5-25 Oct, wknds only. 4 Apr-4 Oct, daily, 11-5.30 (last entry 4).* Fees £13 (ch 3-15 £6, pen £11). Passport ticket for Woburn Abbey and Woburn Safari Park allows one visit to each attraction on same or different days £22.50 (ch £15.50, pen £19). Please phone or check website for further details.* Facilities
🅿 ⛽ 🍽 licensed ⌐ (outdoor) ♿ (partly accessible) (limited access to house, only 3 rooms on ground floor. Other areas can only be accessed by stairs) toilets for disabled shop ⊗

WOBURN

Woburn Safari Park

MK17 9QN

☎ 01525 290407 📠 01525 290489
e-mail: info@woburnsafari.co.uk
web: www.woburn.co.uk
dir: Signed from M1 junct 13

Enjoy a Safari Adventure and see the beauty of wild animals in real close-up. Tour the reserves from the safety of your car and experience the thrill of being alongside white rhino, buffalo, giraffe or Siberian tiger. The Leisure Park has adventure playgrounds, walkthrough areas with wallabies, squirrel monkeys and lemurs, and a full programme of keeper talks. The sea lions and the penguins are very popular. Other attractions include the new Mammoth Play Ark, Great Woburn Railway and the Swanboats.

Times Open 7 Mar-1 Nov 10-5 (last entry), Winter wknds 11-3 (Nov-early Mar).* Fees £10.50-£18.50 (ch 3-15 £8.50-£13.50, pen £8.50-£15). Passport ticket for Woburn Safari Park and Woburn Abbey allows one visit to each attraction on same or different days £22.50 (ch £15.50, pen £16-£19). Please phone or check website for further details.* Facilities ℗ ⌨ 🍽 licensed 卅 (indoor & outdoor) ♿ (partly accessible) (some steeper hills in leisure area) toilets for disabled shop ⊗

BRACKNELL

The Look Out Discovery Centre

Nine Mile Ride RG12 7QW

☎ 01344 354400 📠 01344 354422
e-mail: thelookout@bracknell-forest.gov.uk
web: www.bracknell-forest.gov.uk/be
dir: 3m S of town centre. From M3 junct 3, take A322 to Bracknell and from M4 junct 10, take A329M to Bracknell. Follow brown tourist signs

A hands-on, interactive science and nature exhibition where budding scientists can spend many hours exploring and discovering over 80 fun filled exhibits within five themed zones, linked to the National Curriculum. Zones include Light and Colour, Forces and Movement and the Body and Perception. A new exciting zone, Woodland and Water; has a vortex, stream, ant colony and many more interactive exhibits. Climb the 88 steps to the Look Out tower and look towards Bracknell and beyond or enjoy a nature walk in the surrounding 1,000 hectares of Crown Estate woodland. Interactive shows for the public and schools running throughout the year. Please note the tower is closed when wet.

Times Open all year 10-5 (Closed 24-26 Dec, 11-15 Jan). Fees £5.95 (ch & concessions £3.95). Family (2ad+2ch or 1ad+3ch) £15.85. Prices valid until 31 March 2010.* Facilities ℗ ⌨ 卅 (outdoor) toilets for disabled shop ⊗

HAMPSTEAD NORREYS

The Living Rainforest

RG18 0TN

☎ 01635 202444 📄 01635 202440
e-mail: enquiries@livingrainforest.org
web: www.livingrainforest.org
dir: follow brown tourist signs from M4/A34

By providing education and supporting research into the relationship between humanity and the rainforests, this wonderful attraction hopes to promote a more sustainable future. Visitors to the Living Rainforest will see plants and wildlife that are under threat in their natural habitat, and be encouraged to take part in a large variety of activities, workshops and exhibitions.

Times Open all year daily 10-5. (Closed 24-26 Dec) **Fees** £8.75 (ch 3-4 £5.75, ch 5-14 £6.75, concessions £7.75). Family ticket £27.50*
Facilities 🅿 ⬚ 🌳 (outdoor) ♿ toilets for disabled shop ⊗

LOWER BASILDON

Basildon Park

RG8 9NR

☎ 0118 984 3040 📄 0118 976 7370
e-mail: basildonpark@nationaltrust.org.uk
web: www.nationaltrust.org.uk/basildonpark
dir: 7m NW of Reading on W side of A329 between Pangbourne & Streatley

This 18th-century house, built of Bath stone, fell into decay in the 20th century, but has been beautifully restored by Lord and Lady Iliffe. The classical front has a splendid central portico and pavilions, and inside there are delicate plasterwork decorations on the walls and ceilings. The Octagon drawing room has fine pictures and furniture, and there is a small formal garden. The house more recently featured in the 2005 film adaptation of Jane Austen's Pride and Prejudice. Please contact for details of special events.

Times House open mid Mar-Oct, Wed-Sun & BH Mon 12-5. Park & garden, shop & tea room mid Feb-mid Dec, Wed-Sun & BH Mon 11-3. **Fees** House & grounds £8.80 (ch £4.40). **Facilities** 🅿 🍴 licensed 🌳 (outdoor) ♿ (partly accessible) (grd floor ramped access to exhibition rooms, tea rooms & shop) toilets for disabled shop 🐾

LOWER BASILDON

Beale Park

Lower Basildon RG8 9NH
☎ 0870 777 7160 🖹 0870 777 7120
web: www.bealepark.co.uk
dir: M4 junct 12, follow brown tourist signs to
Pangbourne, A329 towards Oxford

Beale Park is home to an extraordinary collection
of birds and animals including peacocks, swans,
owls and parrots. It also offers a steam railway,
rare breeds of farm animals, a great pet corner,
meerkats, wallabies, ring-tailed lemurs, a deer
park, three splash pools, a huge adventure
playground, acres of gardens, and sculptures in a
traditional, family park beside the Thames. There
are summer riverboat trips and excellent lake and
river fishing.

Times Open Mar-Oct.* Facilities 🅿 ⏛ ⑩
licensed 🎋 (outdoor) toilets for disabled shop ⊗

RISELEY

Wellington Country Park

RG7 1SP
☎ 0118 932 6444 🖹 0118 932 6445
e-mail: info@wellington-country-park.co.uk
web: www.wellington-country-park.co.uk
dir: signed off A33, between Reading &
Basingstoke

350 acres of woodland walks and parkland ideal
for a family outing. Attractions appealing to
younger and older children include; a miniature
railway, a variety of play areas, crazy golf and
nature trails. There is also an 80-acre family
campsite, a nature trail maze and animal corner.

Times Open Feb-Nov, daily 9.30-5 in low season,
9.30-5.30 in high season. Fees £6.50 (ch 2
and under free, 3-15 £5.50, pen £6) Family
ticket (2ad+2ch) £21.50* Facilities 🅿 ⏛ 🎋
(outdoor) ♿ (partly accessible) (most walks are
forest floor but park area stone surface) toilets
for disabled shop ⊗

WINDSOR

LEGOLAND Windsor

Winkfield Rd SL4 4AY

📄 01753 626119

e-mail: customer.services@legoland.co.uk
web: www.legoland.co.uk
dir: on B3022 (Windsor to Ascot road) signed
from M3 junct 3 & M4 junct 6

With over 50 interactive rides, live shows,
building workshops, driving schools and
attractions. Set in 150 acres of beautiful
parkland, LEGOLAND Windsor is a different
sort of family theme park. An atmospheric and
unique experience for the whole family, a visit to
LEGOLAND Windsor is more than a day out, it's a
lifetime of memories.

Times Open daily 12 Mar-5 Nov* **Facilities** 🅿 🅿
🍴 licensed 🎪 (outdoor) toilets for disabled
shop 🚫

WINDSOR

Windsor Castle

SL4 1NJ

☎ 020 7766 7304   📄 020 7930 9625
e-mail: bookinginfo@royalcollection.org.uk
web: www.royalcollection.org.uk
dir: M4 junct 6 & M3 junct 3

Covering 13 acres, Windsor Castle is the official
residence of HM The Queen, and the largest
occupied castle in the world. Begun as a wooden
fort by William the Conqueror, it has been added
to by almost every monarch since. A visit takes
in the magnificent State Apartments, St George's
Chapel, Queen Mary's doll's house, the Drawings
Gallery, and between October and March, the
semi-state rooms created by George IV.

Times Open daily except Good Fri & 25-26 Dec.
Nov-Feb, 9.45-4.15 (last admission 3); Mar-Oct,
9.45-5.15 (last admission 4). May be subject
to change at short notice (24hr info line: 01753
831118) **Fees** £16 (ch under 17 £9.50, under 5's
free, concessions £14.50) Family (2ad+3ch) £42
Facilities 🅿 ♿ toilets for disabled shop 🚫

Bristol Zoo Gardens

Clifton BS8 3HA
☎ 0117 974 7399   📄 0117 973 6814
e-mail: information@bristolzoo.org.uk
web: www.bristolzoo.org.uk
dir: M5 junct 17, take A4018 then follow brown
elephant signs. Also signed from city centre

There are over 450 exotic and endangered species
in the 12-acre grounds of Bristol Zoo. Visit the
primates in Monkey Jungle, stroll through the
lemur garden, and visit the Seal and Penguin
coast. Other favourites include Gorilla Island, the
Asiatic lions, Bug World, Butterfly Forest, Twilight
World, the Reptile House and the children's play
area. Follow the footsteps of jungle adventurers
at the new Explorers' Creek exhibit, home to three
exciting areas; Splash, a water-play area, Forest
of Birds, and feed the Lorikeets, a truly unique
experience.

Times Open all year, daily (ex 25 Dec). 9-5.30
(British Summer Time), 9-5 (standard hrs)*
Fees £12.50 (ch 3-14yrs £7.75, under 3 free,
concessions £11). Family ticket (2ad+2ch)
£36.50.* **Facilities** 🅿 ⛽ 🍴 licensed 🎪
(outdoor) ♿ toilets for disabled shop ⊗

Brunel's ss Great Britain

Great Western Dock, Gas Ferry Rd BS1 6TY
☎ 0117 926 0680   📄 0117 925 5788
e-mail: admin@ssgreatbritain.org
web: www.ssgreatbritain.org
dir: off Cumberland Rd

Built and launched in Bristol in 1843, Isambard
Kingdom Brunel's maritime masterpiece was
the first ocean-going, propeller-driven, iron ship.
Launched in 1843 to provide luxury travel to New
York, the world's first great ocean liner set new
standards in engineering, reliability and speed.
Find out about passengers and crew - from the
rich and famous to those leaving 1850s England
to begin a new life. Steer the ship on a westerly
course, prepare her for sail and climb to the
crow's nest. Descend beneath the glass 'sea'
for a close up view of the ship's giant hull and
propeller and the state-of-the-art equipment
which will save her for the next hundred years.
Another feature is the Dockyard Museum charting
the history of Brunel's Masterpiece. A replica
of the square rigger 'Matthew' is moored at the
same site when in Bristol. Special events are held
all year - please see the website for details.

Times Open all year daily 10-6, 4.30 in winter.
(Closed 17, 24-25 Dec).* **Facilities** 🅿 ⛽ 🚻♿
toilets for disabled shop ⊗

BRISTOL

Explore-At-Bristol

Anchor Rd, Harbourside BS1 5DB
☎ 0845 345 1235 📄 0117 915 7200
e-mail: information@at-bristol.org.uk
web: www.at-bristol.org.uk
dir: from city centre, A4 to Anchor Rd. Located on left opposite Cathedral

Explore-At-Bristol is one of the UK's most exciting hands-on science centres, and is located on Bristol's historic Harbourside. Discover interactive exhibits and special exhibitions, take in a Planetarium show or join the Live Science team for fun experiments and activities. Explore involves people of all ages in an incredible journey through the workings of the world around us.

Times Open all year, term-time wkdays 10-5, wknds & school hols 10-6. (Closed 24-26 Dec).* Fees With Gift Aid £11.90 (ch £7.70, concessions £9.90). Family ticket £34.* Facilities ❷ ℗ 🖵 🚻 (outdoor) ⚹ (partly accessible) toilets for disabled shop ⊗

BRISTOL

HorseWorld

Staunton Manor Farm, Staunton Ln, Whitchurch BS14 0QJ
☎ 01275 540173 📄 01275 540119
e-mail: visitor.centre@horseworld.org.uk
web: www.horseworld.org.uk
dir: A37 Bristol to Wells road, follow brown signs from Maes Knoll traffic lights

Set in beautiful stone farm buildings on the southern edge of Bristol, HorseWorld's Visitor Centre is an award winning attraction that offers a great day for everyone. Meet the friendly horses, ponies and donkeys.

Times Open all year Apr-Oct daily 10-5; Nov-Mar daily (ex Mon & Tue) 10-4. Fees £6.95 (ch 3-15yrs £4.95, concessions £5.95). Family (2ad+2ch) £20.95.* Facilities ❷ 🖵 🍴 licensed 🚻 (indoor & outdoor) ⚹ toilets for disabled shop

AYLESBURY

Tiggywinkles Visitor Centre & Hedgehog World Museum

Aston Rd HP17 8AF
☎ 01844 292511
e-mail: mail@sttiggywinkles.org.uk
web: www.tiggywinkles.com
dir: Turn off A418 towards Haddenham then follow signs to 'Wildlife Hospital'

Look through the glass into bird and mammal nursery wards in the hospital. Find out all about the hospital, the patients and their treatment on education boards dotted around the gardens. See some of the other hospital wards on CCTV monitor. Wander round the world's first Hedgehog Memorabilia Museum, or watch the foxes in their permanent enclosure. Try to catch a glimpse of one of the resident badgers or see the deer in the recovery paddocks. The animals live as natural a life as possible, so don't be surprised if they do not come out to visit.

Times Open Etr-Sep, daily 10-4* Facilities **P**
⊼ shop ⊗

BEACONSFIELD

Bekonscot Model Village and Railway

Warwick Rd HP9 2PL
☎ 01494 672919 📄 01494 675284
e-mail: info@bekonscot.co.uk
web: www.bekonscot.com
dir: M40 junct 2, 4m M25 junct 16, take A355 and follow signs to Model Village

A miniature world, depicting rural England in the 1930s. A Gauge 1 model railway meanders through six little villages, each with their own tiny population. Rides on the sit-on miniature railway take place at weekends and local school holidays. Remote control boats are available.

Times Open 13 Feb-Oct, 10-5. Fees £8 (ch £4.50, concessions £5)* Facilities **P P** **⊡ ⊼** (indoor & outdoor) 🚻 toilets for disabled shop ⊗

CHALFONT ST GILES

Chiltern Open Air Museum

Newland Park, Gorelands Ln HP8 4AB
☎ 01494 871117 📄 01494 872774
e-mail: coamuseum@netscape.net
web: www.coam.org.uk
dir: M25 junct 17, M40 junct 2. Follow brown signs

Chiltern Open Air Museum is an independent charity, established over 30 years ago, with the aim of preserving some of the historic buildings that are unique examples of the heritage of the Chilterns. The museum is now home to more than 30 historic buildings all rescued from demolition and re-erected on this 45-acre woodland and parkland site. Events take place weekends and school holidays throughout the season, please check website for details.

Times Open 27 Mar-29 Oct, daily 10-5 (last admission 3.30). **Fees** £7.50 (ch 5-16 £5, under 5's free), concessions £6.50) Family ticket (2ad+2 ch) £22.* **Facilities** 🅿 ⊑ 🛱 (indoor & outdoor) ♿ (partly accessible) (Some paths/areas and buildings not accessible for all on this 45 acre site - full details on website or phone) toilets for disabled shop ⊗

GREAT MISSENDEN

The Roald Dahl Museum & Story Centre

81-83 High St HP16 0AL
☎ 01494 892192 📄 01494 892191
e-mail: admin@roalddahlmuseum.org
web: www.roalddahlmuseum.org
dir: From London/Amersham turn left off A413 into Great Missenden link road

This award-winning museum is aimed at 6 to 12 year olds and their families. Two interactive and biographical galleries tell the fascinating story of Roald Dahl's life, while the Story Centre puts imagination centre-stage, and encourages everyone (young and old) to dress up, make up stories, words and poems, or get arty in the craft room. Situated in Great Missenden where Dahl lived for over 36 years, it was created as a home for the author's archive (which visitors can see on regular tours) and as a place to inspire creativity and a love of reading in children, about which Dahl was passionate. 13th September every year - Roald Dahl Day national celebrations.

Times Open all year, Tue-Sun & BH Mon 10-5.* **Facilities** 🅿 ⊑ 🛱 (indoor & outdoor) toilets for disabled shop ⊗ 🚐

HIGH WYCOMBE

Hughenden Manor

HP14 4LA

☎ 01494 755573 📠 01494 474284
e-mail: hughenden@nationaltrust.org.uk
web: www.nationaltrust.org.uk
dir: 1.5m N of High Wycombe, on W side of A4128

This fascinating Victorian manor was home to Prime Minister Benjamin Disraeli from 1848 to 1881. Many of his possessions are still on display, along with beautiful gardens designed by his wife Mary-Anne. Other facilities include circular woodland walks, family tracker packs, I-spy sheets in the Manor and an exhibition revealing Hughenden's role in WWII. See website for special event details.

Times House open 17 Feb-Oct, Wed-Sun & BH Mon 12-5 (last admission 4.30); 3 Nov-19 Dec 11-4. Gardens 17 Feb-Oct, 11-5. Park open all year. Fees £8 (ch £4.10). Family ticket £20. Garden only £3.20 (ch £2.20). Park free. Facilities ❷ ⏹ licensed ⛱ (outdoor) ♿ (partly accessible) (Ground floor only fully accessible) toilets for disabled shop ⊗ 🐾

WADDESDON

Waddesdon Manor

HP18 0JH

☎ 01296 653211, 653226 & 653203
📠 01296 653212
e-mail: waddesdonmanor@nationaltrust.org.uk
web: www.waddesdon.org.uk
dir: entrance off A41, 6m NW of Aylesbury

Built in the 19th century by Baron Ferdinand de Rothschild, this French-style chateau was created as a showcase for his fine collection of French decorative arts. The Victorian gardens are known for seasonal displays, a parterre, walks, views, fountains and statues. Special events throughout the year.

Times Gardens: 3 Jan-29 Mar, wknds only; Apr-23 Dec, Wed-Sun & BHs; 27-31 Dec, Wed-Sun & 28-29 Dec, 10-5. House: Apr-1 Nov, Wed-Sun & BHs. Bachelors Wing Apr-1 Nov, Wed-Fri; 11 Nov-23 Dec, Wed-Fri 12-4; Sat-Sun, 21-22 Dec; 27-31 Dec Wed-Sun & 28-29 Dec, Sat-Sun 11-4 & Wed-Fri 12-4.* Fees Gardens, 6 Jan-18 Mar (wknds only) 21 Mar-23 Dec, 27-31 Dec (Wed-Fri) £5.50, (ch £2.75). Family £13.75. 19 Mar-23 Dec, 27-31 Dec (wknds & BHs) £7, (ch £3.50). Family £17.50. House & gardens, 21 Mar-28 Oct (Wed-Fri) £13.20, (ch £9.35), wknds & BHs £15, (ch £11).* Facilities ❷ ⏹ licensed ♿ toilets for disabled shop ⊗ 🐾

DUXFORD

Imperial War Museum Duxford

CB22 4QR

☎ 01223 835000 📄 01223 837267
e-mail: duxford@iwm.org.uk
web: www.iwm.org.uk/duxford
dir: off M11 junct 10, on A505

Duxford is Europe's premier aviation museum with many original buildings such as the control tower and hangars which are still in use, alongside state-of-the-art, award-winning exhibition buildings including AirSpace and the American Air Museum. A collection of nearly 200 aircraft includes over 50 historic aircraft that regularly take to the sky. Duxford also has one of the finest collections of tanks, military vehicles and artillery in the UK. The Museum holds four air shows throughout the summer plus other special events such as American Air Day, Military Vehicle Show and car shows and more.

Times Open all year, 15 Mar-26 Oct, daily 10-6 (last admission 5); 28 Oct-14 Mar, daily 10-4 (last admission 3). Closed 24-26 Dec.* Fees £16 (ch under 16 free, concessions £12.80). Events & airshow prices vary.* Facilities 🅿 ⬜ 🍽 licensed ⌐ (indoor & outdoor) ♿ toilets for disabled shop ⊗

PETERBOROUGH

Flag Fen Archaeology Park

The Droveway, Northey Rd PE6 7QJ

☎ 01733 313414 📄 01733 349957
e-mail: info@flagfen.org
web: www.flagfen.org
dir: From A1139 exit at Boongate junct. At rdbt 3rd exit, through lights, turn right. At T-junct turn right, Flag Fen signed

Although visitors enter this site through a 21st-century roundhouse, the rest of their day will be spent in the Bronze Age, some 3,000 years ago. Flag Fen's Museum contains artefacts found over the last 20 years of excavating on site, and includes among them the oldest wheel in Britain. In the Park there is a reconstructed Bronze Age settlement and Iron Age roundhouse, while in the Preservation Hall visitors can see the excavated Bronze Age processional way that spanned over one mile. The Hall also contains a 60-ft mural depicting the fens in ancient times.

Times Open daily Mar-Oct 10-5 (last admission 4). Fees £5.50 (ch £4.15, concessions £4.95). Family £15.15. Prices include gift aid.* Facilities 🅿 ⬜ ⌐ (outdoor) ♿ toilets for disabled shop ⊗

RAMSEY

Ramsey Abbey Gatehouse

Abbey School PE17 1DH

☎ 01480 301494   🖷 01263 734924

e-mail: ramseyabbey@nationaltrust.org.uk

web: www.nationaltrust.org.uk

dir: SE edge of Ramsey, at Chatteris Road &
B1096 junct

The ruins of this 15th-century gatehouse,
together with the 13th-century Lady Chapel,
are all that remain of the abbey. Half of the
gatehouse was taken away after the Dissolution.
Built in ornate late-Gothic style, it has panelled
buttresses and friezes.

Times Open Apr-Sep, first Sun of the month
1-5 (Group visits by appt only other wknds)*
Fees Free but donations appreciated. Facilities
⊗ ✄

WATERBEACH

The Farmland Museum and Denny Abbey

Ely Rd CB25 9PQ

☎ 01223 860988   🖷 01223 860988

e-mail: info@farmlandmuseum.org.uk

web: www.dennyfarmlandmuseum.org.uk

dir: on A10 between Cambridge & Ely

Explore two areas of rural life at this fascinating
museum. The Abbey tells the story of those who
have lived there, including Benedictine monks,
Franciscan nuns, and the mysterious Knights
Templar. The farm museum features the craft
workshops of a wheelwright, a basketmaker, and
a blacksmith. There is also a 1940s farmworker's
cottage and a village shop. Special events on
Easter, May and August Bank Holidays.

Times Open daily, Apr-Oct, 12-5.* Facilities 🅿
⊑ � (outdoor) ♿ (partly accessible) toilets for
disabled shop

WOODHURST

The Raptor Foundation

The Heath, St Ives Rd PE28 3BT
☎ 01487 741140 📠 01487 841140
e-mail: heleowl@aol.com
web: www.raptorfoundation.org.uk
dir: B1040 to Somersham, follow brown signs

Permanent home to over 250 birds of which there are 40 different varieties. This is a unique opportunity to meet and learn about birds of prey. Depending on weather and time of year flying demonstrations are held, usually three times a day and audiences have the chance to participate in displays. There are nearly 60 birds in the flying team, so each display has a different set of birds. Educational trail linking to new education room. New indoor flying area. Ask about activity days, membership and adoption.

Times Open all year, daily 10-5. Closed 25-26 Dec & 1 Jan.* **Fees** £4.50 (ch £2.75 ages 2-4 £1, concessions £3.50). Family ticket £12.50.*
Facilities 🅿 ⃠🍽 licensed ⋔ (outdoor) ♿ toilets for disabled shop ⊗

CHESTER

Chester Zoo

Upton-by-Chester CH2 1LH
☎ 01244 380280 📠 01244 371273
e-mail: marketing@chesterzoo.org
web: www.chesterzoo.org
dir: 2m N of city centre off A41& M53 junct 10 southbound, junct 12 all other directions

Chester Zoo is the UK's number one charity zoo, with over 7,000 animals and 400 different species, some of them amongst the most endangered species on the planet. There's plenty to see and do, like the Realm of the Red Ape enclosure, home to the Bornean and Sumatran orang-utans. Experience the sights and sounds of Assam, with the herd of Asian Elephants, Hornbills, Tree Shrews and rare fish inside Elephants of the Asian Forest. View the world's fastest land mammal, the cheetah, from the new Bat's Bridge. See a wide variety of beautifully coloured African birds housed in African Aviaries and Philippine crocodiles in their new enclosure in the Tropical Realm.

Times Open all year, daily from 10. Last admission varies with season. (Closed 25-26 Dec). **Fees** £14.95 (ch £11.30). Family £50*
Facilities 🅿 Ⓟ ⃠🍽 licensed ⋔ (indoor & outdoor) ♿ toilets for disabled shop ⊗

CHESTER

Dewa Roman Experience

Pierpoint Ln, (off Bridge St) CH1 1NL
☎ 01244 343407 📠 01244 347737
e-mail: info@dewaromanexperience.co.uk
web: www.dewaromanexperience.co.uk
dir: city centre

Stroll along reconstructed streets experiencing the sights, sounds and smells of Roman Chester. From the streets of Dewa (the Roman name for Chester) you return to the present day on an extensive archaeological 'dig', where you can discover the substantial Roman, Saxon and medieval remains beneath modern Chester. Try on Roman armour, solve puzzles and make brass rubbings and make mosaics in the hands-on/ activity room. Roman soldier patrols available.

Times Open all year, daily Feb-Nov 9-5, Dec-Jan 10-4 . (Closed 25-26 & 31 Dec & 1 Jan).*
Facilities Ⓟ shop

ELLESMERE PORT

Blue Planet Aquarium

Cheshire Oaks CH65 9LF
☎ 0151 357 8800 📠 0151 356 7288
e-mail: info@blueplanetaquarium.co.uk
web: www.blueplanetaquarium.com
dir: M53 junct 10 at Cheshire Oaks, M56 junct 15 follow Aquarium signs

A voyage of discovery on one of the longest moving walkways in the world. Beneath the waters of the Caribbean Reef, see giant rays and awesome sharks pass inches from your face, stroke some favourite fish in the special rock pools, or pay a visit to the incredible world of poisonous frogs. Divers hand feed the fish throughout the day and can answer questions via state of the art communication systems. Home to Europe's largest collection of sharks, including the large sand tiger sharks. We offer at least two special events in each season please check website for details.

Times Open all year, daily from 10. (Closed 25 Dec). Seasonal variations in closing times, please call to confirm. **Fees** £14.50 (ch £10.50, concessions £12.50). Family ticket £48 (2ad+2ch). Groovy grandparent ticket (2+2) £44. Please check website for further details.*
Facilities Ⓟ Ⓟ licensed (outdoor) toilets for disabled shop

ELLESMERE PORT

The National Waterways Museum

South Pier Rd CH65 4FW
☎ 0151 355 5017 📠 0151 355 4079
e-mail: bookings@thewaterwaystrust.org
web: www.nwm.org.uk
dir: M53 junct 9

The National Waterways Museum aims to bring Britain's canal history to life. The fascinating museum is set within a 200-year-old seven acre dock complex and includes the world's largest floating collection of canal craft. With the dock workers cottages, blacksmiths forge, boat trips and events throughout the year there is something for everyone to enjoy. Check website or telephone for details of future events.

Times Open Summer daily 10-5. Winter Thu-Sun 10-4. Closed 1 Jan.* Facilities ℗ 🖵 🍴 (indoor & outdoor) ♿ (partly accessible) (85% of the site is accessible to wheelchairs) toilets for disabled shop

JODRELL BANK VISITOR CENTRE & ARBORETUM

Jodrell Bank Visitor Centre & Arboretum

SK11 9DL
☎ 01477 571339 📠 01477 571695
web: www.manchester.ac.uk/jodrellbank
dir: M6 junct 18, A535 Holmes Chapel to Chelford road

At Jodrell Bank, a scientific and engineering wonder awaits you - the magnificent Lovell telescope, one of the largest radio telescopes in the world. A pathway leads you 180 degrees around the telescope as it towers above you surveying and exploring the universe. Then, the visitor can wander along pathways amongst the trees of the extensive arboretum. The Centre is currently under a redevelopment, which will take 2-3 years to complete.

Times Open daily Nov-mid Mar 10.30-3, wknds 11-4; mid Mar-end Oct 10.30-5.30* Facilities ℗ 🖵 🍴 (outdoor) ♿ toilets for disabled shop ⊗

KNUTSFORD

Tatton Park

WA16 6QN

☎ 01625 374400 & 374435

🖷 01625 374403

e-mail: tatton@cheshireeast.gov.uk

web: www.tattonpark.org.uk

dir: Signed on A556, 4m S of Altrincham.
Entrance to Tatton Park on Ashley Rd, 1.5m NE of
junct A5034 with A50

Tatton Park is one of England's most complete
historic estates, with gardens and a 1,000-acre
country park. The centrepiece is the Georgian
mansion, with gardens by Humphry Repton and
Sir Joseph Paxton. More recently, a Japanese
garden with a Shinto temple was created. The
Tudor Old Hall is the original manor house,
and there is also a working 1930s farm and
a children's adventure playground. Special
events include the RHS flower show and open air
concerts.

Times 28 Mar-4 Oct, 10-7; 5 Oct-26 Mar 11-5*
Fees Car entry £4.50. Each attraction £4.50
(ch £2.50). Family ticket £11.50. Totally Tatton
Ticket (up to 3 attractions) £7 (ch £3.50). Family
£17.* Facilities ❷ ⊙ licensed ⋒ (outdoor) ⅙
(partly accessible) (old hall & areas of farm not
accessible) toilets for disabled shop ⋇

NANTWICH

Stapeley Water Gardens

London Rd, Stapeley CW5 7LH

☎ 01270 623868 & 628628

🖷 01270 624919

e-mail: info@stapeleywg.com

web: www.stapeleywg.com

dir: off M6 junct 16, 1m S of Nantwich on A51

There is plenty to do at Stapeley Water Gardens.
The Palms Tropical Oasis is home to piranhas,
parrots, skunks and exotic flowers, as well
as tamarin monkeys, poisonous frogs and a
crocodile. The two-acre Water Garden Centre
houses a fantastic collection of water-lilies,
as well as Koi carp and other water features.
There is also a large garden centre, and various
children's activities, including 'Meet the Keeper',
which take place during school holidays.

Times Open Summer: Mon-Sat 9-6, BHs 10-6,
Sun 10-4, Wed 9-8; Winter: Mon-Sat 9-5, BHs
10-5, Sun 10-4. The Palms Tropical Oasis open
from 10.* Fees The Palms Tropical Oasis £4.95
(ch £2.95, concessions £4.45). Family ticket
(2ad+2ch) £12.60 (2ad+3ch) £15. Discounts for
groups 15+* Facilities ❷ ⊡ ⊙ licensed ⋒
(outdoor) ⅙ toilets for disabled shop ⊗

NORTHWICH

Salt Museum

162 London Rd CW9 8AB
☎ 01606 271640   📠 01606 350420
e-mail: cheshiremuseums@cheshire.gov.uk
web: www.saltmuseum.org.uk
dir: on A533, 0.5m S of town centre & 0.5m N of A556. Well signed from A556

Britain's only Salt Museum tells the fascinating story of Cheshire's oldest industry. Models, reconstructions, original artefacts and audio-visual programmes throw new light on something we all take for granted. Various temporary exhibitions are held here, please contact for details.

Times Open Tue-Fri 10-5, wknds 2-5 (Sat & Sun, 12-5 in Aug). Open BH & Mons in Aug 10-5.*
Facilities 🅿 ☕ 🍴 (outdoor) ♿ toilets for disabled shop ⊗

STYAL

Quarry Bank Mill & Styal Estate

SK9 4LA
☎ 01625 527468   & 445896
📠 01625 539267
e-mail: quarrybankmill@nationaltrust.org.uk
web: www.quarrybankmill.org.uk
dir: 1.5m N of Wilmslow off B5166, 2.5m from M56 junct 5. Follow signs from A34 & M56

Founded in 1784, Quarry Bank Mill is one of the finest surviving cotton mills of the period. Inside the mill there are hands-on exhibits and demonstrations of how spinning and weaving were transformed by early textile engineers. Using the most powerful working waterwheel in Europe, two mill engines bring the past to life. At the Apprentice House you can discover what life was like for the children who worked in the mill in the 1830s. Visitors can also walk through woods and farmland along the River Bollin.

Times Open Mar-Oct, daily 11-5; Nov-Feb, Wed-Sun 11-4 (last admission 1hr before closing). Apprentice House timed tours. Garden open Mar-Oct.* **Fees** Mill & Apprentice House or Garden £10 (ch £5). Family ticket £24. Mill only £7 (ch £3.70). Family ticket £17.70. **Facilities** 🅿 ☕ 🍴 licensed 🍴 ♿ (partly accessible) (Apprentice House level access to ground floor only) toilets for disabled shop ⊗ 🐾

FALMOUTH

National Maritime Museum Cornwall

Discovery Quay TR11 3QY
☎ 01326 313388   📠 01326 317878
e-mail: enquiries@nmmc.co.uk
web: www.nmmc.co.uk
dir: follow signs from A39 for park/float ride and museum

Recently voted the south west's Visitor Attraction of the Year, this award winning museum offers something for everyone from ever changing exhibitions, hands-on family activities, talks, lectures, displays, events, crabbing and the opportunity to sail and see marine and bird life. Admire the views from the 29 metre tower, descend the depths in one of only three natural underwater viewing galleries in the world and discover Cornwall, journey through time, explore the seas and go mad about boats. The purchase of a full price individual ticket gives you free entry to the Museum for a year.

Times Open daily 10-5. Closed 25-26 Dec.*
Fees £8.75 (ch under 5 free, ch 6-15 & students £6, pen £7). Family ticket £24.* Facilities ⓟ ⓟ ☐ �🍽 licensed ♿ toilets for disabled shop ⊗

FALMOUTH

Pendennis Castle

Pendennis Headland TR11 4LP
☎ 01326 316594   📠 01326 212044
web: www.english-heritage.org.uk
dir: 1m SE

Together with St Mawes Castle, Pendennis forms the end of a chain of castles built by Henry VIII along the south coast as protection from attack from France. Journey through 450 years of history and discover the castle's wartime secrets.

Times Open all year, Apr-Jun & Sep, daily 10-5 (Sat 10-4); Jul-Aug, daily 10-6 (Sat 10-4); Oct-Mar, daily 10-4. Closed 24-26 Dec & 1 Jan.
Fees £5.70 (ch £2.90, concessions £4.80). Family £14.30. Prices and opening times are subject to change in March 2010. Please call 0870 333 1181 for the most up to date prices and opening times when planning your visit. Facilities ⓟ ☐ 🍴♿ (partly accessible) (two steep steps ticket point, spiral staircase, difficult steps to upper floor) toilets for disabled shop ⊗ ▦

GWEEK

National Seal Sanctuary

TR12 6UG

☎ 01326 221361 & 221874

🖷 01326 221210

e-mail: slcgweek@merlin-entertainments.com

web: www.sealsanctuary.co.uk

dir: pass RNAS Culdrose, take A3293, then B3291 to Gweek. Sanctuary signed from village

Britain's first rescue centre dedicated to the rehabilitation and release of grey seals. The Sanctuary offers a unique, educational experience and is a fun opportunity to learn more about the UK's largest mammal. Visit the UK's only Arctic hooded seal and the most diverse collection of pinnipeds (members of the seal family) in the UK, as well as Asian short-clawed otters, goats, ponies and sheep.

Times Open all year, daily from 10. Closed 25 Dec. Fees £12.90 (ch under 3 free, 3-14 £10.75, concessions £11.85). Family ticket (2ad+2ch) £38.70.* Facilities 🅿 ☕ 🍴 (outdoor) ♿ toilets for disabled shop

HELSTON

The Flambards Experience

Culdrose Manor TR13 0QA

☎ 01326 573404   🖷 01326 573344

e-mail: info@flambards.co.uk

web: www.flambards.co.uk

dir: 0.5m SE of Helston on A3083, Lizard road

Three award-winning, all-weather attractions can be visited on one site here. Flambards Victorian Village is a recreation of streets, shops and houses from 1830-1910. Britain in the Blitz is a life-size wartime street featuring shops, a pub and a living room complete with Morrison shelter. The Science Centre is a science playground that brings physics alive for the whole family. Along with the Thunderbolt and Extreme Force, Flambards also offers the Hornet Rollercoaster, the Family Log Flume, Go-Kart circuit, and rides and play areas for the very young. The Wildlife Experience show features lizards, snakes, large spiders and birds of prey. See the website for special events.

Times Open Etr-Nov, summer opening. Nov-Mar, winter opening.* Fees £16 (ch 3-15 £11.50). Family from £36.* Facilities 🅿 ☕ 🍴 (indoor & outdoor) ♿ (partly accessible) (some rivers not accessible) toilets for disabled shop ⊗

Goonhilly Satellite Earth Station Experience

Goonhilly Downs TR12 6LQ
☎ 0800 679593 🖹 01326 221438
e-mail: goonhilly.visitorscentre@bt.com
web: www.goonhilly.bt.com
dir: From Helston follow the brown direction signs

Future World is on the site of what was the largest satellite earth station in the world, with over 60 dishes, which makes a dramatic impression on the Lizard Peninsula landscape. Enter a world of historic predictions, past inventions and ideas and see artefacts from jet packs and space helmets to the Sinclair C5 and the first mobile phones, complete with 'brick' size batteries. Journey into a zone of interactive displays where you can record your own visions of the future. Discover the history and heritage of Goonhilly itself in the main visitors' centre, and learn how international communications have developed over the past 200 years. You an also book a tour into the heart of 'Arthur', the Grade II listed iconic satellite dish.

Times Open 15 Mar-27 Jun & 6 Sep-31 Oct 10-5; 28 Jun-5 Sep 10-6; Nov-27 Mar 11-4.* **Facilities** 🅿 ⬛ 🍽 licensed 🎪 (outdoor) ♿ toilets for disabled shop ⊗

Trevarno Estate Garden & Museum of Gardening

Trevarno Manor, Crowntown TR13 0RU
☎ 01326 574274 🖹 01326 574282
e-mail: enquiry@trevarno.co.uk
web: www.trevarno.co.uk
dir: E of Crowntown. Leave Helston on Penzance road signed B3302

Victorian gardens with the splendid fountain garden conservatory, unique range of crafts and the National Museum of Gardening. In the tranquil gardens and grounds, follow the progress of restoration projects, visit craft areas including handmade soap workshop, explore Britain's largest and most comprehensive collection of antique tools, implements, memorabilia and ephemera, creatively displayed to illustrate how gardens and gardening influences most people's lives. Adventure play area for the youngsters, extended estate walk and viewing platform. Home of the national daffodil collection showgarden (flowering Jan-mid May).

Times Open daily 10.30-5. Closed 25-26 Dec **Fees** £6.50 (ch 5-14 £2.25, concessions £5.75, disabled £3.25). Group 12+* **Facilities** 🅿 ⬛ 🎪 (outdoor) ♿ toilets for disabled shop

LANHYDROCK

Lanhydrock

PL30 5AD
☎ 01208 265950 📄 01208 265959
e-mail: lanhydrock@nationaltrust.org.uk
web: www.nationaltrust.org.uk
dir: 2.5m SE of Bodmin, signed from A30, A38 & B3268

Part-Jacobean, part-Victorian building that gives a vivid picture of life in Victorian times. The 'below stairs' sections have a huge kitchen, larders, dairy, bakehouse, cellars, and servants' quarters. The long gallery has a moulded ceiling showing Old Testament scenes, and overlooks the formal gardens with their clipped yews and bronze urns. The higher garden, famed for its magnolias and rhododendrons, climbs the hillside behind the house.

Times House open 13 Mar-Oct daily (ex Mon) 11-5 (Apr-Sep 5.30), open BH Mon & Mon during school hols. Gardens open all year, daily 10-6. Fees House & Grounds £10.90 (ch £5.40). Family tickets available. Garden & Grounds £6.40 (ch £5.80). Reduced rate when arriving by cycle or public transport. Facilities ● ℗ 🖵 🍽 licensed 🎪 (outdoor) ♿ toilets for disabled shop ⊗ 🐾

LAUNCESTON

Tamar Otter & Wildlife Centre

North Petherwin PL15 8GW
☎ 01566 785646
e-mail: info@tamarotters.co.uk
web: www.tamarotters.co.uk
dir: 5m NW off B3254 Bude road

Visitors to this wildlife centre will see British and Asian short-clawed otters in large natural enclosures. They will also be able to see fallow and Muntjac deer, and wallabies roaming around the grounds. There are also owls, peacocks, and a large selection of waterfowl on two lakes. Otters are fed at noon and 3pm and this is accompanied by an informative talk.

Times Open Apr-Oct, daily 10.30-6 (dates extended in accordance with school hols). Opens Good Fri if earlier than 1 Apr.* Fees £7 (ch 3-15yrs £3.50, concessions £6) Family (2 ad+3 ch) £18* Facilities ● 🖵 🎪 (outdoor) ♿ (partly accessible) (steep slope to otter pens/woodland walk) toilets for disabled shop ⊗

LOOE

The Monkey Sanctuary Trust

St Martins PL13 1NZ
☎ 01503 262532   📠 01503 262532
e-mail: info@monkeysanctuary.org
web: www.monkeysanctuary.org
dir: signed on B3253 at No Man's Land between East Looe & Hessenford

Visitors can see a colony of Amazonian woolly monkeys in extensive indoor and outdoor territory. There are also conservation gardens, children's play area, activity room, a display room and vegetarian cafe. The Monkey Sanctuary Trust is also a rescue centre for ex-pet capuchin monkeys rescued from the UK pet trade. In addition a bat cave is on site where visitors can watch a colony of rare horseshoe bats.

Times Open Sun-Thu from the Sun before Etr-Sep. Also open Autumn Half Term.* Facilities ℗ 🖵 ⊼ (outdoor) ♿ (partly accessible) toilets for disabled shop ⊗

MARAZION

St Michael's Mount

TR17 0HT
☎ 01736 710507 & 710265
📠 01736 719930
e-mail: mail@stmichaelsmount.co.uk
web: www.stmichaelsmount.co.uk
dir: access is by foot at low tide, or by motorboat in summer

In the 11th century, the abbey on St Michael's Mount was granted to the Benedictines and the church on the summit was built. Miracles in the 1260s increased the island's religious attraction to pilgrims. Besieged during the Wars of the Roses, in 1588 it was the place where the first beacon was lit to warn of the arrival of the Spanish Armada, and in the Civil War it was a Royalist stronghold attacked by Cromwell. The island is separated from the mainland by a causeway which is covered by the sea at high tide.

Times Open: Castle 29 Mar-1 Nov 10.30-5. (last entry 45mins before closing). Winter Tue & Fri by guided tour only. Garden May-June, Mon-Fri, Jul-Oct Thu & Fri 10.30-5.* Fees £6.60 (ch £3.30) Family ticket £16.50 (1ad family £9.90). Groups 15+ £5.60. Garden £3 (ch £1). Castle & gardens free to NT members.* Facilities ℗ 🖵🍴 licensed ⊼ (outdoor) shop ⊗ 🐾

NEWQUAY

Blue Reef Aquarium

Towan Promenade TR7 1DU
☎ 01637 878134 📠 01637 872578
e-mail: newquay@bluereefaquarium.co.uk
web: www.bluereefaquarium.co.uk
dir: from A30 follow signs to Newquay, follow Blue Reef Aquarium signs to car park in town centre. Satellite Navigation TR7 1JQ. Disabled access please ring.

Discover Cornish marine life from native sharks and rays to the incredibly intelligent and playful octopus. From here journey through warmer waters to watch the magical seahorses, unusual shape shifting, jet-propelled cuttlefish and the vibrant, swaying tentacles of living sponges and anemones. Here you will encounter the activities of a coral reef alive with shoals of brightly coloured fish and the graceful, black tip reef sharks which glide silently overhead. Daily talks and regular feeding demonstrations bring the experience to life. Events all year, please see website for details.

Times Open all year, daily 10-5. (Closed 25 Dec). Open until 6 during summer holidays. Fees £8.95 (ch £6.95, concessions £7.95).* Facilities ℗ ⬛☂ (outdoor) ♿ (partly accessible) (small area, only accessible via steps) toilets for disabled shop ⊗

NEWQUAY

Dairy Land Farm World

Summercourt TR8 5AA
☎ 01872 510246 📠 01872 510349
e-mail: info@dairylandfarmworld.co.uk
web: www.dairylandfarmworld.com
dir: Signed from A30 at exit for Mitchell/ Summercourt

Visitors can watch while the cows are milked to music on a spectacular merry-go-round milking machine. The life of a Victorian farmer and his neighbours is explored in the Heritage Centre, and a Farm Nature Trail features informative displays along pleasant walks. Children will have fun getting to know the farm animals in the Farm Park. They will also enjoy the playground, assault course and indoor play areas.

Times Open daily, late Mar-Oct 10-5. (Bull pen additional winter openings Thu-Sun & school hols, please telephone for more information)* Facilities 🅿 ⬛☂ (indoor & outdoor) toilets for disabled shop ⊗

NEWQUAY

Newquay Zoo

Trenance Gardens TR7 2LZ
☎ 01637 873342 🖹 01637 851318
e-mail: info@newquayzoo.org.uk
web: www.newquayzoo.org.uk
dir: off A3075 and follow signs to Zoo

Newquay Zoo is set among exotic lakeside gardens with animals from all around the world. Enjoy fascinating talks, animal encounters and feeding times throughout the day. See the otter family playing in the stream in the Oriental Garden, look out for meerkats on sentry duty, try to spot the secretive red panda, and glimpse the endangered lemurs and fossa. Kids will enjoy the Tarzan Trail, the village farm and the dragon maze. Other highlights include penguin, zebra, Sulawesi-crested macaques, tapirs, marmosets, tamarim and a new African Savanna and Philippines exhibits.

Times Open all year Apr-Sep, daily 9.30-6, (last entry 5); Oct-Mar, 10-5. Fees Under review please contact for details. Facilities ℗ Ⓟ 🖵 🍽 licensed ㄇ (outdoor) ♿ (partly accessible) (stairs in Tropical House & upto the Owls & Tarzan Trail) toilets for disabled shop ⊗

PENDEEN

Geevor Tin Mine

TR19 7EW
☎ 01736 788662 🖹 01736 786059
e-mail: bookings@geevor.com
web: www.geevor.com
dir: From Penzance take A3071 towards St Just, then B3318 towards Pendeen. From St Ives follow B3306 to Pendeen

A preserved tin mine and museum provide an insight into the methods and equipment used in the industry that was once so important in the area. The Geevor Tin Mine only actually stopped operation in 1990. Guided tours let visitors see the tin treatment plant, and a video illustrates the techniques employed. A museum of hard rock mining has recently opened, and the underground tour is well worth the trip.

Times Open daily (ex Sat) 9-5 (9-4 Nov-Mar). Closed 21-26 Dec & 1 Jan Fees £8.50 (ch & students £4.50, concessions £7.50) Family ticket £25. Facilities ℗ Ⓟ 🖵 🍽 licensed ㄇ (outdoor) ♿ (partly accessible) (access to new museum, shop & cafe) toilets for disabled shop ⊗

ST AUSTELL

Charlestown Shipwreck & Heritage Centre

Quay Rd, Charlestown PL25 3NJ
☎ 01726 69897   📠 01726 69897
e-mail: admin@shipwreckcharlestown.com
web: www.shipwreckcharlestown.com
dir: signed off A390 from St. Austell close to Eden Project

Charlestown is a small and unspoilt village with a unique sea-lock, china-clay port, purpose built in the 18th century. The Shipwreck and Heritage Centre was originally a dry house for china clay built on underground tunnels. Now it houses the largest display of shipwreck artefacts in the UK, along with local heritage, diving exhibits, and an RMS Titanic display. A recent addition is a Nelson display which commemorates the 200th anniversary of the Battle of Trafalgar.

Times Open Mar-Oct, daily 10-5. (Last admission 1 hour before closing) Fees £5.95 (ch under 10 free if accompanied by paying adult, ch under 16 £2.50, concessions £3.95) group prices on request. Facilities 🅿 🅿 🖵 🍴 licensed 🗜 toilets for disabled shop

ST AUSTELL

The China Clay Country Park

Carthew PL26 8XG
☎ 01726 850362   📠 01726 850362
e-mail: info@chinaclaycountry.co.uk
web: www.chinaclaycountry.co.uk
dir: 2m N on B3274, follow brown signs 'China Clay Museum'

This museum tells the story of Cornwall's most important present-day industry: china clay production. The open-air site includes a complete 19th-century clayworks, with huge granite-walled settling tanks, working water-wheels and a wooden slurry pump. There is a fully interactive gallery, nature trails and a children's adventure trail. Exhibition halls and interactive displays depict the life of claypit workers from 1800 to the present.

Times Open all year 10-6, last admission summer 4, winter 3* Facilities 🅿 🅿 🖵 🍴 licensed 🗜 (outdoor) 🗜 toilets for disabled shop

ST AUSTELL

Eden Project

Bodelva PL24 2SG
☎ 01726 811911 📄 01726 811912
e-mail: information@edenproject.com
web: www.edenproject.com
dir: overlooking St Austell Bay signposted from A390/A30/A391

An unforgettable experience in a breathtaking location, the Eden Project is a gateway into the fascinating world of plants and human society. Space age technology meets the lost world in the biggest greenhouse ever built. Located in a 50 metre deep crater the size of 30 football pitches are two gigantic geodesic conservatories: the Humid Tropics Biome and the Warm Temperate Biome. This is a startling and unique day out. There's an ice-rink in the winter (Nov-Feb) and concerts in the summer - see the website for details.

Times Open Mar-Oct, daily 9-6 (last admission 4.30). Nov-Mar 10-4.30 (last admission 3). 20 Jul-4 Sep open until 8 on Tue, Wed & Thu. Closed 24-25 Dec & 25-26 Jan. Fees £16 (ch £5, under 5's free, student £8 concessions £11). Family ticket (2ad+ up to 3ch) £38. Annual membership available.* Facilities ⓟ ☲ 🍴 licensed ⼀ (indoor & outdoor) ♿ (partly accessible) toilets for disabled shop ⊗

TINTAGEL

Tintagel Castle

PL34 0HE
☎ 01840 770328 📄 01841 772105
web: www.english-heritage.org.uk
dir: on Tintagel Head, 0.5m along uneven track from Tintagel, no vehicles

Overlooking the wild Cornish coast, Tintagel is one of the most spectacular spots in the country and associated with King Arthur and Merlin. Recent excavations revealed Dark Age connections between Spain and Cornwall, alongside the discovery of the 'Arthnou' stone suggesting that this was a royal place for the Dark Age rulers of Cornwall.

Times Open all year, Apr-Sep, daily 10-6; Oct-1 Nov, daily 10-5; 2 Nov-Mar, daily 10-4. Closed 24-26 Dec & 1 Jan. Beach cafe open daily, Apr-Oct (closes 1/2hr before castle) Nov-Mar 11-3.30. Fees £4.90 (concessions £4.20, ch £2.50). Family ticket £12.30. Prices and opening times are subject to change in March 2010. Please call 0870 333 1181 for the most up to date prices and opening times when planning your visit.
Facilities ⓟ shop ⊗ ⌗

WENDRON

Poldark Mine and Heritage Complex

TR13 0ER

☎ 01326 573173   ▤ 01326 563166

e-mail: info@poldark-mine.com

web: www.poldark-mine.com

dir: 3m from Helston on B3297 Redruth road, follow brown signs

The centre of this attraction is the 18th-century tin mine where visitors can join a guided tour of workings which retain much of their original character. The site's Museum explains the history of tin production in Cornwall from 1800BC through to the 19th century and the fascinating story of the Cornish overseas. In addition to the Museum, the audio-visual presentation gives more insight into Cornwall's mining heritage. Ghost tours through July and August, please phone for details.

Times Open Etr-end Oct, 10-5.30 (last tour 4).* **Facilities** 🅿 ⬚ 🍴 licensed ⦿ (indoor & outdoor) ♿ (partly accessible) (surface area only) toilets for disabled shop

BASSENTHWAITE

Trotters World of Animals

Coalbeck Farm CA12 4RD

☎ 017687 76239   ▤ 017687 76598

e-mail: info@trottersworld.com

web: www.trottersworld.com

dir: follow brown signs on A591/A66 from Bassenthwaite Lake

Home to hundreds of friendly creatures including lemurs, wallabies, zebras, otters and other exotic animals along with reptiles and birds of prey and a family of gibbons which will keep families amused for hours. Informative, amusing demonstrations bring visitors closer to the animals. "Clown About" is an indoor play centre with soft play area and ballpools for toddlers upwards.

Times Open all year, except 25 Dec & 1 Jan, 10-5.30 or dusk if earlier.* **Facilities** 🅿 ⬚ 🍴 licensed ⦿ (outdoor) ♿ toilets for disabled shop 🚫

BORROWDALE

Honister Slate Mine

Honister Pass CA12 5XN
☎ 01768 777230 🖷 01768 777958
e-mail: info@honister.com
web: www.honister.com
dir: from Keswick take B5289 through Borrowdale & Rosthwaite, follow road to top of pass. From Cockermouth take B5292 towards Keswick for 4m, turn right onto B5289 to Low Larton & Buttermere. Follow road to top of pass

The last working slate mine in England. Fully guided tours allow you to explore the caverns hacked out by Victorian miners. Learn the history of the famous Honister green slate, how to rive slates, and see local skills in action.

Times Open Mon-Fri 9-5, wknds 10-5. Closed 19 Dec-12 Jan.* Facilities 🅿 ⓟ 🖵 †◎⃒ licensed 🛱 ♿ (partly accessible) toilets for disabled shop

DALTON-IN-FURNESS

South Lakes Wild Animal Park

Crossgates LA15 8JR
☎ 01229 466086 🖷 01229 461310
e-mail: office@wildanimalpark.co.uk
web: www.wildanimalpark.co.uk
dir: M6 junct 36, A590 to Dalton-in-Furness, follow tourist signs

A day you'll never forget at one of Cumbria's top attractions. Hand feed giraffes, penguins and kangaroos every day. Get up close to rhinos, tigers, bears, hippos, monkeys, vultures, and lemurs. There are new aerial walkways and viewpoints, the Wild Things gift shop and Maki restaurant, all overlooking a recreated African Savannah where rhinos, giraffes and baboons wander.

Times Open all year, daily 10-5 (last admission 4.15); Nov-Feb 10-4.30 (last admission 3.45). Closed 25 Dec. Fees £11.50 (ch & concessions £8). Facilities 🅿 ⓟ 🖵 🛱 (indoor & outdoor) ♿ toilets for disabled shop ⊗

HAWKSHEAD

Beatrix Potter Gallery

Main St LA22 0NS

☎ 015394 36269   🖷 015394 36811

e-mail: beatrixpottergallery@nationaltrust.org.uk

web: www.nationaltrust.org.uk

dir: on main street in village centre

An annually changing exhibition of Beatrix Potter's original illustrations from her children's storybooks, housed in the former office of her husband, solicitor William Heelis.

Times Open 13 Feb-25 Mar, Sat-Thu 11-3.30; 27 Mar-Oct, Sat-Thu 10.30-4.30. Admission by timed ticket including NT members. **Fees** £4.20 (ch £2.10). Family ticket (2ad+3ch) £10.50. **Facilities** ℗ ♿ (partly accessible) shop ⊗ ♨

KENDAL

Museum of Lakeland Life

Abbot Hall LA9 5AL

☎ 01539 722464   🖷 01539 722494

e-mail: info@lakelandmuseum.org.uk

web: www.lakelandmuseum.org.uk

dir: M6 junct 36, follow signs to Kendal. Located at south end of Kendal beside Abbot Hall Art Gallery

The life and history of the Lake District is captured by the displays in this museum, housed in Abbot Hall's stable block. The working and social life of the area are well illustrated by a variety of exhibits including period rooms, a Victorian Cumbrian street scene, a farming display, Arts and Crafts movement textiles and furniture and a recreation of Arthur Ransome's study, furnished with many of his personal possessions.

Times Open 13 Jan-12 Dec, Mon-Sat 10.30-5. (Closing at 4 Jan-Mar & Nov-Dec)* **Fees** £4.75 (ch £3.40). Family ticket £13.60.* **Facilities** ℗ ℗ 🖵 ♿ (partly accessible) toilets for disabled shop ⊗

KESWICK

Cars of the Stars Motor Museum

Standish St CA12 5LS
☎ 017687 73757 📄 017687 72090
e-mail: cotsmm@aol.com
web: www.carsofthestars.com
dir: M6 junct 40, A66 to Keswick, continue to town centre, close to Bell Close car park

This unusual museum features celebrity TV and film vehicles. Some notable exhibits to look out for are Chitty Chitty Bang Bang, James Bond's Aston Martin DB5, Harry Potter's Ford Anglia, Del Boy's Robin Reliant, A-Team van and Batmobiles. Each vehicle is displayed in its individual film set. Newly opened - "The Bond Museum".

Times Open Feb half term, daily Etr-Nov (wknds Dec) 10-5 **Fees** £6 (ch £4)* **Facilities** ℗ ₺ shop

KESWICK

Cumberland Pencil Museum

Southey Works, Greta Bridge CA12 5NG

☎ 017687 73626 📄 01900 602489
e-mail: kes_museum@acco.com
web: www.pencilmuseum.co.uk
dir: M6 N onto A66 at Penrith. Left at 2nd Keswick exit, left at T-junct, left over Greta Bridge

Investigating the history and technology of an object most of us take utterly for granted, this interesting museum includes a replica of the Borrowdale mine where graphite was first discovered, the world's longest pencil, children's activity area, and various artistic techniques that use pencils. Artist demonstrations and workshops will take place throughout the year.

Times Open daily 9.30-4 (hours may be extended during peak season). (Closed 25-26 Dec & 1 Jan). **Fees** £3.50 (concessions £2.25). Family ticket (2ad+3ch) £9.25. Annual membership £14.75. **Facilities** ℗ ℗ ⊒ ㅠ (outdoor) ₺ toilets for disabled shop

LAKESIDE

Lakes Aquarium

LA12 8AS

☎ 015395 30153   🖷 015395 30152
e-mail: info@lakesaquarium.co.uk
web: www.lakesaquarium.co.uk
dir: M6, junct 36, take A590 to Newby Bridge.
Turn right over bridge, follow Hawkshead Rd to
Lakeside

The Lakes Aquarium is home to creatures that
live in and around freshwater lakes across
the globe. See things that swim, fly and bite
in beautifully-themed displays. Discover
mischievous otters in the Asia area, piranhas
in the Americas and cheeky marmosets in
the rainforest displays, not forgetting all your
favourite creatures that live a bit closer to home.
This includes diving ducks in the spectacular
underwater tunnel and fresh water rays and
seahorses in the Seashore Discover Zone. Special
themed events take place throughout the year,
please see website for details.

Times Open all year, daily from 9-5 (winter) 9-6
(summer) last admission 1hr prior to closing.
Closed 25 Dec.* Fees £8.75 (ch 3-15 £5.75,
concessions £7.25). Family ticket (2ad+2ch
£24.95)* Facilities 🅿 ⛟ 🍽 licensed ☐
(outdoor) ♿ toilets for disabled shop ⊗

NEAR SAWREY

Hill Top

LA22 0LF

☎ 015394 36269   🖷 015394 36811
e-mail: hilltop@nationaltrust.org.uk
web: www.nationaltrust.org.uk
dir: 2m S of Hawkshead. or 2m from Bowness
Car Ferry.

This small 17th-century house is where Beatrix
Potter wrote many of her famous children's
stories. It remains as she left it, and in each
room can be found something that appears in
one of her books.

Times House open 13 Feb-25 Mar, Sat-Thu
11-3.30; 27 Mar-Oct, Sat-Thu 10.30-4.30. Garden
open 13 Feb-25 Mar, daily 11-4; 26 Mar-Oct,
daily 10-5; Nov-24 Dec, daily 10-4 Fees £6.20
(ch £3.10). Family ticket £15.50 (2ad+3ch).
Entry to garden free on Fri when house is closed.
Facilities 🅿 ♿ (partly accessible) (access by
arrangement) shop ⊗ 🦌

PENRITH

The Rheged Centre

Redhills CA11 0DQ
☎ 01768 868000 🖹 01768 868002
e-mail: enquiries@rheged.com
web: www.rheged.com
dir: M6 junct 40, on A66 near Penrith

Rheged's ten shops reflect the unique nature of the region, while the indoor and outdoor activities provide challenges for children of all ages. The centre has introduced large format 3D films, three films show twice a day. From a relaxed family lunch to a quick coffee and cake, Rheged's three cafes offer fresh food, made on the premises using the finest local ingredients.

Times Open daily 10-5.30. Closed 25-26 Dec & 1 Jan Fees £4.95 (ch £3, pen £3.95). Family ticket £17 3D large format films* Facilities ❷ ⛾ ⓣⓞⓘ licensed ⋒ (outdoor) ♿ toilets for disabled shop ⊗

PENRITH

Wetheriggs Animal Rescue & Conservation Centre FREE

Clifton Dykes CA10 2DH
☎ 01768 866657 🖹 01768 866657
web: www.wetheriggsanimalrescue.co.uk
dir: approx 2m off A6, S from Penrith, signed

Wetheriggs is an animal rescue centre with a mixture of farm and exotic animals. All proceeds go towards rescuing and looking after the animals. You can also learn about the heritage of the steam-powered pottery and engine room, and paint your own pot. There is a newt pond, play area and a petting farm and reptile house, café and gift shop, all set in 7.5 acres of the beautiful Eden Valley.

Times Open daily, Apr-Oct 10-4; Nov-Mar 10-3. Closed 25-26 Dec & 1 Jan.* Facilities ❷ ⛾ ⋒ (outdoor) toilets for disabled shop

39

WINDERMERE

Lake District Visitor Centre at Brockhole

LA23 1LJ

☎ 015394 46601 📄 015394 43523
e-mail: infodesk@lake-district.gov.uk
web: www.lake-district.gov.uk
dir: on A591, between Windermere and Ambleside, follow brown tourist signs

Set in 32 acres of landscaped gardens and grounds, on the shore of Lake Windermere, this house became England's first National Park Visitor Centre in 1969. It offers permanent and temporary exhibitions, lake cruises, an adventure playground and an extensive events programme. Contact the Centre for a copy of their free events guide. Boats available for hire in summer, weekends and school holidays.

Times Open 14 Feb-1 Nov, daily 10-5. Grounds & gardens open all year.* **Facilities** 🅿 🛒 🍽 licensed 🍴 (indoor & outdoor) ♿ toilets for disabled shop

BUXTON

Poole's Cavern (Buxton Country Park)

Green Ln SK17 9DH

☎ 01298 26978 📄 01298 73563
e-mail: info@poolescavern.co.uk
web: www.poolescavern.co.uk
dir: 1m from Buxton town centre, off A6 and A515

Limestone rock, water, and millions of years created this natural cavern containing thousands of crystal formations. A 45-minute guided tour leads the visitor through chambers used as a shelter by Bronze Age cave dwellers, Roman metal workers and as a hideout by the infamous robber Poole. Attractions include the underground source of the River Wye, the Grand Cascade and underground sculpture formations. Set in 100 acres of woodland, Buxton Country Park has leafy trails to Grinlow viewpoint and panoramic peakland scenery.

Times Open Mar-Oct, daily 9.30-5; Nov-Feb wknds 10-4.* **Fees** £7.50 (ch £4.50, concessions £6). Family ticket £22. Please check website or telephone for current details* **Facilities** 🅿 🛒 🍽 licensed 🍴 (outdoor) ♿ (partly accessible) (access to visitor centre & 1st 100mtrs of cave tour to main chamber, no access to woods) toilets for disabled shop ⊗

CASTLETON

Blue-John Cavern & Mine

Buxton Rd S33 8WP
☎ 01433 620638 & 620642
📠 01433 621586
e-mail: lesley@bluejohn.gemsoft.co.uk
web: www.bluejohn.gemsoft.co.uk
dir: follow brown 'Blue-John Cavern' signs from Castleton

A remarkable example of a water-worn cave, over a third of a mile long, with chambers 200ft high. It contains 8 of the world's 14 veins of Blue John stone, and has been the major source of this unique form of fluorspar for nearly 300 years.

Times Open all year, daily, 9.30-5 (or dusk). Guided tours of approx 1hr every 10 mins tour. Closed 25-26 Dec & 1 Jan. Fees £8 (ch £4, pen & students £6) Family ticket £22. Party rates on request.* Facilities ❷ ℗ ⛺ shop

CASTLETON

Peak Cavern

S33 8WS
☎ 01433 620285
e-mail: info@peakcavern.co.uk
web: www.devilsarse.com
dir: on A6187, in centre of Castleton

One of the most spectacular natural limestone caves in the Peak District, with an electrically-lit underground walk of about half a mile. Ropes have been made for over 500 years in the 'Grand Entrance Hall', and traces of a row of cottages can be seen. Rope-making demonstrations are included on every tour.

Times Open all year, daily 10-5. Nov-Mar limited tours, please call in advance for times. Closed 25 Dec.* Fees £7.25 (ch £5.25, other concessions £6.25). Family ticket (2ad+2ch) £22.* Facilities ❷ ℗ ⊓ (indoor & outdoor) ♿ (partly accessible) (number of stairs throughout the cave) shop

CASTLETON

Speedwell Cavern

Winnats Pass S33 8WA
☎ 01433 620512 📄 01433 621888
e-mail: info@speedwellcavern.co.uk
web: www.speedwellcavern.co.uk
dir: A625 becomes A6187 at Hathersage. 0.5m
W of Castleton

Descend 105 steps to a boat that takes you on
a one-mile underground exploration of floodlit
caverns part of which was once a lead mine. The
hand-carved tunnels open out into a network of
natural caverns and underground rivers. See the
Bottomless Pit, a huge subterranean lake in a
huge, cathedral-like cavern.

Times Open all year, daily 10-5 (Closed 25 Dec).
Phone to check winter opening times due to
weather. Last boat 4 Fees £7.75 (ch £5.75).*
Facilities ❷ ℗ ♿ (partly accessible) (105
steps in one flight down to boat & back up again
to surface) shop ⊗

CASTLETON

Treak Cliff Cavern

S33 8WP
☎ 01433 620571 📄 01433 620519
e-mail: treakcliff@bluejohnstone.com
web: www.bluejohnstone.com
dir: 0.75m W of Castleton on A6187

An underground world of stalactites, stalagmites,
flowstone, rock and cave formations, minerals
and fossils. There are rich deposits of the rare
and beautiful Blue John stone, including 'The
Pillar', the largest piece ever found. Show caves
include the Witch's Cave, Aladdin's Cave, Dream
Cave and Fairyland Grotto. These caves contain
some of the most impressive stalactites in the
Peak District. Visitors can also polish their own
Blue John stone in school holidays.

Times Open all year, Mar-Oct, daily 10-last
tour 4.20; Nov-Feb daily - call for special tour
times. All tours are guided & last about 40
mins. Enquire for last tour of day & possible
closures. Closed 24-26 & 31 Dec & 1 Jan. All
dates & times are subject to change without
notice.* Fees £7.95 (ch 5-15 £4). Family ticket
(2ad+2ch) £22.* Facilities ℗ ℗ ⊐ 🍴 (indoor
& outdoor) ♿ (partly accessible) (no wheelchair
access, walking disabled only) shop

CHATSWORTH

Chatsworth

DE45 1PP

☎ 01246 565300 🖷 01246 583536

e-mail: visit@chatsworth.org

web: www.chatsworth.org

dir: 8m N of Matlock off B6012. 16m from M1 junct 29, signposted via Chesterfield, follow brown signs

Home of the Duke and Duchess of Devonshire, Chatsworth contains a massive private collection of fine and decorative arts. There is a splendid painted hall, and a great staircase leads to the chapel, decorated with statues and paintings. There are pictures, furniture and porcelain, and a trompe l'oeil painting of a violin on the music room door. The park was laid out by 'Capability' Brown, but is most famous as the work of Joseph Paxton, head gardener in the 19th century. The park is also home to the Duke and Duchess' personal collection of contemporary sculpture.

Times Open mid Mar-23 Dec, House & Garden 11-5.30, Farmyard 10.30-5.30.* Facilities **P** **P** ⊡ ⏲⊙¹ licensed & (partly accessible) toilets for disabled shop ⊗

CRESWELL

Creswell Crags Museum and Education Centre

Crags Rd, Welbeck S80 3LH

☎ 01909 720378 🖷 01909 724726

e-mail: info@creswell-crags.org.uk

web: www.creswell-crags.org.uk

dir: off B6042, Crags Road, between A616 & A60, 1m E of Creswell village

Creswell Crags, a picturesque limestone gorge with lakes and caves, is one of Britain's most important archaeological sites. The many caves on the site have yielded Ice Age remains, including bones of woolly mammoth, reindeer, hyena and bison, stone tools of Ice Age hunters from over 10,000 years ago and new research has revealed the only Ice Age rock art in Britain (about 13,000 years old). Visit the Museum and Education Centre to learn more about your Ice Age ancestors through an exhibition, touch-screen computers and video. Join a 'Virtually the Ice Age' cave tour, picnic in Crags Meadow, or try the new activity trail. Plenty of special events year round, contact for details.

Times Open all year, Feb-Oct, daily, 10.30-4.30; Nov-Jan, Sun only 10.30-4.30.* Facilities **P** ⊓ & (partly accessible) (accessible round Gorge. Tour may be unsuitable for mobility scooters, due to steps) toilets for disabled shop ⊗

CRICH

Crich Tramway Village

DE4 5DP

☎ 01773 854321   📄 01773 854320
e-mail: enquiry@tramway.co.uk
web: www.tramway.co.uk
dir: off B5035, 8m from M1 junct 28

A mile-long scenic journey through a period street to open countryside with panoramic views. You can enjoy unlimited vintage tram rides, and the exhibition hall houses the largest collection of vintage electric trams in Britain. The village street contains a bar and restaurant, tearooms, a sweet shop, ice cream shop, and police sentry box, among others. There is also a Workshop Viewing Gallery where you can see the trams being restored. Ring for details of special events.

Times Open Apr-Oct, daily 10-5.30 (6.30 wknds Jun-Aug & BH wknds). 10.30-4 until Nov.*
Fees £10.50 (ch 4-15 £5.50, pen £9.50). Family ticket (2ad+3ch)* **Facilities** 🅿 🅿 ⬚ 🍴 licensed 🪑 (outdoor) ♿ toilets for disabled shop

SUDBURY

Sudbury Hall and Museum of Childhood

DE6 5HT

☎ 01283 585305   📄 01283 585139
e-mail: sudburyhall@nationaltrust.org.uk
web: www.nationaltrust.org.uk
dir: 6m E of Uttoxeter at junct of A50 & A515

The country home of the Lords Vernon features exquisite plasterwork, wood carvings, murals based classical stories and fine 17th century craftsmanship. The Great Staircase and Long Gallery are extremely impressive. The Museum of Childhood is a delight for all ages with something for everyone. Explore the childhoods of times gone by, make stories, play with toys and share your childhood with others.

Times Opening details not confirmed for the 2010 edition. Please telephone or see website for details. **Fees** Admission prices not confirmed for the 2010 edition. Please telephone or see website for details. **Facilities** 🅿 🅿 ⬚ 🍴 licensed ♿ (partly accessible) (Access via steps & 4 flights of steps to first floor. Lift to all Museum floors. Grounds partly accessible, grass & loose gravel paths, some steps) toilets for disabled shop
🚫 🐾

BEER

Pecorama Pleasure Gardens

Underleys EX12 3NA
☎ 01297 21542 📄 01297 20229
e-mail: pecorama@btconnect.com
web: www.peco-uk.com
dir: from A3052 take B3174, Beer road, signed

The gardens are high on a hillside, overlooking Beer. A miniature steam and diesel passenger line offers visitors a stunning view of Lyme Bay as it runs through the Pleasure Gardens. Attractions include an aviary, crazy golf, children's activity area and the Peco Millennium Garden. The main building houses an exhibition of railway modelling in various small gauges. There are souvenir and railway model shops, plus full catering facilities. Please telephone for details of events running throughout the year.

Times Open Etr-end Oct , Mon-Fri 10-5.30, Sat 10-1. Open Sun at Etr & 30 May-5 Sep.
Fees £6.60 (ch 4-14 £4.50, concessions £6.10, over 80 & under 4 free)* **Facilities** 🅿 🅟 ⏛ ⦿ licensed ⊟ (outdoor) � (partly accessible) (no wheelchairs on miniature railway) toilets for disabled shop ⊗

BLACKMOOR GATE

Exmoor Zoological Park

South Stowford, Bratton Fleming EX31 4SG
☎ 01598 763352 📄 01598 763352
e-mail: exmoorzoo@btconnect.com
web: www.exmoorzoo.co.uk
dir: off A361 link road onto A399, follow tourist signs

Exmoor Zoo is both personal and friendly. Open since 1982 it is an ideal family venue, catering particularly for the younger generation. The zoo specialises in smaller animals, many endangered, such as the golden-headed lion tamarins. There are new exhibits for animals such as cheetahs, maned wolves, tapirs, sitatungas and of course the "Exmoor Beast".

Times Open daily, Mar-4 May & 16 Sep-2 Nov 10-5; 3 Nov-30 Mar 10-4; 5 May-15 Sep 10-6* **Fees** £8.25 (ch £6, concessions £7.25). Family ticket (2ad+2ch) £26.50.* **Facilities** 🅿 ⏛ ⊟ (outdoor) ⅃ (partly accessible) (tarmac paths on hill) toilets for disabled shop ⊗

Buckfast Butterfly Farm & Dartmoor Otter Sanctuary

TQ11 0DZ

☎ 01364 642916
e-mail: contact@ottersandbutterflies.co.uk
web: www.ottersandbutterflies.co.uk
dir: off A38, at Dart Bridge junct, follow tourist
signs, adjacent to steam railway

Visitors can wander around a specially designed,
undercover tropical garden, where free-flying
butterflies and moths from around the world can
be seen. The otter sanctuary has large enclosures
with underwater viewing areas. Three types of
otters can be seen - the native British otter along
with Asian and North American otters.

Times Open Apr-Oct, daily 10-5 or dusk (if
earlier). For rest of year please see website
Fees £6.95 (ch £4.95, concessions £5.95). Family
ticket £19.95* Facilities ❷ ❷ ⬜ ㅠ (outdoor)
♿ (partly accessible) (fence height around some
otter enclosures can make it difficult for w/chair
users to see) shop ⊗

Canonteign Falls

EX6 7NT

☎ 01647 252434   📠 01647 52617
e-mail: info@canonteignfalls.co.uk
web: www.canonteignfalls.co.uk
dir: off A38 at Chudleigh/Teign Valley junct onto
B3193 and follow tourist signs for 3m

A magical combination of waterfalls, woodlands
and lakes. 3 graded walks marked with colour
ferns.

Times Open summer 10-5. Last admission 1
hour before closing.* Fees £5.75 (ch £4.50,
concessions £4.75). Family £19.50.* Facilities
❷ ⬜ ㅣ⬤l licensed ㅠ (indoor & outdoor) ♿
(partly accessible) (grounds partly accessible but
not up to falls) toilets for disabled shop

CLOVELLY

The Milky Way Adventure Park

EX39 5RY
☎ 01237 431255 📠 01237 431735
e-mail: info@themilkyway.co.uk
web: www.themilkyway.co.uk
dir: on A39, 2m from Clovelly

Adventure park in the country with 5 major rides and live shows. Something fun and educational for everyone. Get close and personal with a bird of prey, lose yourself in a maze or take a trip out of this world whatever the weather. The Cosmic Typhoon is Devon's tallest, fastest and longest rollercoaster. Height restriction but don't worry, there's one for smaller adventurers, The Big Apple. Plenty to do even on rainy days, with indoor attractions from alien adventures on the Clone Zone Ride and Droid Destroyer Dodgems, not to mention the death defying slides and ball pools of the Time Warp and the North Coast's largest indoor play area. Under fives can enjoy ball pools, sand pits, play tractors and more on Fantasy Farm.

Times Open Etr-end Oct, daily 10.30-6. Also open wknds & school hols in winter. **Fees** £10 per person (under 3's free, concessions £8). **Facilities** Ⓟ ☕ ⛩ (indoor & outdoor) ♿ toilets for disabled shop

COMBE MARTIN

Combe Martin Wildlife Park & Dinosaur Park

EX34 0NG
☎ 01271 882486 📠 01271 883869
e-mail: info@dinosaur-park.com
web: www.dinosaur-park.com
dir: M5 junct 27 then A361 towards Barnstaple, turn right onto A399

Come and see the UK's only full-size animatronic Tyrannosaurus Rex, along with a pair of vicious, interacting Meglosaurs, a Velociraptor and Dilophosaurus, the 'Spitting Dinosaur'. Explore 26 acres of stunning gardens with cascading waterfalls and hundreds of exotic birds and animals. There are daily sea lion shows, falconry displays, lemur encounters and handling sessions. Other attractions include the Earthquake Canyon Train Ride, Tomb of the Pharoahs, Tropical House, T Rex photographic studio, and much more.

Times Open Feb half term-7 Nov, daily 10-5 (last admission 3). **Fees** £12 (ch 3-15 £7.50, ch under 3 free, pen £8.50). Family (2ad+2ch) £34.* **Facilities** Ⓟ Ⓟ ☕ ⛩ (outdoor) ♿ (partly accessible) (bottom part of park has sharp decline, not suitable for wheelchairs or severe disabilities) toilets for disabled shop ⊗

DARTMOUTH

Woodlands Leisure Park

Blackawton TQ9 7DQ
☎ 01803 712598 🖃 01803 712680
e-mail: fun@woodlandspark.com
web: www.woodlandspark.com
dir: 5m from Dartmouth on A3122. From A38
follow brown tourist signs

An all-weather attraction packed with variety
for all ages at one inclusive cost. The new
Ninja Towers has three top aerial runways, sky
high rope bridges and incredible slides. The
baffling illusion of the Seascape Mirror Maze has
bewildering pathways and weird sea monsters
that disappear. Great for rainy days with
100,000sq ft of undercover action. Incredible
Zoo-in-a-Farm, amazing night and day creatures,
insects and birds. Get close to the animals and
ride big U-Drive tractors. There is also a falconry
centre with fascinating flying displays; and live
entertainers in the summer holidays.

Times Open daily 27 Mar-7 Nov. Winter wknds
& Devon school holidays only. Fees £11.45-
£12.25 (under 92cms free). Family ticket £43.80
(2ad+2ch).* Facilities ❷ ⯑ ⯑ (indoor &
outdoor) ⯑ (partly accessible) (some rides not
suitable) toilets for disabled shop ⊗

DREWSTEIGNTON

Castle Drogo

EX6 6PB
☎ 01647 433306 🖃 01647 433186
e-mail: castledrogo@nationaltrust.org.uk
web: www.nationaltrust.org.uk
dir: 5m S of A30 Exeter-Okehampton. Coaches
turn off A382 at Sandy Park

India tea baron Julius Drewe's dream house,
this granite castle, built between 1910 and
1930, is one of the most remarkable works of Sir
Edward Lutyens, and combines the grandeur of
a medieval castle with the comfort of the 20th
century. A great country house with terraced
formal garden, woodland spring garden, huge
circular croquet lawn and colourful herbaceous
borders. Standing at more than 900 feet
overlooking the wooded gorge of the River Teign
with stunning views of Dartmoor, and delightful
walks. Lots of events in school holidays, ring for
details.

Times Castle open 14 Mar-1 Nov, daily 11-5;
Garden, tearooms & shop open 14 Mar-1 Nov
10.30-5.30* Facilities ❷ ⯑ ⯑ (outdoor) ⯑
(partly accessible) (Gardens, Hall & Library fully
accessible, other areas only accessible via stairs)
toilets for disabled shop ⊗ ⯑

EXETER

Exeter's Underground Passages

2 Paris St EX1 1GA
☎ 01392 665887 📄 01392 265625
e-mail: underground.passages@exeter.gov.uk
web: www.exeter.gov.uk/passages
dir: Follow signs for city centre

Dating from the 14th century, these medieval passages under Exeter High Street are a unique ancient monument. No similar system of passages can be explored by the public anywhere else in Britain. The passages were built to house the pipes that brought fresh water to the city. Visitors to the Underground Interpretation Centre pass through an exhibition and video presentation before their guided tour. The centre is packed with interactive exhibits but the passages remain the same: narrow, dark and exciting.

Times Open Jun-Sep (incl school hols outside this period), Mon-Sat 9.30-5.30 (last tour 4.30). Sun 10.30-4 (last tour 3). Oct-May (closed Mon), Tue-Fri 11.30-5.30, Sat 9.30-5.30 (last tour 4.30), Sun 11.30-4 (last tour 3).* **Fees** £4.90 (ch 5-18 £3.40, under 5 free access to exhibition only, concessions £3.90). Family ticket (2ad+3ch) £14.65.* **Facilities** ⓟ toilets for disabled shop ⊗

EXMOUTH

The World of Country Life

Sandy Bay EX8 5BU
☎ 01395 274533 📄 01392 227131
e-mail: info@worldofcountrylife.co.uk
web: www.worldofcountrylife.co.uk
dir: M5 junct 30, take A376 to Exmouth. Follow signs to Sandy Bay

All-weather family attraction including falconry displays, and a safari train that travels through a forty acre deer park. Kids will enjoy the friendly farm animals, pets centre and animal nursery. There is also a Victorian street, working models and thousands of exhibits from a bygone age, including steam and vintage vehicles.

Times Open Apr-1 Nov, daily 10-5.* **Fees** £9.85 (ch 3-17 & pen £7.85). Family ticket (2ad+2ch) £32.50, (2ad+3ch) £37.50.* **Facilities** ⓟ ⓟ ⊑ ⓣ⊙� licensed ⋈ (indoor & outdoor) ♿ toilets for disabled shop ⊗

ILFRACOMBE

Watermouth Castle & Family Theme Park

EX34 9SL

☎ 01271 863879 📄 01271 865864
web: www.watermouthcastle.com
dir: 3m NE off A399, midway between Ilfracombe & Combe Martin

A popular family attraction including mechanical music demonstrations, musical water show, dungeon labyrinths, Victorian displays, bygone pier machines, animated fairy tale scenes, tube slide, mini golf, children's carousel, swingboats, aeroplane ride, water fountains, river ride, gardens and a maze.

Times Open Apr-end Oct, closed Sat. (Also closed some Mon & Fri off season). Ring for further details.* Fees £12 (ch £10, under 92cm free & pen £8)* Facilities ❷ ♨ ♒ (outdoor) ♿ (partly accessible) toilets for disabled shop ⊗

KINGSBRIDGE

Cookworthy Museum of Rural Life

The Old Grammar School, 108 Fore St TQ7 1AW
☎ 01548 853235
e-mail: wcookworthy@talk21.com
web: www.kingsbridgemuseum.net
dir: A38 onto A384, then A381 to Kingsbridge, museum at top of town

The 17th-century schoolrooms of this former grammar school are now the setting for another kind of education. Reconstructed room-sets of a Victorian kitchen, a costume room and extensive collection of local historical items are gathered to illustrate South Devon life. A walled garden and farm gallery are also features of this museum, founded to commemorate William Cookworthy, 'father' of the English china clay industry. The Local Heritage Resource Centre with public access databases and microfilm of local newspapers since 1855 is available to visitors. Please ring for details of special events.

Times Open 31 Mar-Sep, Mon-Sat 10.30-5; Oct 10.30-4. Nov-Mar groups by arrangement. Local Heritage Resource Centre open all year, Mon-Thu 10-12 & Wed also 2-4, other times by appointment. Fees £2.50 (ch £1, concessions £2). Family £6 (2ad+ up to 4ch).* Facilities ℗ ♒ (outdoor) ♿ (partly accessible) toilets for disabled shop ⊗

LYDFORD

Lydford Gorge

EX20 4BH

☎ 01822 820320 & 820441

📄 01822 822000

e-mail: lydfordgorge@nationaltrust.org.uk

web: www.nationaltrust.org.uk

dir: off A386, between Okehampton & Tavistock

This lush oak-wooded steep-sided river gorge, with its fascinating history and many legends, can be explored through a variety of short and long walks. See the spectacular White Lady Waterfall, pass over the tumbling water at Tunnel Falls and watch the river bubble in the Devil's Cauldron. There's an abundance of wildlife to spot.

Times Open 14 Mar-Nov, daily 10-5 (Oct & Nov 10-4). Winter opening - please ring for details.*

Facilities 🅿 🅟 ⛽ 🅵 (outdoor) ♿ (partly accessible) toilets for disabled shop ♨

MORWELLHAM

Morwellham Quay

PL19 8JL

☎ 01822 832766 & 833808

📄 01822 833808

e-mail: enquiries@morwellham-quay.co.uk

web: www.morwellham-quay.co.uk

dir: 4m W of Tavistock, off A390. Midway between Gunnislake & Tavistock. Signed

A unique, open-air museum based around the ancient port and copper mine workings in the heart of the Tamar Valley. Journey back into another time as costumed interpreters help you re-live the daily life of a 19th-century mining village and shipping quay. A tramway takes you deep into the workings of the George and Charlotte mine. Special events include music festivals, classic car shows, and a Victorian food festival.

Times Open all year (ex Xmas wk) 10-6 (4.30 Nov-Etr). Last admission 3.30 (2.30 Nov-Etr).*

Facilities 🅿 ⛽ 🍽 licensed 🅵 (indoor & outdoor) toilets for disabled shop

NEWTON ABBOT

Prickly Ball Farm and Hedgehog Hospital

Denbury Rd, East Ogwell TQ12 6BZ
☎ 01626 362319 & 330685
e-mail: enquiries@pricklyballfarm.co.uk
web: www.pricklyballfarm.com
dir: 1.5m from Newton Abbot on A381 towards Totnes, follow brown heritage signs

See, touch and learn about this wild animal. In mid-season see baby hogs bottle feeding. Find out how to encourage hedgehogs into your garden and how they are put back into the wild. Talks on hedgehogs throughout the day, with a big-screen presentation. There is goat walking, pony grooming, lamb feeding (in season), a petting zoo and pig and sheep feeding.

Times Open Apr-Nov, 10-5. (Recommended last admission 3.30)* **Fees** £5.95 (ch 3-14 £5.25, ch under 3 free, concessions £5.50, special needs £4.25). Family ticket £21 (2ad+2ch)* **Facilities** 🅿 ⌷ 🎠 (indoor & outdoor) ♿ toilets for disabled shop ⊗

PAIGNTON

Paignton & Dartmouth Steam Railway

Queens Park Station, Torbay Rd TQ4 6AF
☎ 01803 555872 📄 01803 664313
e-mail: mail@pdsr.eclipse.co.uk
web: www.paignton-steamrailway.co.uk
dir: from Paignton follow brown tourist signs

Steam trains run for seven miles from Paignton to Kingswear on the former Great Western line, stopping at Goodrington Sands, Churston, and Kingswear, connecting with the ferry crossing to Dartmouth. Combined river excursions available. Please ring for details of special events.

Times Open Jun-Sep, daily 9-5.30 & selected days Oct & Apr-May. Santa specials in Dec.*
Fees Paignton to Kingswear £9 (ch £5.50, pen £8). Family £25. Paignton to Dartmouth (including ferry) £11 (ch £6.50, pen £10). Family £30.* **Facilities** 🅿 ⌷♿ toilets for disabled shop

PAIGNTON

Paignton Zoo Environmental Park

Totnes Rd TQ4 7EU

☎ 01803 697500 📄 01803 523457

e-mail: info@paigntonzoo.org.uk

web: www.paigntonzoo.org.uk

dir: 1m from Paignton town centre on A3022 Totnes road. Follow brown signs

Paignton is one of Britain's biggest zoos, set in a beautiful and secluded woodland valley, where new enclosures are spacious and naturalistic. Your visit will take you through some of the world's threatened habitats - Forest, Savannah, Wetland and Desert, with hundreds of species, many of them endangered and part of conservation breeding programmes. There is a new crocodile swamp. There are regular keeper talks, a children's play area, and special events throughout the year.

Times Open all year, daily 10-6 (5 in winter). Last admission 5 (4 in winter). Closed 25 Dec.* Fees £11.35 (ch 3-15 £7.60, concessions £9.35). Family ticket (2ad & 2ch) £34.10. Joint family saver ticket with Living Coasts £49.15.* Facilities ❷ Ⓟ ⬛ †◎¹ licensed 卅 (indoor & outdoor) ♿ (partly accessible) (footpaths have slight gradient, some steep hills) toilets for disabled shop ⊗

PLYMOUTH

National Marine Aquarium

Rope Walk, Coxside PL4 0LF

☎ 01752 600301 📄 01752 600593

e-mail: enquiries@national-aquarium.co.uk

web: www.national-aquarium.co.uk

dir: A38 to Marsh Mills (Sainsbury's) then towards city centre & follow brown signs for Barbican & Coxside car park

Europe's biggest tank has now got Europe's biggest collection of sharks and rays - Atlantic Ocean is the must see exhibit in 2010. Next to this is Ocean Drifters the UK's largest collection of jellyfish. The National Marine Aquarium is noted for being the safest attraction in the South West so come and enjoy the under water world.

Times Open all year daily, mid Mar-Oct 10-6; Nov-mid Mar 10-5* Fees £11 (ch £6.50, under 5's free, concessions £9). Family £30 (2ad+2ch). Facilities Ⓟ ⬛ 卅 (outdoor) ♿ toilets for disabled shop ⊗

SOUTH MOLTON

Quince Honey Farm

EX36 3AZ

☎ 01769 572401 ▯ 01769 574704
e-mail: info@quincehoney.co.uk
web: www.quincehoney.com
dir: 3.5m W of A361, on N edge of South Molton

Follow the story of honey and beeswax from flower to table. The exhibition allows you to see the world of bees close up in complete safety; hives open at the press of a button revealing the honeybees' secret life. After viewing the bees at work, sample the fruits of their labour in the café or shop.

Times Open daily, Apr-Sep 9-6; Oct 9-5; Shop only Nov-Etr 9-5, closed Sun. Closed 25 Dec-4 Jan.* **Fees** £4 (ch 5-16 £3, pen £3.50)* **Facilities** ❷ ▱ ☐ (outdoor) ⛔ (partly accessible) (no lift to exhibition on first floor) toilets for disabled shop ⊗

TORQUAY

Babbacombe Model Village

Hampton Av, Babbacombe TQ1 3LA

☎ 01803 315315 ▯ 01803 315173
e-mail: sw@model-village.co.uk
web: www.model-village.co.uk
dir: follow brown tourist signs from outskirts of town

See the world recreated in miniature. Thousands of miniature buildings, people and vehicles capture the essence of England's past, present and future, set in four acres of award-winning gardens. Various events are planned, please contact for details.

Times Open all year, times vary.* **Fees** Price varies - please contact for current prices.* **Facilities** ❷ ℗ ▱ ⦿ licensed ⛔ ⛔ (partly accessible) (very steep slopes but access is possible) toilets for disabled shop

TORQUAY

Kents Cavern

Cavern House, 91 Ilsham Rd, Wellswood
TQ1 2JF
☎ 01803 215136
e-mail: caves@kents-cavern.co.uk
web: www.kents-cavern.co.uk
dir: 1.25m NE off B3199, follow brown tourist
signs. 1m from Torquay harbour

Probably the most important Palaeolithic site in
Britain and recognised as one of the country's
most significant archaeological areas. This is
not only a world of spectacular natural beauty,
but also a priceless record of past times, where
a multitude of secrets of mankind, animals and
nature have become trapped and preserved
over the last 500,000 years. 170 years after the
first excavations and with over 80,000 remains
already unearthed, modern research is still
discovering new clues to our past. Please visit
website for details of special events.

Times Open all year daily from 10, last tour 3.30
Nov-Feb, 4 Mar-Jun & Sep-Oct, 4.30 Jul-Aug.*
Facilities ❷ ⓟ ⏛ 🍴 licensed ⋔ (outdoor) ♿
(partly accessible) toilets for disabled shop ⊗

TORQUAY

Living Coasts

Beacon Quay TQ1 2BG
☎ 01803 202470 📄 01803 202471
e-mail: info@livingcoasts.org.uk
web: www.livingcoasts.org.uk
dir: once in Torquay follow A379 and brown
tourist signs to harbour

Living Coasts is a coastal zoo that allows visitors
to take a trip around the coastlines of the world
without leaving Torquay. Specially designed
environments are home to fur seals, puffins,
penguins, ducks, rats, and waders among others.
All the animals can be seen above and below
the water, while the huge meshed aviary allows
the birds to fly free over your head. Visitors can
obtain special joint tickets which will allow them
to visit nearby Paignton Zoo. Contact or see
website for details of special events.

Times Open daily from 10. Closed 25 Dec.
Fees £9.20 (ch over 3 £6.90, concessions £7.15).
Family ticket (2ad+2ch) £28.90. Facilities ❷ ⓟ
⏛ 🍴 licensed ♿ toilets for disabled shop ⊗

ABBOTSBURY

Abbotsbury Swannery

New Barn Rd DT3 4JG

☎ 01305 871858 📠 01305 871092

e-mail: info@abbotsbury-tourism.co.uk

web: www.abbotsbury-tourism.co.uk

dir: turn off A35 at Winterborne Abbas near Dorchester. Abbotsbury on B3157 (coastal road), between Weymouth & Bridport

Abbotsbury is the breeding ground of the only managed colony of mute swans. The swans can be seen safely at close quarters, and the site is also home or stopping point for many wild birds. The highlight of the year is the cygnet season, end of May to the end of June, when there may be over 100 nests on site. Visitors can often take pictures of cygnets emerging from eggs at close quarters. There is an audio-visual show, as well as mass feeding at noon and 4pm daily, and an ugly duckling trail. Children's play area available and a new giant maze planted with willow in the shape of a swan. Find your way to the giant egg at the centre!

Times Open 20 Mar-Oct, daily 10-6 (last admission 5). **Fees** £9.50 (ch £6.50 & concessions £9). **Facilities** 🅿 🖵 �🍴 licensed ⅌ (outdoor) ♿ toilets for disabled shop ⊗

BOURNEMOUTH

Oceanarium

Pier Approach, West Beach BH2 5AA

☎ 01202 311993 📠 01202 311990

e-mail: info@oceanarium.co.uk

web: www.oceanarium.co.uk

dir: from A338 Wessex Way, follow Oceanarium tourist signs

Take an underwater adventure around the waters of the world and come face to face with hundreds of awesome creatures. Home to all your favourites from flamboyant clownfish and tiny terrapins, to stunning sharks and the infamous piranha, immerse yourself in a sea of colour, with 10 spectacular recreated environments including the Great Barrier Reef underwater tunnel. Experience the world's first Interactive Dive Cage - take a virtual adventure to discover more about magnificent sea creatures, without getting wet. And don't miss the Global Meltdown experience and find out what would happen if the ice caps melted and your world was flooded with water.

Times Open all year, daily from 10. Late night opening during school summer hols. Closed 25 Dec. **Fees** Please telephone for admission charges or visit website. **Facilities** 🅿 🍴 licensed ♿ toilets for disabled shop ⊗

BOVINGTON CAMP

The Tank Museum

BH20 6JG

☎ 01929 405096   📄 01929 405360
e-mail: info@tankmuseum.org
web: www.tankmuseum.org
dir: off A352 or A35, follow brown tank signs from Bere Regis & Wool

The Tank Museum houses the world's best collection of tanks. From the first tank ever built to the modern Challenger II, the Museum houses examples from all over the world. This definitive collection comprises of over 250 vehicles dating back to 1909. The Tank Museum is the only place where many of these rare and historic vehicles can be seen. You will come face to face with tanks that have seen action in all the major wars of the 20th century. There are plenty of live action displays all year, please see website for details.

Times Open all year, daily 10-5 (limited opening over Xmas).* **Facilities** 🅿 🅟 ⬚ 🍽 licensed 🍴 (outdoor) ♿ toilets for disabled shop ⊗

BROWNSEA ISLAND

Brownsea Island

BH13 7EE

☎ 01202 707744   📄 01202 701635
e-mail: brownseaisland@nationaltrust.org.uk
web: www.nationaltrust.org.uk
dir: located in Poole Harbour

Peaceful island of woodland, wetland and heath with a rich diversity of wildlife. The island is most famous for its rare red squirrels and as the site of the first experimental Scout camp held by Lord Baden-Powell in 1907. 2010 is the Guiding centenary.

Times Open 13 Mar-Oct, daily, 10-5 (13-26 Mar boats from Sandbanks only, 27-31 Mar full boat service from Poole Quay & Sandbanks). **Fees** £4.90 (ch £2.40). Family ticket £12.20. Group £4.20 (ch £2.10)* **Facilities** ⬚ 🍽 licensed 🍴 (outdoor) ♿ (partly accessible) (countryside property with rough terrain in places. Contact ferry operators to discuss carrying of wheelchairs on boats) toilets for disabled shop ⊗ 🐾

CORFE CASTLE

Corfe Castle

BH20 5EZ

☎ 01929 481294   📠 01929 477067

e-mail: corfecastle@nationaltrust.org.uk

web: www.nationaltrust.org.uk

dir: follow A351 from Wareham to Swanage. Corfe Castle approx 5m

Built in Norman times, the castle was added to by King John. It was defended during the Civil War by Lady Bankes, who surrendered after a stout resistance. Parliament ordered the demolition of the castle, and today it is one of the most impressive ruins in England. Please ring for details of special events.

Times Open all year, daily Mar 10-5; Apr-Sep 10-6; Oct 10-5; Nov-Feb 10-4. (Last admission 30 mins before closing). Closed 25-26 Dec. **Fees** £6.20 (ch £3.10). Family ticket (2ad+3ch) £15.50 or (1ad+3ch) £9.30. Groups £5 (ch £2.50). **Facilities** 🅿 🅟 ▯🍴 licensed ♿ (partly accessible) (steep, uneven cobbled paths & steps, wheelchair access restricted to Outer Bailey only) toilets for disabled shop 🐾

DORCHESTER

Dinosaur Museum

Icen Way DT1 1EW

☎ 01305 269880   📠 01305 268885

e-mail: info@thedinosaurmuseum.com

web: www.thedinosaurmuseum.com

dir: off A35 into Dorchester, museum in town centre just off High East St

Britain's award-winning museum devoted to dinosaurs has a fascinating mixture of fossils, skeletons, life-size reconstructions and interactive displays such as the 'feelies', colour box and parasaurlophus sound. There are multi-media presentations providing an all-round family attraction with something new each year. There is a Great Dinosaur Easter Egg Hunt every Easter weekend.

Times Open all year, daily 9.30-5.30 (10-4.30 Nov-Mar). Closed 24-26 Dec. **Fees** £6.95 (ch £5.50, concessions £5.95, under 4's free). Family ticket £22.50* **Facilities** 🅟 ♿ (partly accessible) (ground floor only accessible) shop

DORCHESTER

Teddy Bear Museum

High East St & Salisbury St DT1 1JU
☎ 01305 266040 📠 01305 268885
e-mail: info@teddybearmuseum.co.uk
web: www.teddybearmuseum.co.uk
dir: off A35, museum in town centre near
Dinosaur Museum

Meet Edward Bear and his extended family
of people-sized bears. See them relaxing and
busying themselves in their Edwardian-style
house. From the earliest teddies of 100 years ago
to today's TV favourites, they are all on display in
this family museum.

Times Open daily, 10-5 (4.30 in winter). Closed
24-26 Dec. Fees £5.75 (ch £4, under 4's free,
concessions £5). Family £18.* Facilities ℗
shop ⊗

DORCHESTER

Tutankhamun Exhibition

High West St DT1 1UW
☎ 01305 269571 📠 01305 268885
e-mail: info@tutankhamun-exhibition.co.uk
web: www.tutankhamun-exhibition.co.uk
dir: off A35 into Dorchester town centre

The exhibition recreates the excitement of one
of the world's greatest discoveries of ancient
treasure. A reconstruction of the tomb and
recreations of its treasures are displayed. The
superbly preserved mummified body of the boy
king can be seen, wonderfully recreated in every
detail. Facsimiles of some of the most famous
treasures, including the golden funerary mask
and the harpooner can be seen in the final
gallery.

Times Open all year daily, Apr-Oct, 9.30-5.30;
Nov-Mar, wkdays 9.30-5, wknds 10-4.30. Closed
24-26 Dec.* Fees £6.95 (ch £5.50, under 5
free, concessions £5.95). Family ticket £22.50.*
Facilities ℗ ♿ shop ⊗

59

ORGANFORD

Farmer Palmer's Farm Park

BH16 6EU

☎ 01202 622022 📠 01202 622182
e-mail: info@farmerpalmers.co.uk
web: www.farmerpalmers.co.uk
dir: From Poole, just off A35 straight over rdbt
past Bakers Arms, signed on left, take 2nd turn,
0.5m after rdbt

Family owned and run Farmer Palmers has been
specially designed for families with children 8
years and under. Many activities include meeting
and learning about the animals, climbing the
straw mountain, going for a tractor trailer ride
and exercising in the soft play area. A fun and
busy day for the family.

Times Open 6 Feb-19 Dec, daily 10-5.30 (10-4
outside main season). Closed mid Dec-early
Feb. Fees £6.75 (ch £6.75, under 2 free,
pen £5.95, disabled & carers £5.75). Family
ticket (2ad+2ch) £25.* Facilities 🅿️🅿️ ⛾
🍽️ licensed 🍴 (indoor & outdoor) ♿ (partly
accessible) (woodland walk & outside animal pen
not level) toilets for disabled shop ⊗

PORTLAND

Portland Castle

Castleton DT5 1AZ

☎ 01305 820539 📠 01305 860853
web: www.english-heritage.org.uk
dir: overlooking Portland harbour

Visit one of Henry VIII's finest coastal forts, in
use right up to World War II. Home to the Wrens
and scene of the US troops' embarkation for the
D-Day invasion in 1944. Explore the Captain's
House and Gardens.

Times Open Apr-Jun & Sep, daily 10-5; Jul-Aug,
daily 10-6; Oct-1 Nov, daily 10-4. Closed 2 Nov-
Mar. Fees £4 (concessions £3.40, ch £2). Family
ticket £10. Prices and opening times are subject
to change in March 2010. Please call 0870 333
1181 for the most up to date prices and opening
times when planning your visit. Facilities 🅿️ ⛾
toilets for disabled shop ⊗ ⛩

WEYMOUTH

Weymouth Sea Life Adventure Park & Marine Sanctuary

Lodmoor Country Park DT4 7SX
☎ 0871 423 2110 & 01305 761070
📄 01305 760165
e-mail: slcweymouth@merlinentertainments.biz
web: www.sealifeeurope.com
dir: on A353

A unique mix of indoor and outdoor attractions set in 7 acres. The park offers a day of fun, bringing you face to face with penguins, otters, seals and much more.

Times Open all year, daily from 10. (Closed 25 Dec).* Facilities 🅿 🅿 ⊑ 🍽 licensed 🍴 (indoor & outdoor) ♿ toilets for disabled shop ⊗

WOOL

Monkey World Ape Rescue Centre

Longthorns BH20 6HH
☎ 01929 462537 & 0800 456600
📄 01929 405414
e-mail: apes@monkeyworld.org
web: www.monkeyworld.org
dir: 1m N of Wool on Bere Regis road

Set up in order to rescue monkeys and apes from abuse and illegal smuggling, Monkey World houses over 230 primates in 65 acres of Dorset woodland. There is the largest group of chimps outside Africa, as well as orang-utans, gibbons, woolly monkeys, lemurs, macaques and marmosets. Those wishing to help the centre continue in its quest to rescue primates from lives of misery may like to take part in the adoption scheme which includes free admission to the park for one year. There are keeper talks every half hour, and the south's largest Great Ape Play Area for kids.

Times Open daily 10-5; Jul-Aug, 10-6. (Last admission 1hr before closing). Closed 25 Dec. Fees £10.50 (ch 3-15 & pen £7.25, students £8.25). Family ticket (1ad+2ch) £21.50, (2ad+2ch) £31. Group rates available.* Facilities 🅿 ⊑ 🍽 licensed 🍴 (indoor & outdoor) ♿ (partly accessible) (woodland walk uneven surface) toilets for disabled shop ⊗

61

Beamish Museum

DH9 0RG

☎ 0191 370 4000   ▤ 0191 370 4001
e-mail: museum@beamish.org.uk
web: www.beamish.org.uk
dir: off A693 & A6076. Signed from A1M junct 63.

Set in 300 acres of countryside, award-winning Beamish recreates life in the early 1800s and 1900s. Costumed staff welcome visitors to a 1913 town street, colliery village, farm and railway station; a re-creation of how people lived and worked. Ride on early electric tramcars, take a ride on a replica of an 1825 steam railway and visit Pockerley Manor where a yeoman farmer and his family would have lived.

Times Open Apr-Oct, daily 10-5; Oct-Mar 10-4 (last admission 3). Closed Mon, Fri & part of Dec.* Fees Summer £16 (ch £10, pen £12.50). Winter £6 (ch & pen £6). Winter visit is centered on town, colliery village & tramway only, other areas are closed.* Facilities ❷ ⊑ 🎮 (outdoor) ♿ (partly accessible) (some 1st floor areas inaccessible, some ground floor areas have steeped access & narrow doorways) toilets for disabled shop ⊗

Killhope The North of England Lead Mining Museum

DL13 1AR

☎ 01388 537505   ▤ 01388 537617
e-mail: info@killhope.org.uk
web: www.killhope.org.uk
dir: beside A689 midway between Stanhope & Alston

Equipped with hard hats and lamps, you can explore the working conditions of Victorian lead miners. The lead mine and 19th-century crushing mill have been restored to look as they would have done in the 1870s, and the 34ft water wheel has been restored to working order. There is also a visitor centre and mineral exhibition, a woodland walk, children's play area and red squirrel and bird hides. Please ring for information on workshops and events.

Times Open Apr-Oct, daily10.30-5. Fees Mine & Site: £6.50 (ch £3.50, concessions £6). Family £17. Site: £4.50 (ch £1.50, concessions £4). Family £11.50* Facilities ❷ ⊑ 🎮 (indoor & outdoor) ♿ (partly accessible) (accessible hide for wildlife viewing) toilets for disabled shop

DURHAM

Old Fulling Mill Museum of Archaeology

The Banks DH1 3EB

☎ 0191 334 1823   📄 0191 334 5694
e-mail: archaeology.museum@durham.ac.uk
web: www.dur.ac.uk/fulling.mill
dir: On river bank directly below Cathedral

Once a key part of Durham's cloth making industry, the Old Fulling Mill is now home to Durham University's Museum of Archaeology. The collections on display provide a fascinating insight into the rich heritage of the north east of England, as well as showcasing items from across Europe. Highlights include outstanding Roman collections together with Anglo-Saxon, Medieval and Tudor finds from Durham City and the local area. Up to date details of exhibitions and the lively programme of family activities at weekends and during school holidays can be found on the museum's website.

Times Open Apr-Oct, daily 10-4; Nov-Mar, Fri-Mon 11.30-3.30* Fees £1 (ch & concessions 50p, students free). Family ticket £2.50.* Facilities
Ⓟ ♿ (partly accessible) (ground floor only accessible) shop ⊗

HARTLEPOOL

Hartlepool's Maritime Experience

Maritime Av TS24 0XZ

☎ 01429 860077   📄 01429 867332
e-mail: info@hartlepoolsmaritimeexperience.com
web: www.hartlepoolsmaritimeexperience.com
dir: from N A19 take A179 and follow signs for marina then historic quay. From S A19 take A689 and follow signs for marina then historic quay

Britain's maritime heritage is brought to life, with the sights, sounds and smells of an 1800s quayside. Learn about the birth of the Royal Navy, and visit the Quayside shops, the admiral's house, Europe's oldest warship afloat HMS Trincomalee and the children's Maritime Adventure Centre. Other features include regular demonstrations of sword fighting, and cannon firing. The new HMS Trincomalee exhibition is now open.

Times Open all year daily summer 10-5, winter 11-3. Closed 25-26 Dec & 1 Jan.* Fees £7.75 (ch £4.75, concessions £4.75-£5.75). Family ticket (2ad+3ch) £20. Museum is free.* Facilities
Ⓟ 🖵 🍴 licensed ⅌ (outdoor) ♿ (partly accessible) toilets for disabled shop ⊗

SHILDON

Locomotion: The National Railway Museum at Shildon

DL4 1PQ

☎ 01388 777999   📠 01388 777999
e-mail: info@locomotion.uk.com
web: www.locomotion.uk.com
dir: A1(M) junct 68, take A68 & A6072 to Shildon, attraction is 0.25m SE of town centre

Timothy Hackwood (1786-1850) was an important figure in the development of steam travel. He constructed Puffing Billy for William Hedley, ran Stephenson's Newcastle Works, and also became the first superintendent of the Stockton & Darlington Railway. The museum and house detail Hackwood's life and the steam transport revolution, as well as displaying working models and locomotives from various periods. Steam train rides are available throughout the year, on event days. The Collections building contains 60 vehicles from the National Collection.

Times Open Apr-5 Oct, daily 10-5; 6 Oct-1 Apr, daily, 10-4. Buildings at western end of site are closed Mon & Tue in winter. **Fees** Free, small charge for train rides.* **Facilities** 🅿 Ⓟ ᗡ 🎋 (indoor & outdoor) ♿ toilets for disabled shop ⊗

AUDLEY END

Audley End House & Gardens

CB11 4JF

☎ 01799 522842   📠 01799 521276
web: www.english-heritage.org.uk
dir: 1m W of Saffron Walden on B1383

One of the most significant Jacobean houses in England with 31 opulent rooms on view. Set in a 'Capability' Brown landscaped park, with walled Victorian kitchen garden.

Times Open Apr-Sep, Wed-Sun & BH 11-5 (Sat last admission 2.30); Oct-1 Nov, Wed-Sun 11-4. (Sat last admission 2.30). Closed Nov-Mar except for Festive Fun wknds (21-22, 28-29 Nov & 5-6, 12-13, 19-20 Dec). **Fees** House & Gardens: £10.70 (concessions £9.10, ch £5.40). Family £26.80. Service Wing & Gardens: £7.70 (concessions £6.50, ch £3.90). Family £19.30. Prices & opening times are subject to change in March 2010. Please call 0870 333 1181 for the most up to date prices and opening times. **Facilities** 🅿 ᗡ 🎋 ♿ (partly accessible) (bridges either have a step or steep slope) toilets for disabled shop ⊞

COLCHESTER

Colchester Castle Museum

Castle Park, High St CO1 1TJ
☎ 01206 282939 📠 01206 282925
e-mail: museums@colchester.gov.uk
web: www.colchestermuseums.org.uk
dir: at E end of High St

The largest Norman castle keep in Europe - built over the remains of the magnificent Roman Temple of Claudius which was destroyed by Boudicca in AD60. Colchester was the first capital of Roman Britain, and the archaeological collections are among the finest in the country. Please telephone or visit website for details of a range of events held throughout the year.

Times Open all year, Mon-Sat 10-5, Sun 11-5. Closed Xmas/New Year* Fees £5.50 (ch & concessions £3.50).* Facilities ℗ 🍴 (indoor & outdoor) ♿ (partly accessible) (Roman vaults not accessible) toilets for disabled shop ⊗

COLCHESTER

Colchester Zoo

Stanway, Maldon Rd CO3 0SL
☎ 01206 331292 📠 01206 331392
e-mail: enquiries@colchester-zoo.co.uk
web: www.colchester-zoo.co.uk
dir: turn off A12 onto A1124, follow elephant signs

One of England's finest zoos, Colchester Zoo has over 250 species of animal. Visitors can feed the elephants and giraffes, handle a snake, and see parrots, seals, penguins and birds of prey all appearing in informative daily displays. Enclosures include Spirit of Africa with the breeding group of African elephants, Playa Patagonia where sea lions swim above your head in a 24 metre underwater tunnel, Penguin Shores, Chimp World, and the Kingdom of the Wild, with giraffes, zebras and rhinos. There is also an undercover soft play complex, two road trains, four adventure play areas, eating places and gift shops, all set in 60 acres of gardens. Orangutan Forest is Colchester Zoo's latest new enclosure.

Times Open all year, daily from 9.30. Last admission 5.30 (1hr before dusk out of season). Closed 25 Dec. Fees £14.99 (ch 3-14 £7.99)* Facilities ℗ 🍴 licensed 🍴 toilets for disabled shop ⊗

STANSTED

Mountfitchet Castle Experience

CM24 8SP

☎ 01279 813237 📠 01279 816391
e-mail: office@mountfitchetcastle.com
web: www.mountfitchetcastle.com
dir: off B1383, in village. 2m from M11 junct 8

Come and see a Norman motte and bailey castle
and village reconstructed as it was in Norman
England of 1066, on its original historic site.
A vivid illustration of village life in Domesday
England, complete with houses, church, seige
tower, seige weapons, and many types of animals
roaming freely. Animated wax figures in all the
buildings give historical information to visitors.
Adjacent to the castle is the House on the Hill Toy
Museum, a nostalgic trip through memories of
childhood days. The whole experience is a unique
all-weather, all-in-one heritage entertainment
complex.

Times Open daily, mid Mar-mid Nov, 10-5.
Fees £8.50 (ch £6.50, concessions £8).*
Facilities 🅿 Ⓟ ⊑ 🎋 (outdoor) ♿ (partly
accessible) (partly accessible due to grassy
slopes, cobbled areas & steps) toilets for
disabled shop 🚫

WALTHAM ABBEY

Lee Valley Park Farms

Stubbins Hall Ln, Crooked Mile EN9 2EG
☎ 01992 892781 & 702200
📠 01992 899561
e-mail: hayeshill@leevalleypark.org.uk
web: www.leevalleypark.org.uk
dir: M25 junct 26, follow to Waltham Abbey. 2m
from Waltham Abbey on B914

Lee Valley Park offers a unique visitor experience,
two farms for the price of one. Hayes Hill Farm, a
traditional style farm with a variety of different
animals including pigs, goats and rare breeds,
as well as the Pet Centre which houses small
mammals and reptiles. You can take a stroll or
a tractor and trailer ride to Holyfield Hall Farm, a
modern dairy and arable farm. Visit Rabbit World
with the giant bunnies, explore the paddock
pathways then play in the adventure play area
and the new Bundle Barn soft play area.

Times Open Feb half term-Oct, daily 10-5.
Fees £6.80 (ch 2+ £5.40, concessions £5.40).
Family tickets from £11. Group & season tickets
available. Prices are due for review on 1 April
2010.* Facilities 🅿 Ⓟ ⊑ 🎋 (indoor &
outdoor) ♿ toilets for disabled shop

WALTHAM ABBEY

Royal Gunpowder Mills

Beaulieu Dr EN9 1JY

☎ 01992 707370 📄 01992 707372

e-mail: info@royalgunpowdermills.com

web: www.royalgunpowdermills.com

dir: M25 junct 26. Follow signs for A121 to Waltham Abbey at rdbt, entrance in Beaulieu Drive

Set in 170 acres of natural parkland with 20 buildings of major historic importance, the site mixes fascinating history, exciting science and beautiful surroundings to produce a magical day out for all ages. Over 20 special weekend events with may living history and re-enactments, VE Day celebrations, Steam & Country Show, Rocket & Space event and a Classic Vehicle Show. Easy access, children's activities, exhibitions, guided land train tours, a woodland walk and so much more!

Times Open end Apr-end Sep, 11-5, last entry 3.30. (Wknds, BHs & Wed in summer school hols) Fees £7.20 (ch 5-15 £4.40, concessions £6.20, under 5's free) Family ticket (2ad & 3ch) £23.20* Facilities 🅿 Ⓟ 🖵 🍴 (outdoor) ♿ (partly accessible) (stairs provide access to top of Wildlife Tower. Some paths on nature walk are uneven. Lift available in main exhibition, number of ramps on site) toilets for disabled shop ⊗

BOURTON-ON-THE-WATER

Birdland

Rissington Rd GL54 2BN

☎ 01451 820480 📄 01451 822398

e-mail: simonb@birdland.co.uk

web: www.birdland.co.uk

dir: on A429

Birdland is a natural setting of woodland, river and gardens, which is inhabited by over 500 birds; flamingos, pelicans, penguins, cranes, storks, cassowary and waterfowl can be seen on various aspects of the water habitat. Over 50 aviaries of parrots, falcons, pheasants, hornbills, touracos, pigeons, ibis and many more. Tropical, Toucan and Desert Houses are home to the more delicate species. Only group of king penguins in England.

Times Open all year, Apr-Oct, daily 10-6; Nov-Mar, daily 10-4. (Last admission 1hr before closing). Closed 25 Dec.* Fees £6 (concessions £5). Family ticket (2ad+2ch) £18.* Facilities Ⓟ 🖵 🍴 (indoor & outdoor) ♿ toilets for disabled shop

CIRENCESTER

Corinium Museum

Park St GL7 2BX
☎ 01285 655611
e-mail: museums@cotswold.gov.uk
web: www.cotswold.gov.uk/go/museum
dir: in town centre

Discover the treasures of the Cotswolds at the new Corinium Museum. Two years and over £5 million in the making, it has been transformed into a must-see attraction. Featuring archaeological and historical material from Cirencester and the Cotswolds, from prehistoric times to the 19th century. The museum is known for its Roman mosaic sculpture and other material from one of Britain's largest Roman towns. New on display are Anglo-Saxon treasures from Lechlade bringing to life this little-known period. The museum also houses Medieval, Tudor, Civil War and 18th-19th century displays.

Times Open Mon-Sat 10-5, Sun 2-5 (closes 4pm Nov-Mar). Closed Xmas & New Year. **Fees** £4.25 (ch £2.25, students £2.75, con £3.50). Family ticket £11.50 **Facilities** Ⓟ ☕ 🍽 licensed ♿ toilets for disabled shop 🚫

CLEARWELL

Clearwell Caves Ancient Iron Mines

GL16 8JR
☎ 01594 832535 📠 01594 833362
e-mail: jw@clearwellcaves.com
web: www.clearwellcaves.com
dir: 1.5m S of Coleford town centre, off B4228 follow brown tourist signs

These impressive natural caves have also been mined since the earliest times for paint pigment and iron ore. Today visitors explore nine large caverns with displays of local mining and geology. There is a colour room where ochre pigments are still produced and a blacksmith shop. Deep level excursions available for more adventurous visitors, must be pre-booked. Christmas fantasy event when the caverns are transformed into a world of light and sound.

Times Open Mar-Oct, daily 10-5; Jan-Feb, Sat-Sun 10-5; Xmas Fantasy 1-24 Dec, daily 10-5. **Fees** £5.80 (ch £3.80, concessions £5.30) Family ticket £17.30. **Facilities** 🅟 Ⓟ ☕ 🪑 (outdoor) ♿ (partly accessible) (w/chair need 2 helpers on steep pathway) toilets for disabled shop 🚫

CRANHAM

Prinknash Bird & Deer Park

GL4 8EX

☎ 01452 812727 📠 01452 812727
web: www.thebirdpark.com
dir: M5 junct 11a, A417 towards Cirencester, take 1st exit signed A46 Stroud. Follow brown tourist signs

Nine acres of parkland and lakes make a beautiful home for black swans, geese and other water birds. There are also exotic birds such as white and Indian blue peacocks and crown cranes, as well as tame fallow deer and pygmy goats. The Golden Wood is stocked with ornamental pheasants, and leads to the reputedly haunted monks' fishpond, which contains trout. An 80-year old, free-standing, 16 foot tall Wendy House in the style of a Tudor house is located near the picnic area. A pair of reindeer, the only ones to be found in the Cotswolds, can also be seen.

Times Open all year, summer 10-5, winter 10-4. Closed 25 Dec & Good Fri* Fees £5.50 (ch £3.50, pen £4.50)* Facilities ℗ ℗ ⊑ 🏕 (outdoor) ♿ toilets for disabled shop ⊗

GLOUCESTER

Gloucester Folk Museum **FREE**

99-103 Westgate St GL1 2PG
☎ 01452 396868 & 396869
📠 01452 330495
e-mail: folk.museum@gloucester.gov.uk
web: www.gloucester.gov.uk/folkmuseum
dir: from W - A40 & A48; from N - A38 & M5, from E - A40 & B4073; from S - A4173 & A38

Three floors of splendid Tudor and Jacobean timber-framed buildings dating from the 16th and 17th centuries along with new buildings housing the dairy, ironmonger's shop and wheelwright and carpenter workshops. Local history, domestic life, crafts, trades and industries from 1500 to the present, including Toys and Childhood gallery with hands-on toys and a puppet theatre, the Siege of Gloucester, a Victorian class room, Victorian kitchen and laundry equipment. A wide range of exhibitions, hands-on activities, events, demonstrations and role play sessions are held throughout the year. There is an attractive cottage garden and courtyard for events, often with live animals, and outside games.

Times Open all year, Tue-Sat, 10-5* Facilities ℗ 🏕 (outdoor) ♿ (partly accessible) shop ⊗

69

GLOUCESTER

The National Waterways Museum

Llanthony Warehouse, The Docks GL1 2EH
☎ 01452 318200   📄 01452 318202
e-mail: gloucester@thewaterwaystrust.org.uk
web: www.nwm.org.uk
dir: From M5, A40. In city follow brown signs for historic docks

Based in Gloucester Docks, this museum takes up three floors of a seven-storey Victorian warehouse, and documents the 200-year history of Britain's water-based transport. The emphasis is on hands-on experience, including working models and engines, interactive displays, actual craft, computer interactions and the national collection of inland waterways. Boat trips are also available between Easter and October.

Times Open all year, daily 10-5. (Last admission 4). Closed 25 Dec.* Facilities ℗ ℗ ⊡ 🍽️ licensed ⊓ (outdoor) ♿ toilets for disabled shop ⊗

GUITING POWER

Cotswold Farm Park

GL54 5UG

☎ 01451 850307   📄 01451 850423
e-mail: info@cotswoldfarmpark.co.uk
web: www.cotswoldfarmpark.co.uk
dir: signed off B4077 from M5 junct 9

Meet over 50 breeding flocks and herds of rare farm animals. There are lots of activities for the youngsters, with rabbits and guinea pigs to cuddle, lambs and goat kids to bottle feed, tractor and trailer-rides, battery powered tractors, Touch Barn, Maze Quest, a Jumping Pillow and safe rustic-themed play areas both indoors and outside. Lambing occurs in early May, followed by shearing and then milking demonstrations later in the season. The Cotswold Farm Park also has its own 40-pitch camping and caravanning site.

Times Open mid Mar-mid Sep, daily (then open wknds only until end Oct & Autumn half term 10.30-5).* Fees £6.75 (ch £5.50, concessions £6.25). Family ticket £22.* Facilities ℗ ⊡ ⊓ (outdoor) ♿ (partly accessible) toilets for disabled shop ⊗

MORETON-IN-MARSH

Cotswold Falconry Centre

Batsford Park GL56 9AB
☎ 01386 701043
e-mail: mail@cotswold-falconry.co.uk
web: www.cotswold-falconry.co.uk
dir: 1m W of Moreton-in-Marsh on A44

Conveniently located by the Batsford Park Arboretum, the Cotswold Falconry gives daily demonstrations in the art of falconry. The emphasis here is on breeding and conservation, and over 100 eagles, hawks, owls and falcons can be seen.

Times Open mid Feb-mid Nov, 10.30-5.30. (Last admission 5).* Facilities 🅿 ⬛ 🎋 (outdoor) toilets for disabled shop ⊗

NEWENT

The National Birds of Prey Centre

GL18 1JJ
☎ 0870 9901992 📄 01531 821389
e-mail: kb@nbpc.co.uk
web: www.nbpc.co.uk
dir: follow A40, right onto B4219 towards Newent. Follow brown tourist signs from Newent town

Trained birds can be seen at close quarters in the Hawk Walk and the Owl Courtyard and there are also breeding aviaries, a gift shop, bookshop, picnic areas, coffee shop and children's play area. Birds are flown three times daily in summer and winter, giving an exciting and educational display. There are over 80 aviaries on view with 40 species.

Times Open all year daily 10.30-5.30 (closed 25-26 Dec).* Facilities 🅿 ⬛ 🎋 toilets for disabled shop ⊗

SLIMBRIDGE

WWT Slimbridge

GL2 7BT

☎ 01453 891900 📄 01453 890827
e-mail: info.slimbridge@wwt.org.uk
web: www.wwt.org.uk
dir: off A38, signed from M5 junct 13 & 14

Slimbridge is home to the world's largest collection of swans, geese, ducks and flamingos. An internationally renowned reserve with an astounding array of wildlife from water voles to waders, hares to dragonflies. Facilities include a tropical house, discovery centre, children's outdoor play area, shop and restaurant.

Times Open all year, daily from 9.30-5.30 (winter 5). Closed 25 Dec.* Fees £7.95 (ch £4.35, under 4's free, concessions £6.15). Family £20.50.*
Facilities 🅿 🖵 🍽 licensed 🎪 (outdoor) ♿ toilets for disabled shop ⊗

WESTONBIRT

Westonbirt, The National Arboretum

GL8 8QS

☎ 01666 880220 📄 01666 880559
web: www.westonbirtarboretum.com
dir: 3m S Tetbury on A433

Begun in 1829, this arboretum contains one of the finest and most important collections of trees and shrubs in the world. There are 18,000 specimens, planted from 1829 to the present day, covering 600 acres of landscaped Cotswold countryside. Magnificent displays of Rhododendrons, Azaleas, Magnolias and wild flowers, and a blaze of colour in the autumn from the national collection of Japanese Maples. Special events include the Festival of the Tree (Aug BH) and the Enchanted Christmas Trail (every Fri, Sat, Sun in December until Xmas).

Times Open all year, daily 10-8 or sunset. Visitor centre & shop all year. Closed Xmas & New Year.* Facilities 🅿 🖵 🍽 licensed 🎪 (outdoor) ♿ toilets for disabled shop

ASHTON-UNDER-LYNE

Portland Basin Museum **FREE**

Portland Place OL7 0QA
☎ 0161 343 2878 📠 0161 343 2869
e-mail: portland.basin@tameside.gov.uk
web: www.tameside.gov.uk
dir: M60 junct 23 into town centre. Museum near
Cross Hill Street & car park. Follow brown signs
with canal boat image

Exploring the social and industrial history of
Tameside, this museum is part of the recently
rebuilt Ashton Canal Warehouse, constructed in
1834. Visitors can walk around a 1920s street,
dress up in old hats and gloves, steer a virtual
canal boat, and see the original canal powered
waterwheel that once drove the warehouse
machinery. Portland Basin Museum also features
changing exhibitions and event programme- so
there's always something new to see!

Times Open all year, Tue-Sun 10-5. (Closed
Mon, ex BHs)* Facilities ❷ ⓟ ⦿ licensed 乕
(outdoor) ⑆ toilets for disabled shop ⊗

MANCHESTER

Imperial War Museum North **FREE**

The Quays, Trafford Wharf Rd, Trafford Park
M17 1TZ
☎ 0161 836 4000 📠 0161 836 4012
e-mail: iwmnorth@iwm.org.uk
web: www.iwm.org.uk
dir: M60 junct 9, join Parkway (A5081) towards
Trafford Park. At 1st island take 3rd exit onto
Village Way. At next island take 2nd exit onto
Warren Bruce Rd. Right at T-junct onto Trafford
Wharf Rd. Alternatively, leave M602 junct 3 and
follow signs

Imperial War Museum North features a wide
range of permanent and temporary exhibitions
exploring all the ways people's lives have been
and still are affected by war and conflict. The
award-winning building (designed by architect
Daniel Libeskind) symbolises the world torn apart
by conflict.

Times Open all year, Mar-Oct, daily 10-6; Nov-Feb
10-5. Closed 24-26 Dec. Facilities ❷ ⓟ ⲇ 乕
(indoor) ⑆ toilets for disabled shop ⊗

MANCHESTER

Manchester Museum FREE

The University of Manchester, Oxford Rd
M13 9PL
☎ 0161 275 2634 & 2643
📄 0161 275 2676
e-mail: museum@manchester.ac.uk
web: www.manchester.ac.uk/museum
dir: S of city centre on B5117

Discover the natural wonders of the world and the many cultures it is home to. The objects in the Museum's 15 galleries tell the story of the past, present and future of our planet. Come face to face with live poison dart frogs, fossils of prehistoric creatures and much more besides. Handle objects from the collection, take part in hands-on activities or enjoy a glass of wine or cup of coffee whilst exploring the latest ideas in science, culture and the arts. See website for details of family and adult events.

Times Open all year, Tue-Sat 10-5, Sun-Mon & BHs 11-4. Closed Good Fri.* Facilities ℗ ℗ ☐ ⑪ licensed � (indoor) toilets for disabled shop ⊗

MANCHESTER

Manchester United Museum & Tour Centre

Sir Matt Busby Way, Old Trafford M16 0RA
☎ 0161 868 8000 📄 0161 868 8861
e-mail: tours@manutd.co.uk
web: www.manutd.com
dir: 2m from city centre, off A56

This museum was opened in 1986 and was the first purpose-built British football museum. It covers the history of Manchester United in words, pictures, sound and vision, from its inception in 1878 to the present day. Legends Tours are now available with ex players, see website for full details.

Times Open daily 9.30-5 (open until 30mins before kick off on match days). Closed some days over Xmas & New Year. Most match days the museum is closed due to matchday hospitality. Fees Stadium tour & Museum: £12.50 (ch & concessions £8.50) Family ticket (4) £38, (5) £45. Museum only £9 (ch & concessions £7) Family ticket (4) £28, (5) £35. Facilities ℗ ⑪ licensed � (indoor) ♿ toilets for disabled shop ⊗

MANCHESTER

Museum of Science and Industry

Liverpool Rd, Castlefield M3 4FP
☎ 0161 832 2244 🖷 0161 833 1471
e-mail: marketing@mosi.org.uk
web: www.mosi.org.uk
dir: follow brown tourist signs from city centre

Uncover Manchester's industrial past and learn the fascinating stories of the people who contributed to the history and science of a city which helped shape the modern world. Located on the site of the world's oldest passenger railway station, MoSI's action-packed galleries, working exhibits and costumed characters tell the amazing story of revolutionary discoveries and remarkable inventions both past and present. There is a programme of changing exhibitions, please see the website for details.

Times Open all year, daily 10-5. Last admission 4.30. Closed 24-26 Dec & 1 Jan.* Facilities ℗
℗ ⬚ ⬚ licensed ⋈ (indoor & outdoor) ♿ toilets for disabled shop ⊗

MANCHESTER

Urbis **FREE**

Cathedral Gardens M4 3BG
☎ 0161 605 8200 🖷 0161 605 8201
e-mail: info@urbis.org.uk
web: www.urbis.org.uk
dir: opposite Victoria railway station

Urbis is an exhibition centre about city life. On your visit explore five floors of changing exhibitions, offering a unique insight into the culture of the modern city. Family workshops take place every weekend, see the website for details.

Times Open all year, daily 10-6.* Facilities
℗ ⬚ ⬚ licensed ⋈ (outdoor) ♿ toilets for disabled shop ⊗

75

ANDOVER

Finkley Down Farm Park

SP11 6NF

☎ 01264 352195 📄 01264 363172
e-mail: admin@finkleydownfarm.co.uk
web: www.finkleydownfarm.co.uk
dir: signed from A303 & A343, 1.5m N of A303 &
2m E of Andover

This fun family farm park is jam packed with
things to do. You can join in with feeding
time, groom a pony, or cuddle a rabbit. Lots of
activities are scheduled throughout the day, or
kids can just let off steam in the playground
or on the trampolines. From chipmunks to
chinchillas, pygmy goats to peacocks, and lambs
to llamas, Finkley Down Farm has something for
everyone.

Times Open mid Mar-Oct, daily 10-6 (last
admission 5).* **Fees** £6.75 (ch £5.75, pen £6.25).
Family ticket (2ad+2ch) £24* **Facilities** 🅿 ⬛
🍴 (outdoor) ♿ toilets for disabled shop ⊗

ASHURST

Longdown Activity Farm

Longdown SO40 7EH

☎ 023 8029 2837 📄 023 8029 3376
e-mail: enquiries@longdownfarm.co.uk
web: www.longdownfarm.co.uk
dir: off A35 between Lyndhurst & Southampton

Fun for all the family with a variety of hands-on
activities every day, including small animal
handling and bottle feeding calves and goat kids.
Indoor and outdoor play areas, with trampolines
and ball pools and bumpy tractor rides. Tearoom,
picnic area and excellent gift shop. Farm shop
selling locally sourced produce.

Times Open Feb-Oct & 12-24 Dec, daily; wknds
Nov-mid Dec 10-5.* **Fees** £7 (ch 3-14 &
concessions £6). Saver ticket £24 (2ad+2ch).*
Facilities 🅿 ⬛ 🍴 (indoor & outdoor) ♿ (partly
accessible) (concrete path for wheelchairs)
toilets for disabled shop ⊗

BASINGSTOKE

Milestones - Hampshire's Living History Museum

Basingstoke Leisure Park, Churchill Way West
RG22 6PG
☎ 01256 477766 📄 01256 477784
e-mail: louise.mackay@hants.gov.uk
web: www.milestones-museum.com
dir: M3 junct 6, take ringway road (West). Follow brown Leisure Park signs

Milestones brings Hampshire's recent past to life through stunning period street scenes and exciting interactive areas, all under one roof. Nationally important collections of transport, technology and everyday life are presented in an entertaining way. Staff in period costumes, mannequins and sounds all bring the streets to life. Various events through the year.

Times Open all year, Tue-Fri & BHs 10-5, Sat-Sun 11-5. Closed Mon, 25-26 Dec & 1 Jan.*
Fees £7.50 (ch 5-15 £4.50, concessions £6.75). Family ticket (2ad+2ch) £22. Facilities 🅿 🅟 ⌻ 🛋 (indoor & outdoor) ♿ (partly accessible) toilets for disabled shop ⊗

BEAULIEU

Beaulieu : National Motor Museum
SO42 7ZN
☎ 01590 612345 📄 01590 612624
e-mail: info@beaulieu.co.uk
web: www.beaulieu.co.uk
dir: M27 junct 2, A326, B3054, then follow tourist signs

Set in the heart of William the Conqueror's New Forest, on the banks of the Beaulieu River, stands this 16th-century house. It has become most famous as the home of the National Motor Museum. The site also contains the picturesque abbey building ruins, which have an exhibition on life in the middle ages, and various family treasures and memorabilia. The Secret Army Exhibition tells the story of the secret agents trained at the Beaulieu 'Finishing School' during WWII.

Times Open all year - Palace House & Gardens, National Motor Museum, Beaulieu Abbey & Exhibition of Monastic Life, May-Sep 10-6; Oct-Apr 10-5. Closed 25 Dec.* Fees Please contact for current prices.* Facilities 🅿 🅟 ⌻ 🍴 licensed 🛋 (outdoor) toilets for disabled shop

EXBURY

Exbury Gardens & Railway

Exbury Estate Office SO45 1AZ
☎ 023 8089 1203 📠 023 8089 9940
e-mail: nigel.philpott@exbury.co.uk
web: www.exbury.co.uk
dir: from M27 W junct 2, 3m from Beaulieu, off B3054

A 200-acre landscaped woodland garden on the east bank of the Beaulieu River, with one of the finest collections of rhododendrons, azaleas, camellias and magnolias in the world - as well as many rare and beautiful shrubs and trees. A labyrinth of tracks and paths enable you to explore the beautiful gardens and walks. Year round interest is ensured in various parts of the gardens and a steam railway has several features. Exbury is National Collection holder for Nyssa and Oxydendrum, spectacular trees for autumn colour.

Times Open Mar-mid Nov, daily 10-5; Santa Steam Specials in Dec.* **Fees** £8 (ch under 3 free, ch 3-15 £1.50, concessions £7.50). Family ticket (2ad+3ch) £18.50. Railway £3.50. The railway has 4 carriages accessible to wheelchairs.* **Facilities** 🅿 🅟 🍽 licensed 🎪 (outdoor) ♿ (partly accessible) (most pathways accessible) toilets for disabled shop

FAREHAM

Royal Armouries Fort Nelson

Portsdown Hill Rd PO17 6AN
☎ 01329 233734 📠 01329 822092
e-mail: fnenquiries@armouries.org.uk
web: www.royalarmouries.org
dir: from M27 junct 11, follow brown tourist signs for Royal Armouries

Home to the Royal Armouries' collection of over 350 big guns and cannon, this superbly restored Victorian fort overlooks Portsmouth Harbour. Built in the 1860s to deter a threatened French invasion, there are secret tunnels, underground chambers and grass ramparts to explore with daily guided tours and explosive gun firings. There are free children's activity days on Tuesday and Thursday during school holidays.

Times Open all year, Apr-Oct, daily 10-5 (Wed 11-5); Nov-Mar, daily 10.30-4 (Wed 11.30-4). Closed 24-26 Dec. **Fees** Free. There may be a charge for special events/workshops. **Facilities** 🅿 🚻 🎪 (outdoor) ♿ toilets for disabled shop 🚫

GOSPORT

Explosion! Museum of Naval Firepower

Priddy's Hard PO12 4LE
☎ 023 9250 5600 📠 023 9250 5605
e-mail: info@explosion.org.uk
web: www.explosion.org.uk
dir: M27 junct 11, A32 and follow signs

Explosion! The Museum of Naval Firepower is set in the green Heritage Area of Priddy's Hard in Gosport on the shores of Portsmouth Harbour, telling the story of naval firepower from the days of gunpowder to modern missiles. Come face to face with the atom bomb, the Exocet missile and the Gatling Gun and take a trip into the fascinating story of the men and women who supplied the Royal Navy. Walk around the buildings that were a state secret for 200 years and discover the Grand Magazine, an amazing vault once packed full with gunpowder, now a stunning multimedia film show.

Times Open all year, Sat-Sun only, 10-4.*
Fees £4 (ch £2, concessions £3). Family ticket £10* Facilities 🅿 ⬚ 🍴 licensed 🍴 (outdoor) toilets for disabled shop ⊗

GOSPORT

Royal Navy Submarine Museum

Haslar Rd PO12 2AS
☎ 023 9251 0354 📠 023 9251 1349
e-mail: rnsubs@rnsubmus.co.uk
web: www.rnsubmus.co.uk
dir: M27 junct 11, follow brown tourist signs

Step inside at the Royal Navy Submarine Museum, which overlooks Portsmouth Harbour. Former submariners guide you through where they would work, eat and sleep on board HMS Alliance. Peer into the only surviving X-craft to have seen action during WWII and walk onto the Royal Navy's first submarine Holland 1.

Times Open all year, Apr-Oct 10-5.30; Nov-Mar 10-4.30. (Last tour 1 hour before closing). Closed 24 Dec & 25 Jan.* Fees £9 (ch & concessions £6). Family (2ad+4ch) £20.* Facilities 🅿 🅿 ⬚ 🍴 (outdoor) ♿ (partly accessible) (no wheelchair access to the Alliance WWII submarine - film version of tour available) toilets for disabled shop ⊗

HURST CASTLE

Hurst Castle

SO4 0FF

☎ 01590 642344

web: www.english-heritage.org.uk

dir: on Pebble Spit S of Keyhaven

Built by Henry VIII, Hurst Castle was the pride of Tudor England's coastal defences. Crouched menacingly on a shingle spit, the castle has a fascinating history, including involvement in the smuggling trade in the 17th and 18th centuries.

Times Open 21 Mar-Oct, daily 10.30-5.30.*
Facilities 🖵 ⊗ ♯

MARWELL

Marwell Zoological Park

Colden Common SO21 1JH

☎ 01962 777407   🖹 01962 777511

e-mail: marwell@marwell.org.uk

web: www.marwell.org.uk

dir: M3 junct 11 or M27 junct 5. On B2177, follow brown tourist signs

Marwell has over 200 species of rare and wonderful animals including tigers, snow leopards, rhino, meerkats, hippo and zebra. Highlights include The World of Lemurs, Encounter Village, Tropical World with its rainforest environment, Into Africa for giraffes and monkeys, Penguin World and Desert Carnivores. Recent additions include an exciting new snow leopard enclosure and a walkway that enables visitors to come face to face with the giraffes. Marwell is dedicated to saving endangered species and every visit helps conservation work. With road and rail trains, holiday activities, gift shop and adventure playgrounds Marwell provides fun and interest for all ages.

Times Open all year, daily 10-6 (summer), 10-4 (winter). (Last admission 90 mins before closing). Closed 25 Dec.* Facilities 🅿 🖵 ⭕ licensed ⋈ (outdoor) ♿ (partly accessible) toilets for disabled shop ⊗

MIDDLE WALLOP

Museum of Army Flying

SO20 8DY

☎ 01264 784421   🖷 01264 781694
e-mail: administration@flying-museum.org.uk
web: www.flying-museum.org.uk
dir: on A343, between Andover & Salisbury

One of the country's finest historical collections of military kites, gliders, aeroplanes and helicopters. Imaginative dioramas and displays trace the development of Army flying from before the First World War to more recent conflicts in Ireland, the Falklands and the Gulf. Sit at the controls of a real Scout or Apache attack helicopters and test your skills on the flight simulator, plus children's education centre and 1940s house.

Times Open all year, daily 10-4.30. Closed week prior to Xmas. Evening visits by special arrangement. Private functions welcome.*
Fees £7 (ch £4.50, concessions £5) Family £21.*
Facilities 🅿 ⬚ 🍽 licensed 🎠 (outdoor) ♿ toilets for disabled shop ⊗

NEW ALRESFORD

Watercress Line

The Railway Station SO24 9JG
☎ 01962 733810   🖷 01962 735448
e-mail: info@watercressline.co.uk
web: www.watercressline.co.uk
dir: stations at Alton & Alresford signed off A31, follow brown tourist signs

The Watercress Line runs through ten miles of rolling scenic countryside between Alton and Alresford. All four stations are 'dressed' in period style, and there's a locomotive yard and picnic area at Ropley. Special events throughout the year including Thomas the Tank Engine, War on the Line and Santa Specials.

Times Open Jan-Oct wknds, May-Sep midwk, Aug daily.* **Fees** Unlimited travel for the day, £12 (ch £6). Family ticket £30 (2ad+2ch). Charge for dogs. Pre-booked groups 15+ discount available.
Facilities 🅿🅿 ⬚ 🍽 licensed 🎠 (outdoor) ♿ (partly accessible) (ramp access to trains) toilets for disabled shop

OWER

Paultons Park

SO51 6AL

☎ 023 8081 4442   ▤ 023 8081 3025
e-mail: guestservices@paultons.co.uk
web: www.paultonspark.co.uk
dir: exit M27 junct 2, near junct A31 & A36

Paultons Park offers a great day out for all the family with over 50 different attractions. Many fun activities include the Edge Cobra ride, drop rides, roller coaster, 6-lane astroglide, teacup ride, log flume, pirate ship swingboat, dragon roundabout, and wave-runner coaster. Attractions for younger children include Water Kingdom, Tiny Tots Town, Rabbit Ride, the Magic Forest where nursery rhymes come to life, Wonderful World of Wind in the Willows and the Ladybird ride. In beautiful parkland setting with extensive 'Capability' Brown gardens landscaped with ponds and aviaries for exotic birds; lake and hedge maze. There is also the Village Life Museum. Something for everyone.

Times Open mid Mar-Oct, daily 10-6; Nov & Dec, wknds only until Xmas.* **Fees** £17.50 (adults & ch over 1mtr tall) (Free entry only for children under 1mtr tall). Range of Family Supersavers.* **Facilities** ℗ ⊑ ⑩ licensed 🎹 (outdoor) ♿ (partly accessible) (some rides accessible for disabled guests) toilets for disabled shop ⊗

PORTSMOUTH

Charles Dickens' Birthplace Museum

393 Old Commercial Rd PO1 4QL
☎ 023 9282 7261   ▤ 023 9287 5276
e-mail: mvs@portsmouthcc.gov.uk
web: www.charlesdickensbirthplace.co.uk
dir: M27/M275 into Portsmouth, from M275 turn left at 'The News' rdbt. Signed

A small terraced house built in 1805 which became the birthplace and early home of the famous novelist, born in 1812. On display are items pertaining to Dickens' work, portraits of the Dickens' family, and the couch on which he died. Dickens readings are given in the exhibition room on the first Sunday of each month at 3pm.

Times Open Apr-Sep, daily 10-5.30 (Last admission 5).* **Facilities** ℗ shop ⊗

PORTSMOUTH

D-Day Museum & Overlord Embroidery

Clarence Esplanade PO5 3NT
☎ 023 9282 7261   📄 023 9287 5276
e-mail: mvs@portsmouthcc.gov.uk
web: www.ddaymuseum.co.uk
dir: M27/M275 or M27/A2030 into Portsmouth, follow signs for seafront then D-Day museum name signs

Portsmouth's D-Day Museum tells the dramatic story of the Allied landings in Normandy in 1944. The centrepiece is the magnificent 'Overlord Embroidery', 34 individual panels and 83 metres in length. Experience the world's largest ever seaborne invasion, and step back in time to scenes of wartime Britain. Military equipment, vehicles, landing craft and personal memories complete this special story.

Times Open all year, Apr-Sep, daily 10-5.30; Oct-Mar, 10-5. Closed 24-26 Dec* Facilities 🅿 🅟 ⏍ 🍴 (outdoor) ♿ toilets for disabled shop ⊗

PORTSMOUTH

Portsmouth Historic Dockyard

HM Naval Base PO1 3LJ
☎ 023 9283 9766   📄 023 9283 8228
e-mail: enquiries@historicdockyard.co.uk
web: www.historicdockyard.co.uk
dir: M27/M275 & follow brown historic waterfront and dockyard signs

Portsmouth Historic Dockyard is home to the world's greatest historic ships: Mary Rose - King Henry VIII's favourite ship, HMS Victory - Lord Nelson's flagship at the Battle of Trafalgar and HMS Warrior - the first iron-hulled warship. In addition, the Royal Naval Museum has the most significant, permanent collections relating to Nelson and the Battle of Trafalgar, and Action Stations gives an interactive insight into the modern day Royal Navy.

Times Open Apr-Oct, daily 10-6 (last entry 4.30); Nov-Mar, daily 10-5.30 (last entry 4).* Fees All inclusive ticket: £18 (ch & students £13.50 under 5 free, concessions £16) Family £50.50.* Facilities 🅿 🅟 ⏍ 🍴 licensed 🍴 (outdoor) ♿ (partly accessible) toilets for disabled shop ⊗

PORTSMOUTH

Spinnaker Tower

Gunwharf Quays PO1 3TT
☎ 023 9285 7520 📠 023 9229 8726
e-mail: info@spinnakertower.co.uk
web: www.spinnakertower.co.uk
dir: From M275 follow tourist signs for Tower

Elegant, sculptural and inspired by Portsmouth's maritime heritage, the Spinnaker Tower is a new national icon - a 'must-see' landmark for visitors worldwide. Soaring 170 metres above Portsmouth Harbour, with three viewing decks, the Spinnaker Tower is now open to view. Take the high speed internal lift and step right out into the best view in the country. Dare you 'walk on air' on the glass floor, the largest in Europe? Watch history unfold through the unique 'Time Telescopes'.

Times Open daily Feb-Jul & Sep-Jan 10-6, Aug 10-8. **Fees** £7 (ch 3-15 £5.50, ch under 3 free, concessions £6.20). **Facilities** 🅿 ⬛ ♿ (partly accessible) (view deck 3 has no wheelchair access) toilets for disabled shop ⊗

RINGWOOD

Moors Valley Country Park

Horton Rd, Ashley Heath BH24 2ET
☎ 01425 470721 📠 01425 471656
e-mail: moorsvalley@eastdorset.gov.uk
web: www.moors-valley.co.uk
dir: 1.5m from Ashley Heath rdbt on A31 near Three Legged Cross

One thousand acres of forest, woodland, heathland, lakes, river and meadows provide a home for a wide variety of plants and animals, and there's a Visitor Centre, Adventure Playgrounds, picnic area, Moors Valley Railway, Tree Top Trail and 'Go Ape'- high ropes course (book on 0845 643 9215). Cycle hire is also available.

Times Open all year, 8-dusk (8pm at latest). Visitor centre open 9-4.30 (later in summer). Closed 25 Dec. **Fees** No admission charge but parking up to £8 per day. **Facilities** 🅿 ⬛ 🍴 licensed ﬤ (outdoor) ♿ (partly accessible) (some footpaths in forest unaccessible) toilets for disabled shop

WEYHILL

The Hawk Conservancy and Country Park

SP11 8DY

☎ 01264 773850 📠 01264 773772

e-mail: info@hawkconservancy.org

web: www.hawkconservancy.org

dir: 3m W of Andover, signed from A303

The Hawk Conservancy Trust is a registered charity and award winning visitor attraction that has for many years been working in the fields of conservation, education, rehabilitation and the research of birds of prey. The Trust is set in 22 acres of woodland and wild flower meadow, where there are over 150 birds of prey on view from the tiny Pygmy Owl to the impressive European Black Vulture. A day at the Trust has a packed itinerary including three flying demonstrations that see owls, kites, hawks, falcons and eagles showing off their skills. The birds come really close and there is even an opportunity for visitors to hold a British bird of prey!

Times Open all year, mid Feb-Oct daily 10-5.30. Nov-mid Feb wknds only 10-4.30. **Fees** £10 (ch £6, pen £9.25, students £9). Family ticket (2ad+2ch) £32.* **Facilities** 🅿 ⛄ 🍽 licensed 🍴 (indoor & outdoor) ♿ toilets for disabled shop 🚫

WINCHESTER

INTECH - Family Science Centre

Telegraph Way, Morn Hill SO21 1HZ

☎ 01962 863791 📠 01962 868524

e-mail: htct@intech-uk.com

web: www.intech-uk.com

dir: M3 junct 10 (S) or junct 9 (N) onto A31 then B3404 (Alresford road)

This purpose-built, all weather family attraction houses 100 interactive exhibits, which demonstrate the science and technology of the world around us in an engaging and exciting way. The philosophy is most definitely 'hands-on', and the motto of the centre is 'Doing is Believing'. Activities and science shows take place during school holidays. INTECH also has the UK's largest capacity planetarium. This digital cinema has a 17 metre dome making the audience feel it is floating through the universe. Dramatic, awesome and entertaining.

Times Open all year, daily 10-4. Closed 3 days at Xmas. **Fees** £6.95 (ch £4.65, pen £5.50) Family ticket (2ad+2ch) £20.86* **Facilities** 🅿 ⛄ 🍴 (outdoor) ♿ toilets for disabled shop 🚫

ST ALBANS

Verulamium Museum

St Michaels AL3 4SW
☎ 01727 751810 📄 01727 859919
e-mail: museum@stalbans.gov.uk
web: www.stalbansmuseums.org.uk
dir: follow signs for St Albans, museum signed

Verulamium was one of the largest and most important Roman towns in Britain - by the 1st century AD it was declared a `municipium', giving its inhabitants the rights of Roman citizenship, the only British city granted this honour. A mosaic and underfloor heating system can be seen in a separate building, and the museum has wall paintings, jewellery, pottery and other domestic items. On the second weekend of every month legionaries occupy the galleries and describe the tactics and equipment of the Roman Imperial Army and the life of a legionary.

Times Open all year Mon-Fri 10-5.30, Sun 2-5.30. Closed 25-26 Dec.* **Facilities** 🅿 🎪 (outdoor) ♿ toilets for disabled shop ⊗

BEKESBOURNE

Howletts Wild Animal Park

Beekesbourne Rd CT4 5EL
☎ 0844 8424 647 📄 01303 264944
e-mail: info@howletts.net
web: www.totallywild.net
dir: Signposted off A2, 3m S of Canterbury, follow brown tourist signs

Set in 90 acres, Howletts includes the largest group of western lowland gorillas in captivity in the world, and the largest herd of African elephants in the UK. A number of glass-fronted tiger enclosures allow for amazing views of the Sumatran and Indian tigers. In addition, Howletts is home to assorted primates, clouded leopards, tapirs, Javan langurs, black rhinos and Iberian wolves. There are plenty of other rare and endangered species from around the world. Visitors can walk in an open air enclosure where a family of amazingly agile and lively lemurs roam freely.

Times Open all year, daily 10-6 summer (last admission 4.30), 10-5 winter (last admission 3.30). Closed 25 Dec.* **Fees** £16.95 (ch £12.95 4-16yrs (must be accompanied by an adult), under 4's free, NUS card student £13.95 over 16yrs, pen £14.95). Family Ticket £54.00 (2ad+2ch)* **Facilities** 🅿 🖵 🍽 licensed 🎪 (outdoor) ♿ toilets for disabled shop ⊗

BELTRING

The Hop Farm

TN12 6PY
☎ 01622 872068   📠 01622 872630
e-mail: info@thehopfarm.co.uk
web: www.thehopfarm.co.uk
dir: on A228 at Paddock Wood

The Hop Farm is set among the largest collection of Victorian oast houses, and its attractions include museums and exhibitions, indoor and outdoor play areas, animal farm and shire horses, and restaurant and gift shop. The recently opened Driving School and Jumping Pillows offer non-stop fun for children, and for the adults there is Legends in Wax and the story of the Hop Farm. The new Great Goblin Hunt transports children into a fantasy world with 3D attractions. Events and shows all year such as the renowned War and Peace Show, Kent County Fair, The Hop Festival and Paws in the Park. For further details see website.

Times Open Apr-Nov, daily 10am. **Fees** £13. Supersaver for 4 £45, for 5 £55.* **Facilities** ♿ ▭ ⏻ licensed ⼓ (outdoor) ♿ toilets for disabled shop ⊗

CANTERBURY

The Canterbury Tales

St. Margaret's St CT1 2TG
☎ 01227 479227   📠 01227 765584
e-mail: info@canterburytales.org.uk
web: www.canterburytales.org.uk
dir: In heart of city centre, located in St Margaret's St

Step back in time to experience the sights, sounds and smells of the Middle Ages in this reconstruction of 14th-century England. Travel from the Tabard Inn in London, to St. Thomas Becket's Shrine in Canterbury with Chaucer's colourful pilgrims. Their tales of chivalry, romance and intrigue are brought vividly to life along the way.

Times Open all year, Mar-Jun 10-5, Jul-Aug 9.30-5, Sep-Oct 10-5 & Nov-Feb 10-4.30. Closed 25 & 26 Dec, 1 Jan **Fees** £7.75 (ch £5.75, concessions £6.75) Valid until 31/01/2010.* **Facilities** ♿ ♿ toilets for disabled shop ⊗

CHATHAM

Dickens World

Leviathan Way ME4 4LL
☎ 01634 890421 📠 01634 891972
e-mail: enquiries@dickensworld.co.uk
web: www.dickensworld.co.uk
dir: Signposted from junct 1, 3, & 4 of the M2, follow brown anchor signs

Dickens World is an exciting indoor complex themed around the life, books and times of Charles Dickens. It takes visitors on a fascinating journey through the author's lifetime as you step back into Dickensian England and are immersed in the streets, sounds and smells of the 19th century. Dickens World includes The Great Expectations boat ride; The Haunted Man; Victorian School Room; a 4D Hi-def show in Peggotty's Boathouse; Fagin's Den, a soft play area for younger children; and The Britannia Theatre, an animatronic stage show.

Times Open all year, daily from 10, closing time varies seasonally. Closed 25 Dec. **Fees** £12.20 (ch 5-15 £7.30, concessions £10.20)* **Facilities** 🅿 Ⓟ ⌨ ⭕ licensed ♿ (partly accessible) (to board boat ride, wheelchair users must be able to get in/out of chair unaided) toilets for disabled shop ⊗

CHATHAM

The Historic Dockyard Chatham

ME4 4TZ
☎ 01634 823807 & 823800
📠 01634 823801
e-mail: info@chdt.org.uk
web: www.thedockyard.co.uk
dir: M29 junct 6, M2 junct 3 onto A229 towards Chatham. Then A230 and A231, following brown tourist signs. Brown anchor signs lead to visitors entrance

Costumed guides bring this spectacular maritime heritage site alive. Discover over 400 years of maritime history as you explore the most complete dockyard of the Age of Sail, set in a stunning 80-acre estate. Various special events take place throughout the year, please see the website for details.

Times Open daily mid Feb-end Oct, Nov wknds only.* **Facilities** 🅿 Ⓟ ⌨ ⭕ licensed ⛩ (indoor & outdoor) ♿ (partly accessible) toilets for disabled shop

EYNSFORD

Eagle Heights

Lullingstone Ln DA4 0JB
☎ 01322 866466   📠 01322 861024
e-mail: office@eagleheights.co.uk
web: www.eagleheights.co.uk
dir: M25 junct 3/A20 towards West Kingsdown.
Right after 2 rdbts onto A225. Follow brown signs

Eagle Heights is an impressive display of birds
of prey from all over the world. Many are flown
out across the Darenth valley twice daily. There
are also owls, pygmy goat and rabbits in the
paddock. New Africa show including cheetah.

Times Open Mar-Oct daily 10.30-5. Nov, Jan-Feb
wknd only 11-4. **Fees** £8.50 (ch £5, concessions
£7).* **Facilities** 🅿 ⓟ 🖵 ⌱ (outdoor) ♿ toilets
for disabled shop ⊗

LYMPNE

Port Lympne Wild Animal Park

CT21 4LR
☎ 0844 8424 647   📠 01303 264944
e-mail: info@howletts.net
web: www.totallywild.net
dir: M20 junct 11, follow brown tourist signs

An historic mansion and landscaped gardens
set in 600 acres, Port Lympne Park also houses
the largest breeding herd of black rhino outside
Africa as well as African elephants, Siberian
and Indian tigers, small cats, monkeys, Malayan
tapirs, Barbary lions and many more rare and
endangered species. Other exciting features
include the 'African Experience', Livingstone
Safari Lodge, Day and Sunset safaris, Enrichment
Centre Workshops and the chance to be a
keeper for a day (subject to availability and at
an additional charge) Pre-booking essential for
some activities, please see website.

Times Open all year, daily 10-6 (summer, last
admission 4.30) 10-5 (winter, last admission
3.30). Closed 25 Dec.* **Fees** Please phone for
prices or see website.* **Facilities** 🅿 🖵 🍽
licensed ⌱ (outdoor) ♿ (partly accessible)
(very limited access for disabled, special route
available) toilets for disabled shop ⊗

MAIDSTONE

Leeds Castle

ME17 1PL

☎ 01622 765400   🖷 01622 735616
e-mail: enquiries@leeds-castle.co.uk
web: www.leeds-castle.com
dir: 7m E of Maidstone at junct 8 of M20/A20, clearly signed

With over 900 years of fascinating history, the castle has been a Norman stronghold, a royal residence for six medieval queens of England, a favourite palace of Henry VIII and a grand country house. Its blend of history and heritage, glorious gardens, maze and grotto, dog collar museum, craft centre and children's playground, make it the perfect choice for a day out. Special events all year, contact for details or visit the website.

Times Open all year, Grounds: Apr-Sep, daily 10-6 (Castle 10.30-5.30) Last admission 4.30. Grounds: Oct-Mar 10-4 (Castle 10.30-4) Last admission 3. Last entry to the castle is 30min after the last admission time. **Fees** £16.50 (ch £9.50, under 4 free, concessions £13.50). Every ticket purchased for entry to Leeds Castle is valid for unlimited use for an entire year (excluding special ticketed events). Prices are valid until 31 March 2010 **Facilities** 🅿 🍴 licensed 🍴 (outdoor) ♿ (partly accessible) (only ground floor of castle accessible) toilets for disabled shop ⊗

BLACKPOOL

Blackpool Zoo

East Park Dr FY3 8PP

☎ 01253 830830   🖷 01253 830800
e-mail: info@blackpoolzoo.org.uk
web: www.blackpoolzoo.org.uk
dir: M55 junct 4, follow brown tourist signs

This multi-award-winning zoo, built in 1972, houses over 1500 animals within its 32 acres of landscaped gardens. There is a miniature railway, lots of close encounters and animals in action, a children's play area, animal feeding times and keeper talks throughout the day. New animal attractions include Giraffe Heights and Penguin Pool. Many special events throughout the year.

Times Open all year daily, summer 10-6; winter 10-dusk. Jul-Aug, Wed 10-9. Closed 25 Dec.*
Fees £12.95 (ch £8.95, concessions £10.95, disabled & carers £6.50). Family (2ad+2ch) £39, (2ad+3 ch) £47.* **Facilities** 🅿 🅿 ⊒ 🍴 licensed 🍴 (outdoor) ♿ toilets for disabled shop ⊗

LEYLAND

British Commercial Vehicle Museum

King St PR25 2LE
☎ 01772 451011 📄 01772 451015
e-mail: enquiries@bcvm.co.uk
web: www.bcvm.co.uk
dir: 0.75m from M6 junct 28 in town centre

A unique line-up of historic commercial vehicles and buses spanning a century of truck and bus building. There are more than 50 exhibits on permanent display, and plenty of special events including transport model shows, transport shows, and the Ford Cortina Mk I gathering.

Times Open Apr-Sep, Sun, Tue-Thu & BH Mon (Oct open Tue & Sun only); 10-5.* **Facilities** 🅿 🅿 ⏦ ♿ toilets for disabled shop ⊗

PRESTON

National Football Museum **FREE**

Sir Tom Finney Way, Deepdale PR1 6PA
☎ 01772 908442 📄 01772 908444
e-mail: enquiries@nationalfootballmuseum.com
web: www.nationalfootballmuseum.com
dir: 2m from M6 juncts 31, 31A or 32. Follow brown tourist signs

Take an amazing journey through football history. Discover the world's biggest football museum, packed full of great footballing moments, stories and objects -from the World Cup ball used in the first ever final in 1930, to the ball used in the 1966 World Cup final. There are fun interactive opportunities and the brilliant penalty shoot-out game Goalstriker. Plus events, activities and exhibitions all year round means there's always something new to see and do.

Times Open all year, Tue-Sat 10-5, Sun 11-5. Closed Mon ex BHs and school hols. (Museum closed 15 mins before 'kick off' on match days)* **Facilities** 🅿 🅿 ⏦ ♿ toilets for disabled shop ⊗

COALVILLE

Snibston Discovery Museum

Ashby Rd LE67 3LN

☎ 01530 278444 📄 01530 813301
e-mail: snibston@leics.gov.uk
web: www.snibston.com
dir: 4.5m from M1 junct 22 or from A42/M42
junct 13 on A511 on W side of Coalville

Award winning attraction and up-to-date science centre. In the Extra Ordinary hands-on gallery visitors can see how technology has affected everyday life, by lifting up a Mini Cooper. The Fashion Gallery has a wide selection of historic and modern costumes, while the underground life of a miner can be explored in the colliery tour. There are also rides on a diesel locomotive, or fun in the adventure play area. The Country Park is free, and has two fishing lakes, picnic spots and the Grange Nature Reserve.

Times Open all year, Apr-Oct, daily 10-5; Nov-Mar 10-3. School hols & wknds 10-5. Closed 2 weeks in Jan for maintenance. **Fees** £6.75 (ch £4.50, concessions £4.75). Family ticket £20.* **Facilities** 🅿 🅟 🖵 🍴 (indoor & outdoor) ♿ toilets for disabled shop ⊗

LEICESTER

National Space Centre

Exploration Dr LE4 5NS

☎ 0845 605 2001 📄 0116 258 2100
e-mail: info@spacecentre.co.uk
web: www.spacecentre.co.uk
dir: off A6, 2m N of city centre midway between Leicester's central & outer ring roads. Follow brown rocket signs from M1 (junct 21, 21a or 22) & all arterial routes around Leicester

The award-winning National Space Centre offers a great family day out, with six interactive galleries, a full-domed Space Theatre, a 42-metre high Rocket Tower, and the new Human Spaceflight Experience with 3D SIM ride. Explore the universe, orbit Earth, join the crew on the lunar base, and take the astronaut fitness tests, all without leaving Leicester! Project Apollo is the latest interactive experience celebrating the 40th anniversary of the Apollo moon landing. Throughout the year there are numerous events relating to space reality and science fiction, so contact the Centre for more details.

Times Open during school term: Tue-Fri, 10-4, Sat-Sun 10-5. During school hols: daily, 10-5.* **Fees** £13 (ch 4-16yrs & concessions £11). Family of 4 £40, of 5 £50. All tickets valid for a full year. **Facilities** 🅿 🖵 🍴 licensed 🍴 (outdoor) ♿ toilets for disabled shop ⊗

LOUGHBOROUGH

Great Central Railway

Great Central Rd LE11 1RW
☎ 01509 230726　📠 01509 239791
e-mail: sales@gcrailway.co.uk
web: www.gcrailway.co.uk
dir: signed from A6, follow brown tourist signs

This private steam railway runs over eight miles
from Loughborough Central to Leicester North,
with all trains calling at Quorn & Woodhouse and
Rothley. The locomotive depot and museum are
at Loughborough Central. A buffet car runs on
most trains.

Times Open all year daily, trains run every wknd
& BHs throughout the year, May-Sep, Wed; Jun,
Jul & Aug daily ex Fri.* **Fees** Runabout (all day
unlimited travel) £12 (ch £7 & concessions £10).
Family ticket (2ad+3ch) £30 (1ad+3ch) £20*
Facilities 🅿 🅟 　🖵🍽 licensed 🍴 (outdoor) ♿
toilets for disabled shop

MARKET BOSWORTH

Bosworth Battlefield Visitor Centre & Country Park

Ambion Hill, Sutton Cheney CV13 0AD
☎ 01455 290429　📠 01455 292841
e-mail: bosworth@leics.gov.uk
web: www.leics.gov.uk
dir: follow brown tourist signs from A447, A444
& A5

The Battle of Bosworth Field was fought in
1485 between the armies of Richard III and
the future Henry VII. The visitor centre offers a
comprehensive interpretation of the battle, with
exhibitions, models and a film theatre. Special
medieval attractions are held in the summer
months.

Times Open: Country Park daily Apr-Sep,
8.30-5.30, Oct-Mar 8.30-4.40. Heritage Centre
open daily Apr-Oct, 10-5, Nov-Mar, 10-4 (last
admission 1hr before closing). Closed Jan &
24-27 Dec.* **Fees** £6 (ch 3-16 yrs £3, ch under
3 free, concessions £4). Family ticket (2ad+2ch)
£15.* **Facilities** 🅿 🅟 　🖵🍽 licensed 🍴
(outdoor) toilets for disabled shop

MOIRA

Conkers

Millennium Av, Rawdon Rd DE12 6GA

☎ 01283 216633 📠 01283 210321

e-mail: info@visitconkers.com

web: www.visitconkers.com

dir: on B5003 in Moira, signed from A444 and M42

Explore over one hundred indoor interactive exhibits, together with 120 acres that contain lakeside walks and trails, habitats, an assault course, adventure play areas and a miniature train. There are also events in the covered amphitheatre, and many other opportunities for you and your family to be entertained and educated.

Times Open all year, daily, summer 10-6, autumn 10-5, winter 10-4.30. Closed 25 Dec.* **Fees** £7.95 (ch 3-15yrs £5.95, ch under 3 free, concessions £6.95). Family ticket (2ad+2ch) £24.95. Prices include a 10% donation to The Heart of the National Forest. **Facilities** 🅿 ☐ 🍴 licensed 🎪 (indoor & outdoor) ♿ toilets for disabled shop ⊗

TWYCROSS

Twycross Zoo

CV9 3PX

☎ 01827 880250 📠 01827 880700

web: www.twycrosszoo.org

dir: on A444 Burton to Nuneaton road, directly off M42 junct 11

Twycross Zoo appeals to all ages and spans some 50 acres that are home to around 1000 animals, including the most comprehensive collection of primate species in the world. Twycross is the only zoo in Great Britain to house bonobos - humanity's 'closest living relative'. While at the zoo, visitors can visit a genuine Borneo Longhouse, brought to life in the Leicestershire countryside, where many exotic birds, animal species and traditional artefacts can be seen. See also the new Asian elephant walkway and a new children's area with adventure playground, rides for little explorers and pets from around the world.

Times Open all year, daily 10-5.30 (4 in winter). Closed 25 Dec. **Fees** £9.50 (ch £6, pen £7). Family Ticket £29.* **Facilities** 🅿 ☐ 🎪 (outdoor) ♿ toilets for disabled shop ⊗

CLEETHORPES

Pleasure Island Family Theme Park

Kings Rd DN35 0PL
☎ 01472 211511 📄 01472 211087
e-mail: reception@pleasure-island.co.uk
web: www.pleasure-island.co.uk
dir: M180 then A180, follow signs to park

Pleasure Island is packed with over seventy rides and attractions. Hold on tight as the colossal wheel of steel rockets you into the sky at a G-force of 2.5, then hurtles you around 360 degrees, sending riders into orbit and giving the sensation of complete weightlessness. It's not just grown ups and thrill seekers who are catered for at Pleasure Island. For youngsters there's hours of fun in Tinkaboo Town, an indoor themed area full of rides and attractions. There's also five family shows.

Times Open 4 Apr-Oct, daily from 10.30. Plus wknds during Sep-Oct. Park closed Mon-Tue during quiet times. Call for further info.
Fees £16.50 (ch under 4 free, concessions £9.50). Facilities ⓟ ⚋ 🍽 licensed ⋒ (outdoor) ♿ (partly accessible) (shops & restaurants are wheelchair accessible) toilets for disabled shop

GRIMSBY

Fishing Heritage Centre

Alexandra Dock DN31 1UZ
☎ 01472 323345 📄 01472 323555
web: www.nelincs.gov.uk/leisure/museums
dir: follow signs off M180

Sign on as a crew member for a journey of discovery, and experience the harsh reality of life on board a deep sea trawler built inside the Centre. Through interactive games and displays, your challenge is to navigate the icy waters of the Arctic in search of the catch.

Times Open Nov-Apr, Mon-Fri 10-4, Wknds & BHs 11-9* Facilities ⓟ ⓟ ⚋ toilets for disabled shop ⊗

SKEGNESS

Skegness Natureland Seal Sanctuary

North Pde PE25 1DB
☎ 01754 764345   📄 01754 764345
web: www.skegnessnatureland.co.uk
dir: N end of seafront

Natureland houses seals, penguins, tropical birds, aquarium and reptiles, as well as a pets' corner. Also free-flight tropical butterflies (Apr-Oct). Natureland is well known for its rescue of abandoned seal pups, and has successfully reared and returned to the wild a large number of them. The hospital unit incorporates a public viewing area, and a large seascape seal pool (with underwater viewing).

Times Open all year, daily at 10. Closing times vary according to season. Closed 25-26 Dec & 1 Jan. **Fees** £6.20 (ch £4, pen £5). Family ticket £18.40 (2ad+2ch)* **Facilities** ℗ ⊡ ᵀᴼ⎮ licensed ⋒ (outdoor) ᕦ toilets for disabled shop

SPALDING

Butterfly & Wildlife Park

Long Sutton PE12 9LE
☎ 01406 363833 & 363209
📄 01406 363182
e-mail: info@butterflyandwildlifepark@.co.uk
web: www.butterflyandwildlifepark.co.uk
dir: off A17 at Long Sutton

The Park contains one of Britain's largest walk-through tropical gardens, in which hundreds of butterflies from all over the world fly freely. The tropical gardens are also home to crocodiles, snakes and lizards. Outside are 15 acres of butterfly and bee gardens, wildflower meadows, nature trail, farm animals, a pets' corner and a large adventure playground. At The Lincolnshire Birds of Prey Centre, there are daily birds of prey displays. In the ant room visitors can observe leaf-cutting ants in their natural working habitat.

Times Open 15 Mar-2 Nov, daily 10-5. Sep & Oct 10-4* **Facilities** ℗ ⊡ ⋒ (outdoor) ᕦ toilets for disabled shop ⊗

WOOLSTHORPE

Woolsthorpe Manor

23 Newton Way NG33 5PD
☎ 01476 862826 📠 01476 860338
e-mail: woolsthorpemanor@nationaltrust.org.uk
web: www.nationaltrust.org.uk
dir: 7m S of Grantham, 1m W of A1

Isaac Newton was born in this modest manor
house in the mid 1600s and he made many
of his most important discoveries about light
and gravity here. A complex figure, Newton
notched up careers as diverse as Cambridge
Professor and Master of the Royal Mint; spent
years studying alchemy and the Bible as well as
science, and was President of the Royal Society,
which celebrates its 350th anniversary in 2010.
You can still see the famous apple tree from
Isaac's bedroom window and enjoy the brand new
Discovery Centre.

Times Open 27 Feb-29 Mar & 4-26 Oct, Sat & Sun
1-5; Apr-28 Jun & 2-27 Sep, Wed-Sun (open BHs)
1-5; 2 Jul-Aug, Sat & Sun 11-5; Wed-Fri, 1-5;
2 Oct -1 Nov, Fri-Sun 1-5* **Fees** With Gift Aid
donation: £5.80 (ch £2.90). Family ticket £14.50*
Facilities 🅿 ♿ (partly accessible) (narrow
doorways & small rooms, ramps available. Stairs
to other floors. Grounds partly accessible, uneven
& loose gravel paths, some steps) toilets for
disabled shop ⊗ 🐾

E2

V & A Museum of Childhood **FREE**

Cambridge Heath Rd E2 9PA
☎ 020 8983 5200 📠 020 8983 5225
e-mail: moc@vam.ac.uk
web: www.museumofchildhood.org.uk
dir: Underground - Bethnal Green

The V&A Museum of Childhood re-opened
following an extensive transformation a few
years ago. There is a stunning new entrance,
fully updated galleries and displays, a brand new
gallery and expanded public spaces. Galleries
include Creativity, Moving Toys and Childhood
Galleries. There is also a full programme of
activities. Exhibitions include Sit Down, Seating
for kids.

Times Open all year, daily 10-5.45. Closed 25-26
Dec & 1 Jan. **Facilities** 🅿 ♿🍴 (outdoor) ♿
toilets for disabled shop ⊗

E14

Museum of London Docklands

No 1 Warehouse, West India Quay E14 4AL
☎ 020 7001 9844
e-mail: info@museumoflondon.org.uk
web: www.museumoflondon.org.uk/docklands
dir: Signposted from West India Quay DLR

From Roman settlement to Docklands'
regeneration, unlock the history of London's
river, port and people, in this historic warehouse.
Discover a wealth of objects from whale bones
to WWII gas masks in state-of-the-art galleries,
including Mudlarks, an interactive area for kids;
Sailortown, an atmospheric recreation of 19th
century riverside Wapping; and London, Sugar &
Slavery, which reveals the city's involvement in
the transatlantic slave trade.

Times Open all year, daily 10-6. Closed 24-26
Dec. Fees £5 (ch16 free, concessions £3)*
Facilities ℗ ⊑ ⦿ licensed ⋒ (indoor) ﻉ
toilets for disabled shop ⊗

EC2

Museum of London FREE

150 London Wall EC2Y 5HN
☎ 0870 444 3851 ▤ 0870 444 3853
e-mail: info@museumoflondon.org.uk
web: www.museumoflondon.org.uk
dir: Underground - St Paul's, Barbican. N of
St Paul's Cathedral at the end of St Martins le
Grand and S of the Barbican. S of Aldersgate St

Dedicated to the story of London and its people,
the Museum of London exists to inspire a passion
for London in all who visit it. As well as the
permanent collection, the Museum has a varied
exhibition programme with major temporary
exhibitions and topical displays each year. There
are also smaller exhibitions in the foyer gallery.
A wide programme of lectures and events explore
London's history and its evolution into the city
of today.

Times Open all year, Mon-Sat 10-5.50, Sun
12-5.50. Last admission 5.30.* Facilities ❶ ℗
⊑ ⋒ toilets for disabled shop ⊗

EC3

The Monument

Monument St EC3R 8AH
☎ 020 7626 2717 ▤ 020 7403 4477
e-mail: enquiries@towerbridge.org.uk
web: www.towerbridge.org.uk
dir: Underground - Monument

Designed by Wren and Hooke and erected in 1671-7, the Monument commemorates the Great Fire of 1666 which is reputed to have started in nearby Pudding Lane. The fire destroyed nearly 90 churches and about 13,000 houses. This fluted Doric column stands 202ft high (Pudding Lane is exactly 202ft from its base) and you can climb the 311 steps to a platform at the summit, and receive a certificate as proof of your athletic abilities.

Times Open all year, daily, 9.30-5.* Facilities ⊗

EC3

Tower of London

Tower Hill EC3N 4AB
☎ 0870 756 6060
web: www.hrp.org.uk
dir: Underground - Tower Hill

Perhaps the most famous castle in the world, the Tower of London has played a central part in British history. Discover the stories of this awesome fortress; from gruesome tales of torture and escape to fascinating traditions that can still be seen today. Learn the legend of the ravens and be dazzled by the Crown Jewels. Join a Yeoman Warder tour and listen to their captivating tales of pain and passion, treachery and torture, all delivered with a smile and a swagger!

Times Open all year, Mar-Oct, Sun-Mon 10-5.30, Tue-Sat 9-5.30 (last admission 5); Nov-Feb, Tue-Sat 9-4.30, Sun-Mon 10-4.30 (last admission 4). Closed 24-26 Dec & 1 Jan.* Fees £17 (ch £9.50 under 5s free, children must be accompanied by an adult) concessions: full-time student, over 60 with ID £14.50). Family ticket (2ad+3ch) £47.* Facilities ℗ ⊑ ¶⊙ licensed toilets for disabled shop ⊗

NW1

Madame Tussauds

Marylebone Rd NW1 5LR
☎ 0870 400 3000
e-mail: csc@madame-tussauds.com
web: www.madame-tussauds.com
dir: Underground - Baker Street

Madame Tussaud's world-famous waxwork collection was founded in Paris in 1770. It moved to England in 1802 and found a permanent home in London's Marylebone Road in 1884. The 21st century has brought new innovations and new levels of interactivity. Listen to Kylie Minogue whisper in your ear, become an A-list celeb in the 'Blush' nightclub, and take your chances in a high security prison populated by dangerous serial killers.

Times Open all year 9.30-5.30 (9-6 wknds/summer). Closed 25 Dec. **Fees** £25 (ch under 16 £21. (Includes entry into Stardome & The Wonderful World of Stars).* **Facilities** ℗ ⑪ licensed ♿ toilets for disabled shop ⊗

NW1

ZSL London Zoo

Regents Park NW1 4RY
☎ 020 7449 6231   📄 020 7586 6177
e-mail: marketing@zsl.org
web: www.zsl.org
dir: Underground - Camden Town or Regents Park

ZSL London Zoo is home to over 12,000 animals, insects, reptiles and fish. First opened in 1828, the Zoo can claim the world's first aquarium, insect and reptile house. Get closer to your favourite animals, learn about them at the keeper talks and watch them show off their skills at special events. Enjoy Gorilla Kingdom, a walk through the rainforest where you can get close to a group of Western Lowland gorillas. The newest exhibit is Giants of the Galapagos, featuring three Galapagos tortoises.

Times Open all year, daily from 10, (closing time dependant on time of year). Closed 25 Dec.* **Facilities** 🅿 ℗ ⬚ ⑪ licensed ♠ toilets for disabled shop ⊗

SE1

Golden Hinde Educational Trust

182 Pickfords Wharf, Clink St SE1 9DG
☎ 020 7403 0123 ▤ 020 7407 5908
e-mail: info@goldenhinde.org
web: www.goldenhinde.org
dir: On the Thames path between Southwark
Cathedral and the new Globe Theatre

An authentic replica of the galleon in which
Sir Francis Drake sailed around the world in
1577-1580. This ship has travelled over 140,000
miles, many more than the original. She is now
permanently berthed on London's South Bank.

Times Open all year, daily 10-5.30. Visitors are
advised to check opening times as they may vary
due to closures for functions.* Facilities ⓟ 🚻
(partly accessible) (stairs on main deck so no
access to wheelchairs) shop ⊗

SE1

HMS Belfast

Morgans Ln, Tooley St SE1 2JH
☎ 020 7940 6300 ▤ 020 7403 0719
e-mail: hmsbelfast@iwm.org.uk
web: www.iwm.org.uk/hmsbelfast
dir: Underground - London Bridge/Tower Hill/
Monument. Rail - London Bridge

Europe's last surviving big gun armoured
warship from the Second World War, HMS Belfast
was launched in 1938 and served in the North
Atlantic and Arctic with the Home Fleet. She
led the Allied naval bombardment of German
positions on D-Day, and was saved for the
nation in 1971. A tour of the ship will take you
from the Captain's Bridge through nine decks to
the massive Boiler and Engine Rooms. You can
visit the cramped Mess Decks, Officers' Cabins,
Galley, Sick Bay, Dentist and Laundry.

Times Open all year, daily. Mar-Oct 10-6 (last
admission 5); Nov-Feb 10-5 (last admission
4). Closed 24-26 Dec.* Fees £10.70 (ch under
15 free, concessions £8.60).* Facilities ⊑ 🍴
(indoor) 🚻 (partly accessible) (wheelchair access
to main decks, but not all decks) toilets for
disabled shop ⊗

SE1

Imperial War Museum

Lambeth Rd SE1 6HZ
☎ 020 7416 5320 & 5321
🖷 020 7416 5374
e-mail: mail@iwm.org.uk
web: www.iwm.org.uk
dir: Underground - Lambeth North, Elephant & Castle or Waterloo

Founded in 1917, this museum illustrates and records all aspects of the two World Wars and other military operations involving Britain and the Commonwealth since 1914. There are always special exhibitions and the programme of special and family events includes film shows and lectures. The museum also has an extensive film, photography, sound, document and art archive as well as a library, although some reference departments are open to the public by appointment only.

Times Open all year, daily 10-6. Closed 24-26 Dec.* Fees Free admission (charges apply for some temporary exhibitions)* Facilities ℗ ⬜ ⍩ licensed ⟁ (indoor & outdoor) ♿ toilets for disabled shop ⊗

SE1

London Aquarium

County Hall, Riverside Building, Westminster Bridge Rd SE1 7PB
☎ 020 7967 8000 🖷 020 7967 8029
e-mail: info@londonaquarium.co.uk
web: www.londonaquarium.co.uk
dir: Underground-Waterloo & Westminster. On south bank next to Westminster Bridge, nr Big Ben & London Eye

The London Aquarium is one of Europe's largest displays of global aquatic life with over 350 species in over 50 displays, ranging from the mystical seahorse to the deadly stonefish. The huge Pacific display is home to a variety of jacks, stingrays and seven sharks. Come and witness the spectacular Atlantic feed where a team of divers hand-feed rays and native British sharks. The rainforest feed incorporates a frenzied piranha attack with the amazing marksmanship of the archerfish. There is also a range of education tours and literature to enhance any visit.

Times Open all year, daily 10-6. (Last admission 1hr before closing). Closed 25 Dec. Late opening over summer months.* Facilities ℗ ⬜ toilets for disabled shop ⊗

SE1

London Eye

Riverside Building, County Hall, Westminster
Bridge Rd SE1 7PB
☎ 0870 500 0600 📄 0870 990 8882
e-mail: customer.services@londoneye.com
web: www.londoneye.com
dir: Underground - Waterloo/Westminster

The London Eye is one of the most inspiring and
visually dramatic additions to the London skyline.
At 135m/443ft high, it is the world's tallest
observation wheel, allowing you to see one of the
world's most exciting cities from a completely
new perspective. The London Eye takes you
on a gradual, 30 minute, 360 degree rotation,
revealing parts of the city, which are simply
not visible from the ground. For Londoners and
visitors alike, it is the best way to see London and
its many celebrated landmarks. The London Eye
provides the perfect location for private parties
and entertaining, and offers a wide variety of
'in-flight' hospitality packages, like champagne
and canapés, which are available to enjoy in the
privacy of your own capsule.

Times Open all year, daily, Oct-May 10-8;
Jun-Sep, 10-9. Closed 25 Dec & annual
maintenance.* **Facilities** Ⓟ 🚻 toilets for
disabled shop ⊗

SE1

Shakespeare's Globe Theatre Tours & Exhibition

21 New Globe Walk, Bankside SE1 9DT
☎ 020 7902 1500 📄 020 7902 1515
e-mail: info@shakespearesglobe.com
web: www.shakespeares-globe.org
dir: Underground - London Bridge, walk along
Bankside. Mansion House, walk across Southwark
Bridge. St Pauls, walk across Millennium Bridge

Guides help to bring England's theatrical
heritage to life at the 'unparalleled and
astonishing' recreation of this famous theatre.
Discover what an Elizabethan audience would
have been like, find out about the rivalry between
the Bankside theatres, the bear baiting and
the stews, hear about the penny stinkards and
find out what a bodger is. Housed beneath the
reconstructed theatre, the exhibition explores
the remarkable story of the Globe, and brings
Shakespeare's world to life using a range of
interactive display and live demonstrations.

Times Open all year, May-early Oct, daily
9-12 (1-5 Rose Theatre tour); Oct-Apr 10-5.*
Fees £10.50 (ch 5-15 £6.50, pen & students
£8.50). Family ticket (2ad+3ch) £28.* **Facilities**
Ⓟ 🚻 ❯❮ licensed ♿ toilets for disabled shop
⊗

SE1

The Tower Bridge Exhibition

Tower Bridge Rd SE1 2UP
☎ 020 7940 3985 📠 020 7357 7935
e-mail: enquiries@towerbridge.org.uk
web: www.towerbridge.co.uk
dir: Underground - Tower Hill or London Bridge

One of the capital's most famous landmarks, its glass-covered walkways stand 142ft above the Thames, affording panoramic views of the river. Much of the original machinery for working the bridge can be seen in the engine rooms. The Tower Bridge Exhibition uses state-of-the-art effects to present the story of the bridge in a dramatic and exciting fashion.

Times Open all year, Apr-Sep 10-6.30 (last ticket 5.30); Oct-Mar 9.30-5.30 (last ticket 5)*
Facilities ℗ ♿ toilets for disabled shop ⊗

SE10

National Maritime Museum

Romney Rd SE10 9NF
☎ 020 8312 6565 📠 020 8312 6632
e-mail: RScates@nmm.ac.uk
web: www.nmm.ac.uk
dir: central Greenwich A206

Britain's seafaring history is displayed in this impressive modern museum. Themes include exploration and discovery, Nelson, trade and empire, passenger shipping and luxury liners, maritime London, costume, art and the sea, and the future of the sea. There are interactive displays for children.

Times Open all year, daily 10-5 Closed 24-26 Dec. (Partial closures 31 Dec, 1 Jan & Marathon day). **Fees** Free, except some special exhibtions. **Facilities** ℗ ⊡ ⴲ (outdoor) ♿ toilets for disabled shop ⊗

SE10

Royal Observatory Greenwich

Greenwich Park, Greenwich SE10 8XJ
☎ 020 8312 6565 📠 020 8312 6632
e-mail: bookings@nmm.ac.uk
web: www.nmm.ac.uk
dir: off A2, Greenwich Park, enter from
Blackheath Gate only

Charles II founded the Royal Observatory in
1675 'for perfecting navigation and astronomy'.
It stands at zero meridian longitude and is
the original home of Greenwich Mean Time.
Astronomy galleries and the Peter Harrison
Planetarium house an extensive collection
of historic timekeeping, astronomical and
navigational instruments.

Times Open all year, daily 10-5. (Partial closures
31 Dec, 1 Jan and Marathon day) Fees Free,
except for Planetarium shows from £6 (ch
£4). Facilities 🅿 ⛄ 🎋 (outdoor) ♿ (partly
accessible) (narrow staircase to Octagon room)
toilets for disabled shop ⊗

SE18

Firepower Royal Artillery Museum

Royal Arsenal, Woolwich SE18 6ST
☎ 020 8855 7755 📠 020 8855 7100
e-mail: info@firepower.org.uk
web: www.firepower.org.uk
dir: A205, right at Woolwich ferry onto A206,
attraction signed

Firepower is the Royal Artillery Museum in the
historic Royal Arsenal. It spans 2000 years of
artillery and shows the development from Roman
catapult to guided missile to self-propelled gun.
Put science into action with touchscreen displays
and be awed by the big guns.

Times Open all year, Wed-Sun & BHs 11-5.30.
Phone for winter opening times.* Facilities 🅿
🅟 🎋 toilets for disabled shop ⊗

SE18

Thames Barrier Information & Learning Centre

1 Unity Way SE18 5NJ
☎ 020 8305 4188 📄 020 8855 2146
e-mail: learningcentre@environment-agency.gov.uk
web: www.environment-agency.gov.uk
dir: Turn off A102(M) onto A206, turn onto Eastmoor St and follow signs

Spanning a third of a mile, the Thames Barrier is the world's largest movable flood barrier. The visitors' centre and exhibition on the South Bank explains the flood threat and the construction of this £535 million project, now valued at £1 billion. Each month a test closure of all ten gates, lasting over 2 hours, is carried out and the annual full day closure of all ten gates takes place in the autumn.

Times Open Apr-Sep, 10.30-4.30; Oct-Mar, 11-3.30. Closed 25 Dec-3 Jan. **Fees** £3.50 (ch £2, pen £3). **Facilities** ℗ ☒ ☷ (outdoor) ♿ toilets for disabled shop ⊗

SW1

The Household Cavalry Museum

Horse Guards, Whitehall SW1A 2AX

☎ 020 7930 3070
e-mail: museum@householdcavalry.co.uk
web: www.householdcavalrymuseum.org.uk
dir: Underground - Charing Cross, Embankment & Westminster

The Household Cavalry Museum is unlike any other military museum because it offers a unique 'behind-the-scenes' look at the work that goes into the ceremonial duties and operational role of the Household Cavalry. Watch troopers working with their horses in the original 18th-century stables (via a glazed screen) and hear accounts of their demanding training. Plus children's trails, activity packs and dressing up areas.

Times Open all year daily, Mar-Sep 10-6, Oct-Feb 10-5.* **Fees** £6 (ch 5-16 & concessions £4). Family ticket (2ad+3ch) £15. Group rate 10% discount.* **Facilities** ℗ ♿ toilets for disabled shop ⊗

SW1

The Royal Mews

Buckingham Palace, Buckingham Palace Rd
SW1W 0QH
☎ 020 7766 7302   ▤ 020 7930 9625
e-mail: bookinginfo@royalcollection.org.uk
web: www.royalcollection.org.uk
dir: Underground - Victoria, Green Park, St. James
Park. Entrance in Buckingham Palace Road

Designed by John Nash and completed in 1825,
the Royal Mews houses the State Coaches,
horse-drawn carriages and motor cars used for
Coronations, State Visits, Royal Weddings and
the State Opening of Parliament. These include
the Gold State Coach made in 1762, with panels
painted by the Florentine artist Cipriani. As one of
the finest working stables in existence, the Royal
Mews provides a unique opportunity for you to see
a working department of the Royal Household.

Times Open daily ex Fri. Mar-Oct 11-4; Aug-Sep
10-5. (Last admission 3.15, Aug-Sep 4.15).
Fees £8 (ch under 17 £5, ch under 5 free,
concessions £7) Family (2ad+3ch) £21.50.
Facilities ⓟ ♿ toilets for disabled shop ⊗

SW7

The Natural History Museum

Cromwell Rd SW7 5BD
☎ 020 7942 5000   ▤ 020 7942 5075
e-mail: feedback@nhm.ac.uk
web: www.nhm.ac.uk
dir: Underground - South Kensington

This vast and elaborate Romanesque-style
building, with its terracotta tiles showing
relief mouldings of animals, birds and fishes,
covers an area of four acres. Holding over 70
million specimens from all over the globe, from
dinosaurs to diamonds and earthquakes to ants,
the museum provides a journey into Earth's past,
present and future. Discover more about the
work of the museum through a daily programme
of talks from museum scientists or go behind
the scenes of the Darwin Centre, the museum's
scientific research centre.

Times Open all year, daily 10-5.50 (last
admission 5.30). Closed 24-26 Dec. Fees Free.
Charge made for some special exhibitions.
Facilities ⓟ ♲⟊⊙⟊ licensed ⋔ (indoor) ♿
(partly accessible) (top floor/one gallery not
accessible) toilets for disabled shop ⊗

SW7

Science Museum

Exhibition Rd, South Kensington SW7 2DD
☎ 0870 870 4868 📄 020 7942 4421
e-mail: sciencemuseum@sciencemuseum.org.uk
web: www.sciencemuseum.org.uk
dir: Underground - South Kensington, signed from tube stn

See iconic objects from the history of science, from Stephenson's Rocket to the Apollo 10 command module; be amazed by a 3D IMAX movie; take a ride in a simulator; visit an exhibition; and encounter the past, present and future of technology in seven floors of free galleries, including the famous hands-on section where children can have fun investigating science with the Museum's dedicated Explainers. The Museum is free, but charges apply to the IMAX cinema, special exhibitions and simulators.

Times Open all year, daily 10-6. Closed 24-26 Dec. **Fees** Admission free. Charges apply for IMAX 3D cinema, simulators & some special exhibitions. **Facilities** Ⓟ 🖵 †Ⓞ licensed 🎋 (indoor) ♿ toilets for disabled shop ⊗

SW7

Victoria and Albert Museum

Cromwell Rd, South Kensington SW7 2RL
☎ 020 7942 2000
e-mail: vanda@vam.ac.uk
web: www.vam.ac.uk
dir: Underground - South Kensington, Museum situated on A4, Buses C1, 14, 74, 414 stop outside the Cromwell Road entrance

The V&A is the world's greatest museum of art and design. It was established in 1852 to make important works of art available to all, and also to inspire British designers and manufacturers. The Museum's rich and diverse collections span over three thousand years of human creativity from many parts of the world, and include ceramics, furniture, fashion, glass, jewellery, metalwork, sculpture, textiles and paintings. Highlights include the British Galleries 1500-1900, the Jameel Gallery of Islamic Art, and the magnificent John Madejski Garden.

Times Open all year, daily 10-5.45. Fri 10am-10pm* **Facilities** Ⓟ 🖵 †Ⓞ licensed 🎋 (outdoor) toilets for disabled shop ⊗

SW13

London Wetland Centre

Queen Elizabeth Walk SW13 9WT
☎ 020 8409 4400 📠 020 8409 4401
e-mail: info.london@wwt.org.uk
web: www.wwt.org.uk
dir: A306 (underground - Hammersmith)

An inspiring wetland landscape that stretches over 105 acres, almost in the heart of London. Thirty wild wetland habitats have been created from reservoir lagoon to ponds, lakes and reedbeds and all are home to a wealth of wildlife. The visitor centre includes a café, gift shop, cinema, large glass viewing observatory and optics shop. There is a new Explore adventure centre for 3-11s.

Times Openall year: winter 9.30-5 (last admission 4); summer 9.30-6 (last admission 5).* Fees £9.50 (ch £5.25, concessions £7.10). Family ticket £26.55. Facilities 🅿 ⏚ ⍲ licensed ☶ (outdoor) ♿ toilets for disabled shop ⊗

SW19

Wimbledon Lawn Tennis Museum

Museum Building, The All England Club, Church Rd SW19 5AE
☎ 020 8946 6131 📠 020 8947 8752
e-mail: museum@aeltc.com
web: www.wimbledon.org/museum
dir: Underground - Southfields, 15mins walk. By road - from central London take A3 Portsmouth road, just before Tibbet's Corner left onto A219 towards Wimbledon, down Parkside, left onto Church Rd

Visitors to the Wimbledon Lawn Tennis Museum are invited to explore the game's evolution from a garden party pastime to a multi-million dollar professional sport played worldwide. Highlights include the Championship Trophies, a cinema that captures the Science of Tennis using CGI special effects, film and video footage of some of the most memorable matches, an extensive collection of memorabilia dating back to 1555, and a holographic John McEnroe who walks through a recreated 1980s changing room.

Times Open all year, daily 10-5. Closed middle Sun of Championships, Mon immediately following the Championships, 24-26 Dec & 1 Jan. Fees £10 (ch £5.50, ch under 5 free, concessions £8.75). Party 15+. Facilities 🅿 🅿 ⏚♿ toilets for disabled shop ⊗

W1

Pollock's Toy Museum

1 Scala St W1T 2HL
☎ 020 7636 3452
e-mail: pollocks@btconnect.com
web: www.pollockstoytheatre.com
dir: Underground - Goodge St

Teddy bears, wax and china dolls, dolls' houses, board games, toy theatres, tin toys, mechanical and optical toys, folk toys and nursery furniture, are among the attractions to be seen in this appealing museum. Items from all over the world and from all periods are displayed in two small, interconnecting houses with winding staircases and charming little rooms.

Times Open all year, Mon-Sat 10-5. Closed BH, Sun & Xmas.* Facilities Ⓟ ♿ (partly accessible) shop

W1

Royal Academy Of Arts

Burlington House, Piccadilly W1J 0BD
☎ 020 7300 5729 📄 020 7300 8032
e-mail: maria.salvatierra@royalacademy.org.uk
web: www.royalacademy.org.uk
dir: Underground - Piccadilly Circus, head towards Green Park

Known principally for international loan exhibitions, the Royal Academy of Arts was founded in 1768 and is Britain's oldest Fine Arts institution. Two of its founding principles were to provide a free school and to mount an annual exhibition open to all artists of distinguished merit, now known as the Summer Exhibition. The Royal Academy's most prized possession, Michelangelo's Tondo, 'The Virgin and Child with the Infant St John', one of only four marble sculptures by the artist outside Italy, is on permanent display in the Sackler Wing. The John Madejski Fine Rooms are a suite of six rooms displaying the highlights from the RA collection.

Times Open all year, daily 10-6. Late night opening Fri 10am-10pm. Closed 24-25 Dec. Fees £7-£12 (ch, concessions & group visitors reduced price). Prices vary for each exhibition. Free entry to permanent collection. Facilities Ⓟ 💻 🍴 licensed ♿ toilets for disabled shop ⊗

WC1

British Museum

Great Russell St WC1B 3DG
☎ 020 7323 8000 📄 020 7323 8616
e-mail: information@britishmuseum.org
web: www.thebritishmuseum.ac.uk
dir: Underground - Russell Sq, Tottenham Court Rd, Holborn

Of the world and for the world, the British Museum brings together astounding examples of universal heritage, for free. Enter through the largest covered square in Europe. Pick up your audio guide, children's pack or What's On programme. Then discover the world through objects like the Aztec mosaics, the Rosetta Stone, El Anatsui's African textiles or the colossal Ramesses II. And if you want a more intimate look, a fantastic evening meal or some world cinema, come late - every Thursday and Friday.

Times Open all year, Gallery: 10-5.30 selected galleries open late Thu-Fri until 8.30. Great Court: Sun-Wed 9-6, Thu-Sat 9am-11pm. Closed Good Fri, 24-26 Dec & 1 Jan.* Facilities ℗ 🚻 🍽 licensed ⊼ (indoor) toilets for disabled shop ⊗

WC2

London Transport Museum

The Piazza, Covent Garden WC2E 7BB

☎ 020 7379 6344 & 7565 7299
📄 020 7565 7250
e-mail: enquiry@ltmuseum.co.uk
web: www.ltmuseum.co.uk
dir: Underground - Covent Garden, Leicester Sq, Holborn or Charing Cross

Situated in the old Victorian flower market, London Transport Museum tells the story of the development of London, its transport system and how it shaped the lives of people living and working in the Capital. One of the world's best collections of graphic art and design is showcased in the 'Design for Travel' gallery including Harry Beck's famous Underground map, iconic transport posters, architecture and the story of a pioneering corporate identity. The museum also features past and present public transport including the Routemaster bus and the world's first Underground steam train.

Times Open all year Sat-Thu 10-6, Fri 11-6 (last admission 5.15). See website for Xmas & New Year opening times.* Fees With voluntary Gift Aid donation: £10 (under 16 free, pen £8, concessions £6).* Facilities ℗ 🚻 ⊼ (indoor) ♿ toilets for disabled shop ⊗

BARNET

Museum of Domestic Design & Architecture

Middlesex University, Cat Hill EN4 8HT
☎ 020 8411 5244 📠 020 8411 6639
e-mail: moda@mdx.ac.uk
web: www.moda.mdx.ac.uk
dir: from M25, junct 24 signed A111 Cockfosters to Cat Hill rdbt, straight over onto Chase side. Entrance 1st right opposite Chicken Shed Theatre on Cat Hill Campus

MoDA is a museum of the history of the home. It holds one of the world's most comprehensive collections of decorative design for the period 1870 to 1960, and is a rich source of information on how people decorated and lived in their homes. MoDA has two galleries, a lecture theatre for study days, a seminar room with practical workshops for both adults and children, and a study room which gives visitors access to the collections.

Times Open all year, Tue-Sat 10-5, Sun 2-5. Closed Mon, Etr, Xmas & New Year. Fees Free entrance. Charges for study days, workshop & group tours Facilities ♿ 🅿 toilets for disabled shop ⊗

CHESSINGTON

Chessington World of Adventures

Leatherhead Rd KT9 2NE
☎ 0871 663 4477
web: www.chessington.com
dir: M25 junct 9/10, on A243

Explore Chessington - it's a whole world of adventures! Soar on the Vampire roller coaster through the depths of Transylvania, take a fiery spin round Dragon's Fury or discover the mystery of Tomb Blaster in Forbidden Kingdom. Take a walk on the wild side with tigers, lions and gorillas in the Trail of the Kings and come face to face with sharks and curious stingrays in the park's very own Sea Life Centre - all in one place!

Times Open 28 Mar-2 Nov, times vary (main season). Zoo only days wknds from 7 Nov & daily from 12-31 Dec 10-3. Closed 25 Dec.*
Fees Prices not confirmed for 2010. Please telephone for details. Facilities 🅿 ⬛ 🍴 licensed ⊓ (outdoor) ♿ toilets for disabled shop ⊗

HAMPTON COURT

Hampton Court Palace

KT8 9AU

☎ 0870 752 7777   📄 020 8781 9669

e-mail: hamptoncourt@hrp.org.uk

web: www.hrp.org.uk

dir: A3 to Hook underpass then A309. Train from Waterloo - Hampton Court, 2mins walk from station

Step into a living Tudor world at Henry VIII's favourite palace. Creep along the eerie Haunted Gallery, relax in the acres of beautiful gardens running alongside the River Thames, and lose yourself in the world famous Maze.

Times Open all year, palace & maze 29 Mar-24 Oct, daily 10-6. Last ticket sold at 5, last entry into the maze 5.15 ; 25 Oct -27 Mar, daily 10-4.30. Last ticket sold at 3..30, last entry into the maze: 3.45. Closed 24-26 Dec.* **Fees** £14 (ch £7 under 5's free, children must be accompanied by an adult, concessions full-time student, over 60 with ID £11.50). Family ticket (2ad+3ch) £38.* **Facilities** 🅿 Ⓟ 🖵 🍴 licensed 🛏 🛗 toilets for disabled shop ⊗

KEW

Kew Gardens (Royal Botanic Gardens)

TW9 3AB

☎ 020 8332 5655   📄 020 8332 5197

e-mail: info@kew.org

web: www.kew.org

dir: 1m from M4 on South Circular (A205)

Kew Gardens is a paradise throughout the seasons. Lose yourself in the magnificent glasshouses and discover plants from the world's deserts, mountains and oceans. Wide-open spaces, stunning vistas, listed buildings and wildlife contribute to the Gardens' unique atmosphere. As well as being famous for its beautiful gardens, Kew is world renowned for its contribution to botanical and horticultural science.

Times Open all year, Gardens daily 9.30. Closing times vary (seasonal, phone to verify). Closed 24-25 Dec.* **Fees** £13 (ch under 17 free, concessions £11).* **Facilities** 🅿 Ⓟ 🖵 🍴 licensed 🛗 (partly accessible) (access restricted in Palm House basement & galleries, Temperate House & steps to upper level in the Princess of Wales Conservatory) toilets for disabled shop ⊗

TWICKENHAM

World Rugby Museum & Twickenham Stadium Tours

Twickenham Stadium, Rugby Rd TW1 1DZ
☎ 020 8891 8877 🖷 020 8892 2817
e-mail: museum@rfu.com
web: www.rfu.com/museum/
dir: A316, follow signs to Twickenham Stadium

Combine a behind-the-scenes guided tour of the world's most famous rugby stadium with a visit to the World Rugby Museum. The tour includes breathtaking views from the top of the Stand, a visit to the England dressing room and ends by walking through the players tunnel to pitch side. The multi-media museum appeals to enthusiasts of all ages and charts the history and world-wide growth of rugby. You can also test your skills on the scrum machine. 100 years of Twickenham Stadium 2009/2010 season.

Times Open all year, Tue-Sat 10-5 (last museum admission 4.30), Sun 11-5 (last admission 4.30). Closed post Twickenham match days, Etr Sun, 24-26 Dec & 1 Jan. On match days museum only available to match ticket holders. Please pre book all tours. Fees Museum & Tour £14 (concessions £8). Family (2ad+up to 3ch) £40. Facilities 🅿 🖵 🍴 licensed ♿ toilets for disabled shop ⊗

LIVERPOOL

Liverpool Football Club Museum and Stadium Tour

Anfield Rd L4 0TH
☎ 0151 260 6677 🖷 0151 264 0149
e-mail: Stephen.done@liverpoolfc.tv
web: www.liverpoolfc.tv

Touch the famous "This is Anfield" sign as you walk down the tunnel to the sound of the crowd at the LFC museum and tour centre. Celebrate all things Liverpool, past and present. Bright displays and videos chart the history of one of England's most successful football clubs.

Times Open all year: Museum daily 10-5 last admission 4. Closed 25-26 Dec. Match days 9 until last admission - 1hr before kick off. Museum & Tour - tours are run subject to daily demand. Advance booking is essential to avoid disappointment.* Facilities 🅿 🅿 🍴 licensed toilets for disabled shop ⊗

LIVERPOOL

National Conservation Centre
FREE

Whitechapel L1 6HZ
☎ 0151 478 4999 🖹 0151 478 4990
web: www.liverpoolmuseums.org.uk
dir: follow brown tourist signs to Whitechapel

Award-winning centre, the only one of its kind, gives the public an insight into the world of museum and gallery conservation. There is a regular changing exhibition programme.

Times Open all year, daily 10-5 & 24 Dec 10-2. Closed 25-26 Dec & 1 Jan. Facilities 🅿 Ⓟ ▱ ♿ toilets for disabled shop ⊗

PRESCOT

Knowsley Safari Park

L34 4AN
☎ 0151 430 9009 🖹 0151 426 3677
e-mail: safari.park@knowsley.com
web: www.knowsley.com
dir: M57 junct 2. Follow 'safari park' signs

A five-mile drive through the reserves enables visitors to see lions, tigers, elephants, rhinos, monkeys and many other animals in spacious, natural surroundings. Also a children's amusement park, reptile house, pets' corner plus sealion shows. Other attractions include an amusement park and a miniature railway.

Times Open all year, Mar-Oct, daily 10-4; Nov-Feb, 11-3. Closed 25 Dec. Fees £12 (ch & concessions £9).* Facilities 🅿 ▱ 🛋 (outdoor) ♿ toilets for disabled shop ⊗

BANHAM

Banham Zoo

The Grove NR16 2HE
☎ 01953 887771 & 887773
🖹 01953 887445
e-mail: info@banhamzoo.co.uk
web: www.banhamzoo.co.uk
dir: on B1113, signed off A11 and A140. Follow brown tourist signs

Set in 35 acres of magnificent parkland, see hundreds of animals ranging from big cats to birds of prey and siamangs to shire horses. Tiger Territory is a purpose-built enclosure for Siberian tigers, including a rock pool and woodland setting. See also Lemur Island and Tamarin and Marmoset Islands. The Heritage Farm Stables and Falconry displays Norfolk's rural heritage with majestic shire horses and birds of prey. Other attractions include Children's Farmyard Barn and Adventure Play Area.

Times Open all year, daily from 10. (Last admission 1 hour before closing). Closed 25 & 26 Dec.* Facilities 🅿 🅿 ⛲ 🍽 licensed 🗯 toilets for disabled shop ⊗

FAKENHAM

Penstborpe Nature Reserve & Gardens

Penstborpe NR21 0LN
☎ 01328 851465   🖹 01328 855905
e-mail: info@penstborpe.com
web: www.penstborpe.co.uk
dir: 1m from Fakenham on the A1067 to Norwich

Explore the beautiful lakes, nature trails and gardens designed by Chelsea Flower Show gold medallists, and look out for the large collection of cranes in the recently opened Conservation Centre. Penstborpe is currently host to the BBC Springwatch programme.

Times Open Jan-Mar, daily 10-4. Apr-Dec, 10-5. Closed 25-26 Dec* Fees £8.50 (ch 4-16 £5, concessions £7). Family ticket (2ad+2ch) £23. Please telephone or see website for more details.* Facilities 🅿 ⛲ 🗯 (outdoor) ♿ (partly accessible) (suitable paths around some of the reserve) toilets for disabled shop ⊗

GREAT YARMOUTH

Merrivale Model Village

Marine Pde NR30 3JG
☎ 01493 842097
web: www.merrivalemodelvillage.co.uk
dir: Marine parade seafront, next to Wellington Pier

Set in more than an acre of attractive landscaped gardens, this comprehensive miniature village is built on a scale of 1:12, and features streams, a lake and waterfalls. Among the models are a working fairground, a stone quarry, houses, shops, and a garden railway. At some times of the year there are illuminations at dusk. The Penny Arcade gives you the chance to play old amusements.

Times Open Etr-Oct, daily from 10. Fees Please telephone for details Facilities ℗ ⊡ 肩 (outdoor) ♿ toilets for disabled shop

GREAT YARMOUTH

Time and Tide Museum of Great Yarmouth Life

Tower Curing Works, Blackfriar's Rd NR30 3BX
☎ 01493 743930   📠 01493 743940
e-mail: yarmouth.museums@norfolk.gov.uk
web: www.museums.norfolk.gov.uk
dir: from A12 & A47 follow brown signs

An award-winning museum set in a Grade II listed Victorian herring-curing factory. Time and Tide tells Great Yarmouth's fascinating story, from prehistoric times to the present day; displays include fishing, wreck and rescue, seaside holidays, port and trade, and the World Wars. It also brings to life the herring curing industry and the lives of the people who worked here. The Museum's unique collections are interpreted using both traditional and interactive technology.

Times Open all year, Apr-Oct daily, 10-4; Nov-Mar, Mon-Fri 10-4, Sat & Sun12-4.* Facilities ℗ ⊡♿ toilets for disabled shop ⊗

117

LENWADE

Dinosaur Adventure Park

Weston Park NR9 5JW
☎ 01603 876310 📄 01603 876315
e-mail: info@dinosaurpark.co.uk
web: www.dinosaurpark.co.uk
dir: From A47 or A1067 follow brown signs to Park

Visitors can help the Ranger 'Track: T-Rex' on the Dinosaur Trail and meet giants from the past including the new spinosaurus. They can also make friends with animals from hedgehogs to wallabies, or bugs and snakes in the secret animal garden. There is also an adventure play area including a Climb-o-saurus, Raptor Racers, Jurassic Putt Crazy Golf, and the Lost World Amazing Adventure.

Times Open daily from 10 Sep & Oct half term; 11 Sep-22 Oct, Fri-Sun.* Facilities 🅿 ⛱ ⛲ (indoor & outdoor) toilets for disabled shop ⊗

NORWICH

Air Defence Radar Museum

RAF Neatishead NR12 8YB
☎ 01692 631485
e-mail: curator@radarmuseum.co.uk
web: www.radarmuseum.co.uk
dir: follow brown signs from A1062 at Horning

This multi-award winning Museum, housed in the original 1942 Radar Operations building, features the Battle of Britain Room, 1942 Ground Controlled Interception Room, Radar Engineering, Military Communications Systems, Cold War Operations Room, Royal Observer Corps, Space Defence, Bloodhound Missiles and Original Mobile Radar Vehicles. The newest addition is the RAF Coltishall Memorial Room.

Times Open year round 2nd Sat each month; Apr-Oct, Tue & Thu & BH Mons 10-5* Fees £4.50 (ch £3.50, under 13 free, concessions £4)* Facilities 🅿 ⛱ ⛲ (outdoor) ♿ (partly accessible) (two rooms not accessible to wheelchairs) toilets for disabled shop ⊗

SANDRINGHAM

Sandringham House, Gardens & Museum

PE35 6EN
☎ 01553 612908 📠 01485 541571
e-mail: visits@sandringhamestate.co.uk
web: www.sandringhamestate.co.uk
dir: off A148

The private country retreat of Her Majesty The Queen, this neo-Jacobean house was built in 1870 for King Edward VII. The main rooms used by the Royal Family when in residence are all open to the public. Sixty acres of glorious grounds surround the House and offer beauty and colour throughout the season. Sandringham Museum contains fascinating displays of Royal memorabilia. The ballroom exhibition changes each year.

Times Open Etr Sat-mid Jul & early Aug-Oct. House open 11-4.45, Museum 11-5 & Grounds 10.30-5.* Fees House, Museum & Grounds: £10 (ch £5, pen £8). Family ticket £25. Facilities ℗ ⊡ ⊧◉ licensed ♒ (outdoor) ⅙ toilets for disabled shop ⊗

WEST RUNTON

Hillside Shire Horse Sanctuary

Sandy Ln NR27 9QH
☎ 01603 736200
e-mail: contact@hillside.org.uk
web: www.hillside.org.uk
dir: off A149 in village of West Ranton half-way between Cromer & Sheringham, follow brown signs for Shire Horse Sanctuary

Come and see the heavy horses, ponies and donkeys as well as sheep, pigs, rabbits, ducks, hens, goats and many more rescued animals in their home in the beautiful north Norfolk countryside. Visit the museum and relive the farming days of yesteryear surrounded by an extensive collection of carts, wagons and farm machinery. There is lots of space for children to play in the activity areas. Try 'animal friendly' refreshments in the cafe and take home a souvenir from the gift shop. You may even 'adopt' a rescued animal.

Times Open 28 Mar-28 Oct daily; Apr-May after Etr closed Fri & Sat; Jun-Aug closed Sat; Sep-Oct closed Fri & Sat Fees £5.95 (ch £3.95, pen £4.95). Family ticket (2ad+2ch) £18.* Facilities ℗ ⊡ ♒ (outdoor) toilets for disabled shop ⊗

ALNWICK
Alnwick Castle

NE66 1NQ
☎ 01665 510777 📄 01665 510876
e-mail: enquiries@alnwickcastle.com
web: www.alnwickcastle.com
dir: off A1 on outskirts of town, signed

Set in a stunning landscape, Alnwick Castle overlooks the historic market town of Alnwick. Although it was originally built for the Percy family, who have lived here since 1309, -the current Duke and Duchess of Northumberland being the current tenants- the castle is best known as one of the locations that served as Hogwarts School in the Harry Potter movies. The castle is full of art and treasures and there are plenty of activities for all the family.

Times Open Etr-Oct, daily 10-6 (last admission 4.30). Fees £11.95 (ch 5-16yrs £4.95, concessions £9.95). Family ticket (2ad+4ch) £29.95. Party 14+ £7.95.* Facilities Ⓟ 🖵 🍽 licensed 🛱 (outdoor) ♿ (partly accessible) (Some areas not suitable for wheelchair users) toilets for disabled shop ⊗

BAMBURGH
Bamburgh Castle

NE69 7DF
☎ 01668 214515 & 214208
web: www.bamburghcastle.com
dir: A1 Belford by-pass, E on B1342 to Bamburgh

Rising dramatically from a rocky outcrop, Bamburgh Castle is a huge, square Norman castle. Last restored in the 19th century, it has an impressive hall and an armoury with a large collection of armour from the Tower of London. These formidable stone walls have witnessed dark tales of royal rebellion, bloody battles, spellbinding legends and millionaire benefactors. Experience the sights, stories and atmosphere of over two thousand years of exhilarating history.

Times Open Mar-Oct, daily 10-5 (last admission 4).* Fees £8 (ch under 5 free, ch 5-15yrs £4 & pen £7). Facilities Ⓟ Ⓟ 🖵 🛱 (outdoor) ♿ (partly accessible) (5 castle rooms accessible to wheelchairs) toilets for disabled shop ⊗

BARDON MILL

Vindolanda (Chesterholm)

Vindolanda Trust NE47 7JN
☎ 01434 344277   📄 01434 344060
e-mail: info@vindolanda.com
web: www.vindolanda.com
dir: signed from A69 or B6318

Vindolanda was a Roman fort and frontier town.
It was started well before Hadrian's Wall, and
became a base for 500 soldiers. The civilian
settlement lay just west of the fort and has been
excavated. The excellent museum in the country
house of Chesterholm nearby has displays and
reconstructions. There are also formal gardens
and an open-air museum with Roman Temple,
shop, house and Northumbrian croft.

Times Open Feb-Mar, daily 10-5; Apr-Sep, 10-6;
Oct & Nov 10-5. Limited winter opening, please
contact site for further details.* Facilities 🅿
⊡ 🍴 (outdoor) ♿ (partly accessible) (please
contact for further info) toilets for disabled
shop ⊗

GREENHEAD

Roman Army Museum

Carvoran CA8 7JB
☎ 016977 47485
e-mail: info@vindolanda.com
web: www.vindolanda.com
dir: follow brown tourist signs from A69 or B6318

Situated alongside the Walltown Grags Section
of Hadrian's Wall, the museum is a great
introduction to the Roman Army. Find out about
Roman weapons, training, pay, off-duty activities
and much more. See if you can be persuaded to
join up by watching the recruitment film, or view
the Eagle's Eye film and soar with the eagle over
Hadrian's Wall.

Times Open Feb-Mar & Oct-Nov, 10-5; Apr-Sep
10-6 (closed mid Nov-mid Feb)* Facilities 🅿 🅿
⊡ 🍴 (outdoor) ♿ toilets for disabled shop ⊗

WARKWORTH

Warkworth Castle & Hermitage

NE66 0UJ

☎ 01665 711423

web: www.english-heritage.org.uk

The magnificent eight-towered keep of Warkworth Castle stands on a hill high above the River Coquet, dominating all around it. A complex stronghold, it was home to the Percy family, which at times wielded more power in the North than the King himself.

Times Open all year. Castle: Apr-Sep, daily 10-5; Oct-1 Nov, daily 10-4; 2 Nov-Mar, Sat-Mon 10-4. Hermitage: Apr-Sep, Wed, Sun & BH 11-5. Closed 24-26 Dec & 1 Jan. **Fees** Castle: £4.20 (concessions £3.60, ch £2.10). Family ticket £10.50. Hermitage: £3 (concessions £2.60, ch £1.50). Prices and opening times are subject to change in March 2010. Please check web site or call 0870 333 1181 for the most up to date prices and opening times when planning your visit. **Facilities** ℗ ﴾ (partly accessible) (limited access, steps) toilets for disabled shop ⊞

WYLAM

George Stephenson's Birthplace

NE41 8BP

☎ 01661 853457

e-mail: georgestephensons@nationaltrust.org.uk

web: www.nationaltrust.org.uk

dir: 1.5m S of A69 at Wylam

Birthplace of the world famous railway engineer, this small stone tenement was built around 1760 to accommodate mining families. The furnishings reflect the year of Stephenson's birth here in 1781, his whole family living in one room.

Times Open 15 Mar-2 Nov, Thu-Sun, 12-5 & BH Mons.* **Facilities** ℗ ⊑ ﴾ toilets for disabled ⊗ ⛟

EDWINSTOWE

Sherwood Forest Country Park & Visitor Centre **FREE**

NG21 9HN

☎ 01623 823202 & 824490

🖷 01623 823202

e-mail: sherwood.forest@nottscc.gov.uk

web: www.nottinghamshire.gov.uk/
sherwoodforestcp

dir: on B6034 N of Edwinstowe between A6075
and A616

At the heart of the Robin Hood legend is
Sherwood Forest. Today it is a country park and
visitor centre with 450 acres of ancient oaks and
shimmering silver birches. Waymarked pathways
guide you through the forest. A year round
programme of events includes the spectacular
annual Robin Hood Festival.

Times Open all year. Country Park: open daily
dawn to dusk. Visitor Centre: open daily 10-5
(4.30 Nov-Mar). Closed 25 Dec.* Facilities 🅿 🅟
🍴 🎪 (outdoor) toilets for disabled shop

FARNSFIELD

White Post Farm

NG22 8HL

☎ 01623 882977 & 882026

🖷 01623 883499

e-mail: admin@whitepostfarm.co.uk

web: www.whitepostfarm.co.uk

dir: 12m N of Nottingham on A614

With over 25 acres there's lots to see and do at
the White Post Farm. There are more than 3000
animals including pigs, goats and sheep, along
with more exotic animals like deer, reptiles and
wallabies. The new indoor play area is ideal for
small children, and there's also a sledge run,
trampolines and pedal go-karts.

Times Open daily from 10* Fees £8.50 (ch 2-16
£7.75, under 2s free)* Facilities 🅿 🅟 🍴
🍴 licensed 🎪 (indoor & outdoor) 🦽 toilets for
disabled shop 🚫

NEWARK-ON-TRENT

Vina Cooke Museum of Dolls & Bygone Childhood

The Old Rectory, Cromwell NG23 6JE
☎ 01636 821364
e-mail: info@vinasdolls.co.uk
web: www.vinasdolls.co.uk
dir: 5m N of Newark off A1

All kinds of childhood memorabilia are displayed in this 17th-century house: prams, toys, dolls' houses, costumes and a large collection of Victorian and Edwardian dolls including Vina Cooke hand-made character dolls.

Times Open Apr-Sep, Tue, Thu, Sat-Sun & BH 10.30-4.30. Mon, Wed, Fri and Oct-Mar by appointment, please telephone. **Fees** £3 (ch £1.50, pen £2.50).* **Facilities** 🅿 ℗ ⌐ (outdoor) ♿ (partly accessible) (5 steps to front door with handrail on both sides) ⊗

NOTTINGHAM

Galleries of Justice

The Shire Hall, High Pavement, Lace Market NG1 1HN
☎ 0115 952 0555   📄 0115 993 9828
e-mail: info@nccl.org.uk
web: www.nccl.org.uk
dir: follow signs to city centre, brown heritage signs to Lace Market & Galleries of Justice

The Galleries of Justice are located on the site of an original Court and County Gaol. Recent developments include the arrival of the HM Prison Service Collection, which will now be permanently housed in the 1833 wing. Never before seen artefacts from prisons across the country offer visitors the chance to experience some of Britain's most gruesome, yet often touching, reminders of what prison life would have been for inmates and prison staff over the last three centuries.

Times Open all year, Tue-Sun & BH Mon 10-5 (also open Mon in school hols). (Last admission one hour before closing). Contact for Xmas opening times.* **Facilities** ℗ ⊡ ⌐ (indoor) toilets for disabled shop ⊗

SOUTHWELL

The Workhouse

Upton Rd NG25 0PT

☎ 01636 817250 📄 01636 817251
e-mail: theworkhouse@nationaltrust.org.uk
web: www.nationaltrust.org.uk
dir: 13m from Nottingham on A612

Meet the Reverend Becher, the founder of the Workhouse, by watching the introductory film and immerse yourself in the unique atmosphere evoked by the audio guide. Based on real archive records, the guide helps bring the 19th-century inhabitants back to life. Explore the segregated work yards, day rooms, dormitories, master's quarters and cellars, then see the recreated working 19th-century garden and find out what food the paupers would have eaten.

Times Open 28 Feb15 Mar, Sat -Sun 11-5; 18 Mar-1 Nov, Wed-Sun 12-5. Open BH Mons & Good Fri. (Last admission 1hr before closing, normal house admission from noon)* **Fees** With Gift Aid donation: £6.10 (ch £3.15). Family ticket (2ad+3ch) £15.35. Family ticket (1ad) £9.25.* **Facilities** 🅿 🅟 ♿ (partly accessible) (Ground floor accessible, stairs to other floors. Not suitable for motorised wheelchairs. Grounds partly accessible, loose gravel paths) toilets for disabled ⊗ ♨

BURFORD

Cotswold Wildlife Park

OX18 4JP

☎ 01993 823006 📄 01993 823807
web: www.cotswoldwildlifepark.co.uk
dir: on A361 2m S of A40 at Burford

This 160-acre landscaped zoological park, surrounds a listed Gothic-style manor house. There is a varied collection of animals from all over the world, many of which are endangered species such as Asiatic lions, leopards, white rhinos and red pandas. There's an adventure playground, a children's farmyard, and train rides during the summer. The park has also become one of the Cotswolds' leading attractions for garden enthusiasts, with its exotic summer displays and varied plantings offering interest all year.

Times Open all year, daily from 10, (last admission 4.30 Mar-Sep, 3.30 Oct-Feb). Closed 25 Dec. **Fees** £11.50 (ch 3-16 & over 65's £8). **Facilities** 🅿 ⊡ 🍴 licensed 🎪 (indoor & outdoor) ♿ toilets for disabled shop

DIDCOT

Didcot Railway Centre

OX11 7NJ

☎ 01235 817200 📄 01235 510621
e-mail: info@didcotrailwaycentre.org.uk
web: www.didcotrailwaycentre.org.uk
dir: M4 junct 13, A34, located on A4130 at Didcot Parkway Station

Based around the original GWR engine shed, the Centre is home to the biggest collection anywhere of Great Western Railway steam locomotives, carriages and wagons. A typical GWR station has been re-created and a section of Brunel's original broad gauge track relaid, with a replica of Fire Fly locomotive of 1840. There is a full programme of steamdays, including the now-traditional Thomas the Tank and Santa specials. Contact for a timetable.

Times Open all year, Sat-Sun; daily 14-22 Feb; 4-19 Apr ; 23-31 May; 20 Jun-6 Sep; 24 Oct-1 Nov; 27 Dec-3 Jan. Day out with Thomas 6-8 Mar, 2-4 Oct & 5-23 Dec, Fri-Sun.* Fees £5-£10 depending on event (ch £4-£9, concessions £4.50-£9.50).* Facilities ℗ ⌨ ⑪ licensed 🪑 (outdoor) ⚒ (partly accessible) (18 awkward steps at entrance) toilets for disabled shop

HENLEY-ON-THAMES

River & Rowing Museum

Mill Meadows RG9 1BF
☎ 01491 415600 📄 01491 415601
e-mail: museum@rrm.co.uk
web: www.rrm.co.uk
dir: off A4130, signed to Mill Meadows

Discover The River Thames, the sport of rowing and the town of Henley-on-Thames at this award-winning museum, a contemporary building overlooking the river and bordered by meadows. You can also meet Mr Toad, Ratty, Badger and Mole at the Wind in the Willows exhibition. E.H. Shepard's famous illustrations are brought to life by 3-D models of their adventures. See Ratty and Mole's picnic on the riverbank, get lost in the Wild Wood or watch the weasels at Toad Hall.

Times Open: May-Aug 10-5.30; Sep-Apr 10-5. Closed 24-25 & 31 Dec & 1 Jan.* Facilities ℗ ⌨ ⑪ licensed ⚒ (partly accessible) toilets for disabled shop ⊗

OXFORD

Ashmolean Museum of Art & Archaeology **FREE**

Beaumont St OX1 2PH
☎ 01865 278000 📄 01865 278018
web: www.ashmolean.org
dir: city centre, opposite The Randolph Hotel

The oldest museum in the country, opened in 1683, the Ashmolean contains Oxford University's priceless collections. Many important historical art pieces and artefacts are on display, including work from Ancient Greece through to the twentieth century. The museum has undergone a massive redevelopment, including the building of 39 new galleries, an education centre, conservation studios and a walkway.

Times Open all year, Tue-Sun 10-5, BH Mons 10-5. Closed during St.Giles Fair (7-9 Sept) Xmas & 1 Jan. Facilities Ⓟ 🖵 🍽 licensed ♿ toilets for disabled shop ⊗

OXFORD

Museum of the History of Science **FREE**

Broad St OX1 3AZ
☎ 01865 277280 📄 01865 277288
e-mail: museum@mhs.ox.ac.uk
web: www.mhs.ox.ac.uk
dir: next to Sheldonian Theatre in city centre, on Broad St

The first purpose-built museum in Britain, containing the world's finest collection of early scientific instruments used in astronomy, navigation, surveying, physics and chemistry. Various events through the year.

Times Open all year, Tue-Fri 12-5, Sat 10-5, Sun 2-5. Closed Xmas and Etr Sun. Facilities Ⓟ ♿ (partly accessible) (lift to basement) toilets for disabled shop ⊗

OXFORD

Pitt Rivers Museum **FREE**

South Parks Rd OX1 3PP
☎ 01865 270927 📄 01865 270943
e-mail: prm@prm.ox.ac.uk
web: www.prm.ox.ac.uk
dir: 10 min walk from city centre, visitors
entrance on Parks Rd through the Oxford
University Museum of Natural History

The museum is one of the city's most popular
attractions. It is part of the University of Oxford
and was founded in 1884. The collections held at
the museum are internationally acclaimed, and
contain many objects from different cultures of
the world and from various periods, all grouped
by type, or purpose. The upper gallery, housing
the weapons and armour displays, will be closed
until Spring 2010.

Times Open all year, Tue-Sun & BH Mon 10-4.30,
Mon 12-4.30. Contact museum at Christmas &
Easter to check times. The upper gallery, housing
the weapons and armour displays, will be closed
until Spring 2010. **Facilities** Ⓟ ♿ toilets for
disabled shop ⊗

WOODSTOCK

Blenheim Palace

OX20 1PP
☎ 08700 602080 📄 01993 810570
e-mail: operations@blenheimpalace.com
web: www.blenheimpalace.com
dir: M40 junct 9, follow signs to Blenheim Palace,
on A44 8m N of Oxford

Home of the Duke and Duchess of Marlborough
and birthplace of Sir Winston Churchill, Blenheim
Palace is an English Baroque masterpiece. Fine
furniture, sculpture, paintings and tapestries
are set in magnificent gilded staterooms that
overlook sweeping lawns and formal gardens.
'Capability' Brown landscaped the 2100-acre
park, which is open to visitors for pleasant walks
and beautiful views. Please telephone for details
of events throughout the year.

Times Open Palace & Gardens 13 Feb-12 Dec
(ex Mon-Tue in Nov & Dec) daily 10.30-6. (last
admission 4.45). Park daily all year 9-6 (last
admission 4.45) Closed 25 Dec. **Fees** Palace,
Park & Gardens £12.30-£17.50 (ch £6.75-£10,
concessions £10.80-£14). Family £46. Park &
Gardens £6.90-£10 (ch £3.30-£5, concessions
£5.70-£7.50). Family £25. **Facilities** Ⓟ Ⓟ ⊑
⊙ licensed ⋒ (outdoor) ♿ (partly accessible)
(Wheelchair access via lift in Palace) toilets for
disabled shop ⊗

WOODSTOCK

Oxfordshire Museum **FREE**

Fletcher's House, Park St OX20 1SN
☎ 01993 811456   📄 01993 813239
e-mail: oxon.museum@oxfordshire.go.uk
web: www.tomocc.org.uk
dir: A44 Evesham-Oxford, follow signs for
Blenheim Palace. Museum opposite church

Situated in the heart of the historic town of
Woodstock, the award-winning redevelopment
of Fletcher's House provides a home for the new
county museum. Set in attractive gardens, the
new museum celebrates Oxfordshire in all its
diversity and features collections of local history,
art, archaeology, landscape and wildlife as well
as a gallery exploring the County's innovative
industries from nuclear power to nanotechnology.
Interactive exhibits offer new learning
experiences for visitors of all ages. The museum's
purpose-built Garden Gallery houses a variety
of touring exhibitions of regional and national
interest. A new display of dinosaur footprints
from Ardley Quarry and a replica megalosaurus,
are located in the walled garden.

Times Open all year, Tue-Sat 10-5, Sun 2-5.
Closed Good Fri, 25-26 Dec & 1 Jan. Galleries
closed on Mon, but open BH Mons, 2-5. **Facilities**
Ⓟ ⊑ ⏐◎⏐ licensed ⊓ (outdoor) ♿ toilets for
disabled shop ⊗

COSFORD

The Royal Air Force Museum

TF11 8UP
☎ 01902 376200   📄 01902 376211
e-mail: cosford@rafmuseum.org
web: www.rafmuseum.org
dir: on A41, 1m S of M54 junct 3

The Royal Air Force Museum Cosford has one of
the largest aviation collections in the UK, with 70
historic aircraft on display. Visitors will be able
to see Britain's V bombers - Vulcan, Victor and
Valiant and other aircraft suspended in flying
attitudes in the national Cold War exhibition,
housed in a landmark building covering
8000sqm.

Times Open all year daily, 10-6 (last admission
4). Closed 24-26 Dec & 1 Jan, 7-11 Jan.*
Facilities Ⓟ ⊑ ⏐◎⏐ licensed ⊓ (outdoor) ♿
toilets for disabled shop ⊗

IRONBRIDGE

Ironbridge Gorge Museums

Coach Rd TF8 7DQ
☎ 01952 884391　& 0800 590258
📄 01952 884391
e-mail: tic@ironbridge.org.uk
web: www.ironbridge.org.uk
dir: M54 junct 4, signed

Ironbridge is the site of the world's first iron bridge. It was cast and built here in 1779, to span a narrow gorge over the River Severn. Now Ironbridge is the site of a remarkable series of museums relating the story of the bridge, recreating life in Victorian times and featuring ceramics and social history displays.

Times Open all year, 10-5. Some small sites closed Nov-Mar. Telephone for exact winter details. Fees A passport ticket allowing repeat visits to all museums for 12 months is available call 01952 884391or see website for details.* Facilities 🅿 🅟 ⬜ 🍴 licensed 🛋 (outdoor) ♿ toilets for disabled shop 🚫

TELFORD

Hoo Farm Animal Kingdom

Preston-on-the-Weald Moors TF6 6DJ
☎ 01952 677917　📄 01952 677944
e-mail: info@hoofarm.com
web: www.hoofarm.com
dir: M54 junct 6, follow brown tourist signs

Hoo Farm is a real children's paradise where there is always something happening. A clean, friendly farm that appeals to all ages and offers close contact with a wide variety of animals from fluffy chicks and lambs to foxes, llamas, deer and ostriches. A daily programme of events encourages audience participation in the form of bottle feeding lambs, pig feeding, ferret racing and collecting freshly-laid eggs. There are junior quad bikes and a rifle range, pony rides, powered mini-tractors as well as indoor and outdoor play areas and a games room. Please telephone for details of special events throughout the year.

Times Open 25 Mar-9 Sep, Tue-Sun 10-6; 10 Sep-24 Nov, Tue-Sun, 10-5. 25; Nov-24 Dec, daily 10-5. Closes at 1 on 24 Dec. Closed 25 Dec to mid March.* Facilities 🅿 ⬜ 🛋 (indoor & outdoor) ♿ (partly accessible) toilets for disabled shop 🚫

WESTON-UNDER-REDCASTLE

Hawkstone Historic Park & Follies

SY4 5UY
☎ 01948 841700 📠 01939 200335
e-mail: enquiries@hawkstone.co.uk
web: www.principal-hayley.co.uk
dir: 3m from Hodnet off A53, follow brown
heritage signs

Created in the 18th century by the Hill family,
Hawkstone is one of the greatest historic
parklands in Britain. After almost 100 years of
neglect it has now been restored and designated
a Grade I historic landscape. Experience the
magical world of intricate pathways, arches
and bridges, towering cliffs and follies, and an
awesome grotto. The park covers nearly 100
acres of hilly terrain and visitors are advised to
wear sensible shoes and clothing and to bring
a torch. Allow 3-4 hours for the tour, which is
well signposted - a route map is included in the
admission price.

Times Open from 10 Mar, Sat & Sun; Apr-May, &
Sep-Oct, Wed-Sun; Jun-Aug, daily. Closed Nov-
Mar.* Fees Wkdays £6 (ch £4 pen & students
£5). Family ticket £17.* Facilities ℗ 🖵 🍴
licensed 🎪 (outdoor) ♿ (partly accessible)
(access to tearooms, gift shop and grand valley)
toilets for disabled shop

BATH

Bath Postal Museum

27 Northgate St BA1 1AJ
☎ 01225 460333 📠 01225 460333
e-mail: info@bathpostalmuseum.org
web: www.bathpostalmuseum.org
dir: On entering city fork left at mini rdbt. After
all lights into Walcot St. Podium car park facing

The first letter sent with a stamp was sent from
Bath, and this museum helps you to discover
how 18th-century Bath influenced and developed
the Postal System, including the story of the
Penny Post. Visitors can explore the history of
written communication from ancient Egyptian
clay tablets, to the first Airmail flight from Bath
to London in 1912. See the Victorian Post Office
and watch continuous video films including the
in-house production entitled 'History of Writing'.
The museum is full of hands-on and interactive
features to engage the whole family.

Times Open all year, Mon-Sat 11-5. (Last
admission Mar-Oct 4.30, Nov-Feb 4).*
Fees £3.50 (ch under 5 free, ch £1.50,
concessions £3, students £1.50). Family and
Party 10+ tickets available.* Facilities ℗ ♿
shop 🚫

131

BATH

Fashion Museum

Bennett St BA1 2QH
☎ 01225 477173 🖷 01225 477743
e-mail: fashion_bookings@bathnes.gov.uk
web: www.fashionmuseum.co.uk
dir: Museum near city centre. Parking in
Charlotte Street Car park.

The Fashion Museum showcases a world-class
collection of historical and contemporary dress
and includes opportunities to try on replica
corsets and crinolines. It is housed in Bath's
famous 18th-century Assembly Rooms designed
by John Wood the Younger in 1771. Entrance to
the Assembly Rooms is free. Special exhibitions
are held every summer in the Ballroom.

Times Open all year, daily Jan-Feb 10.30-4;
Mar-Oct, 10.30-5; Nov-Dec, 10.30-4. Closed
25-26 Dec.* Fees £7 (ch £5). Family ticket £20.
Combined ticket with Roman Baths, £14.50 (ch
£8.70).* Facilities ⓟ ⊑ ♿ toilets for disabled
shop ⊗

BATH

Roman Baths & Pump Room

Abbey Church Yard BA1 1LZ
☎ 01225 477785 🖷 01225 477743
e-mail: romanbaths_bookings@bathnes.gov.uk
web: www.romanbaths.co.uk
dir: M4 junct 18, A46 into city centre

The remains of the Roman baths and temple
give a vivid impression of life nearly 2,000 years
ago. Built next to Britain's only hot spring, the
baths served the sick, and the pilgrims visiting
the adjacent Temple of Sulis Minerva. Above the
Temple Courtyard, the Pump Room became a
popular meeting place in the 18th century. The
site still flows with natural hot water and no visit
is complete without a taste of the famous hot spa
water. Costumed characters every day.

Times Open all year, Mar-Jun & Sep-Oct, daily
9-5; Jul & Aug, daily 9am-9pm; Jan-Feb & Nov-
Dec, daily 9.30-4.30. Closed 25-26 Dec. (Last
exit 1hr after these times).* Fees £11 (£11.50
Jul-Aug) (ch £7.20). Family ticket £32. Combined
ticket with Fashion Museum £14.50 (ch £8.70).*
Facilities ⓟ ⏺ licensed ♿ (partly accessible)
(lift to lower museum) toilets for disabled shop
⊗

CRICKET ST THOMAS

The Wildlife Park at Cricket St Thomas

TA20 4DB

☎ 01460 30111 & 30892 🖹 01460 30817
e-mail: wildlifepark.cst@bourne-leisure.co.uk
web: www.wild.org.uk
dir: 3m E of Chard on A30, follow brown heritage signs.

The Wildlife Park offers you the chance to see more than 500 animals at close quarters. Visitors can learn about what is being done to save endangered species, take a walk through the Lemur Wood, or ride on the Safari Train. During peak season, park mascot Larry the Lemur stars in his own show.

Times Open all year, daily 10-6, last admission 4; winter 10-4.30, last admission 3. Closed 25 Dec.* Fees £8.75 (ch 3-14 £6.50, under 3's free, concessions £7.50). Family ticket £27.50 (2ad+3ch).* Facilities ❷ ⬜ 🍽 licensed 🏛 (outdoor) ♿ (partly accessible) toilets for disabled shop ⊗

SPARKFORD

Haynes International Motor Museum

BA22 7LH

☎ 01963 440804 🖹 01963 441004
e-mail: info@haynesmotormuseum.co.uk
web: www.haynesmotormuseum.co.uk
dir: from A303 follow A359 towards Castle Cary, museum clearly signed

More than 400 cars and bikes stunningly displayed, dating from 1886 to the present day, this is the largest international motor museum in Britain. If you want a nostalgic trip down memory lane the museum offers a host of familiar names such as Austin, MG and Morris, while for those seeking something more exotic there is a vast array of performance cars, from modern classics such as the Dodge Viper, Jaguar XJ220 and the Ferrari 360, plus the classic Jaguar E Type and AC Cobra. Also on show is a large collection of American cars, including the jewels in the Haynes crown, the V16 Cadillac, and the million-dollar Duesenberg.

Times Open all year, Apr-Sep, daily 9.30-5.30; Oct-Mar, 10-4.30. Closed 24-26 Dec & 1 Jan. Fees £7.95 (ch £4.25, concessions £6.95). Family £10.95 (1ad+1ch), £25.75 (2ad+3ch). Facilities ❷ ⬜ 🏛 (outdoor) ♿ toilets for disabled shop ⊗

WASHFORD

Cleeve Abbey

TA23 0PS
☎ 01984 640377 📠 01984 641348
web: www.english-heritage.org.uk
dir: 0.25m S of A39

This 13th-century monastic site features some of the finest cloister buildings in England; medieval wall paintings, a mosaic tiled floor and an interesting exhibition.

Times Open Apr-Jun & Sep, daily 10-5; Jul-Aug, daily 10-6; Oct-1 Nov, daily 10-4. Closed 2 Nov-Mar. **Fees** £3.80 (concessions £3.20, ch £1.90). Prices and opening times are subject to change in March 2010. Please check web site or call 0870 333 1181 for the most up to date prices and opening times when planning your visit. **Facilities** ❷ 🛱 shop ♿

WESTON-SUPER-MARE

The Helicopter Museum

The Heliport, Locking Moor Rd BS24 8PP
☎ 01934 635227 📠 01934 645230
e-mail: helimuseum@btconnect.com
web: www.helicoptermuseum.co.uk
dir: outskirts of town on A371, nr M5 junct 21, follow propellor signs

The world's largest rotary-wing collection and the only helicopter museum in Britain, home of the Queen's Royal flight helicopters. More than 70 helicopters and autogyros are on display - including examples from France, Germany, Poland, Russia and the United States, from 1935 to the present day - with displays of models, engines and other components explaining the history and development of the rotorcraft. Special events include 'Open Cockpit Days', when visitors can learn more about how the helicopter works. Helicopter flights available on set dates throughout the year.

Times Open all year, Nov-Mar, Wed-Sun 10-4.30; Apr-Oct 10-5.30. Open daily during Etr & summer school hols 10-5.30. Closed 24-26 Dec & 1 Jan. **Fees** £5.50 (ch under 5 free, ch 5-16 £3.50, concessions £4.50). Family ticket (2ad+2ch) £15.50, (2ad+3ch) £17.50. Party 12+.* **Facilities** ❷ 🖵 🛱 (outdoor) ♿ toilets for disabled shop

WOOKEY HOLE

Wookey Hole Caves & Papermill

BA5 1BB

☎ 01749 672243   📄 01749 677749

e-mail: witch@wookey.co.uk

web: www.wookey.co.uk

dir: M5 junct 22 follow signs via A38 & A371, from Bristol & Bath A39 to Wells then 2m to Wookey Hole

Britain's most spectacular caves and legendary home of the infamous Witch of Wookey. The 19th-century paper mill houses a variety of fascinating attractions including a Cave Museum, Victorian Penny Arcade, Magical Mirror Maze, Haunted Corridor of Crazy Mirrors, and the Wizard's Castle play area. Visitors can also see paper being made in Britain's only surviving handmade paper mill. Puppet theatre shows, magic lessons, an enchanted fairy garden and Dinosaur Valley round off this family day out in Wookey Gorge.

Times Open all year daily Apr-Oct 10-5; Nov-Mar 10-4; Dec-Jan, open wknds & sch hol. Closed 25-26 Dec.* Fees £15 (ch 4-14 & concessions £10, under 3's free)* Facilities ❷ 🚻🍴 licensed 🪑 (outdoor) ♿ (partly accessible) (papermill only accessible) toilets for disabled shop ⊗

YEOVILTON

Fleet Air Arm Museum

Royal Naval Air Station BA22 8HT

☎ 01935 840565   📄 01935 842630

e-mail: info@fleetairarm.com

web: www.fleetairarm.com

dir: on B3151, just off junct of A303 and A37

The Fleet Air Arm Museum is where museum meets theatre! You'll 'fly' by helicopter to the replica flight deck of aircraft carrier HMS Ark Royal. You'll see fighter aircraft and two enormous projection screens showing jet fighters taking off and landing, and even a nuclear bomb. The Museum has Europe's largest collection of naval aircraft and the first British-built Concorde. Go on board and visit the cockpit. There's an adventure playground, and the museum is located alongside Europe's busiest military air station at RNAS Yeovilton.

Times Open all year: Apr-Oct, daily 10-5.30; Nov-Mar, Wed-Sun 10-4.30 (Closed 24-26 Dec)* Fees £11 (ch under 17 £8, under 5 free, concessions £9). Family (2ad+3ch) £35.* Facilities ❷ ❷ 🚻🍴 licensed 🪑 (outdoor) ♿ toilets for disabled shop ⊗

ALTON

Alton Towers

ST10 4DB

☎ 08705 204060 📄 01538 704097
e-mail: info@alton-towers.com
web: www.altontowers.com
dir: from S - M1 junct 23a or M6 junct 15. From
N - M1 junct 24a or M6 junct 16

Alton Towers is a fantastic day out for all the
family. With world first rides and attractions
as well as some beautiful gardens, this is
more than just a theme park. The Alton Towers
Resort is a popular UK short break destination
for families. With a unique combination of
rides and attractions suitable for all ages, the
Resort consists of the Alton Towers Theme Park,
waterpark, spa, two fully themed hotels and two
nine-hole golf courses.

Times Open daily 14-22 Feb & 28 Mar-1 Nov.
Hotels, waterpark, spa and golf open all year.*
Facilities 🅿 ⊑ 🍴 licensed ⋔ (outdoor) ᴋ
toilets for disabled shop ⊗

LEEK

Blackbrook Zoological Park

Winkhill ST13 7QR

☎ 01538 308293 📄 01538 308293
e-mail: enquiries@blackbrookzoologicalpark.
co.uk
web: www.blackbrookzoologicalpark.co.uk
dir: off A523 Leek to Ashbourne road

Blackbrook Zoological Park is a fun and
educational day for all. A continually growing
attraction, always with something new to see.
The zoo features: mammals, rare birds, reptiles,
insects and aquatics; owl flights, pelican,
penguin and lemur feeds. Blackbrook Zoological
Park is fully accessible for pushchairs and
wheelchairs.

Times Open daily 10-5.30; winter 10.30-dusk
(last admission 4)* **Facilities** 🅿 ⊑ ⋔ (outdoor)
ᴋ toilets for disabled shop ⊗

SHUGBOROUGH

Shugborough Estate

ST17 0XB

☎ 01889 881388   🖹 01889 881323
e-mail: shugborough.promotions@staffordshire.
gov.uk
web: www.shugborough.org.uk
dir: 6m E of Stafford off A513, signed from M6
junct 13

Discover a bygone era as costumed living history
characters bring the past to life. The story begins
in the walled garden - meet the gardeners of
1805 and find out how fruit and vegetables are
grown on the estate. At the farm the servants
are busy making butter and cheese and the farm
hands tend to the animals. Cooks and kitchen
maids scurry about, preparing food on the range,
starching the whites in the laundry and brewing
ale in the wood-fired brewery. The Mansion House
completes the story, where the 1805 Viscount and
Lady Anson are often present. Please contact or
see website for details of special events.

Times Open 18 Mar-28 Oct, daily 11-5. Site open
all year to pre-booked parties.* Fees £12 (ch £7,
under 5 free, concessions £9.50). Family ticket
(2ad+3ch) £30, (1ad+1ch £15). Facilities ❷ ☐
🍽 licensed ⋒ (outdoor) ♿ (partly accessible)
(steps to house, stairclimber available) toilets for
disabled shop ⊗ ♣

STOKE ON TRENT

Ceramica

Market Place, Burslem ST6 3DS
☎ 01782 832001   🖹 01782 823300
e-mail: info@ceramicauk.com
web: www.ceramicauk.com
dir: A4527 (signposted Tunstall). After 0.5m right
onto B5051 for Burslem. Ceramica is in Old Town
Hall in centre of town.

A unique experience for all the family, Ceramica
is housed in the Old Town Hall in the centre of
Burslem, Mother Town of the Potteries. Explore
the hands-on activities in Bizarreland, and
learn how clay is transformed into china. Dig
into history with the time team and take a
magic carpet ride over the town. Discover the
past, present and future of ceramics with the
interactive displays in the Pavillions. Explore
the Memory Bank and read the local news on
Ceramica TV.

Times Open all year, Mon-Sat 9.30-5, Sun
10.30-4.30. For Xmas opening please telephone.*
Facilities ❷ ℗ ⋒ (indoor) toilets for disabled
shop ⊗

137

TAMWORTH

Drayton Manor Theme Park

B78 3TW

☎ 0844 4721950 & 0844 4721960

🖹 01827 288916

e-mail: info@draytonmanor.co.uk

web: www.draytonmanor.co.uk

dir: M42 junct 9, on A4091. Exit at T2 of M6 toll

A popular family theme park with over 100 rides and attractions suitable for all the family, set in 280 acres of parkland and lakes. Drayton Manor has been run by the same family for 60 years, and features world-class rides like rollercoaster sensation G-Force, Apocalypse- the world's first stand-up tower drop, Stormforce 10 and Shockwave - Europe's only stand-up rollercoaster. There's an award-winning zoo and a penny slot machine museum plus plenty of special events throughout the year.

Times Park & Rides open mid Mar-2 Nov. Rides from 10.30-5, 6 or 7. Zoo open all year. 'ThomasLand' also open 28 Nov-3 Jan (excl 24-26 Dec).* **Fees** £25 (ch under 4 free, 4-11 £21, pen 60+ £12, disabled & helper £19 each).* **Facilities** 🅿 ⬜ 🍴 licensed 🎄 (indoor & outdoor) ♿ (partly accessible) (some rides limited access due to steps, ramps or lifts to most rides) toilets for disabled shop ⊗

TRENTHAM

Trentham Monkey Forest

Trentham Estate, Southern Entrance, Stone Rd ST4 8AY

☎ 01782 659845 🖹 01782 644699

e-mail: info@monkey-forest.com

web: www.monkey-forest.com

dir: M6 junct 15, 5 mins drive to A34 in direction of Stone

A unique experience for everyone - come to the only place in Britain where you can walk amongst 140 Barbary macaques roaming free in 60 acres of forest. Walking in the park, you are transported into a different world through close contact with the monkeys. Guides are situated all along the path to give information and there are feeding talks every hour.

Times Open Feb-Mar & Nov, wknds & school hols, 10-4; daily Apr-Oct 10-5 (school summer hols 10-6). **Fees** £6 (ch under 3 free, ch 3-14 £4.50). Groups 20+ £5 (ch £3.50).* **Facilities** 🅿 Ⓟ ⬜ 🎄 (outdoor) ♿ (partly accessible) (hills in forest) toilets for disabled shop ⊗

EASTON

Easton Farm Park

IP13 0EQ

☎ 01728 746475

e-mail: info@eastonfarmpark.co.uk
web: www.eastonfarmpark.co.uk
dir: signed from A12 at Wickham Market, and from A1120

Award-winning farm park on the banks of the River Deben. There are lots of breeds of farm animals, including Suffolk Punch horses, ponies, pigs, lambs, calves, goats, rabbits, guinea pigs and poultry. Chicks hatching and egg collecting daily. Free hug-a-bunny and pony rides every day.

Times Open Mar-end Sep, daily 10.30-6. Also open Feb & Oct half term hols and wknds in Dec.* Fees £6.75 (ch 1-16 £5.50, under 1's free, concessions £6.25). Family £23.* Facilities 🅿️ ⛶🍴 (indoor & outdoor) ♿ (partly accessible) (mainly hard standing surfaces) toilets for disabled shop

LOWESTOFT

East Anglia Transport Museum

Chapel Rd, Carlton Colville NR33 8BL

☎ 01502 518459   🖷 01502 584658

e-mail: enquiries@eatm.org.uk
web: www.eatm.org.uk
dir: 3m SW of Lowestoft, follow brown signs from A12, A146 & A1117

A particular attraction of this museum is the reconstructed 1930s street scene which is used as a setting for working vehicles: visitors can ride by tram, trolley bus and narrow gauge railway. Other motor, steam and electrical vehicles are exhibited. There is also a woodland picnic area served by trams.

Times Open: Apr-Sep, Sun and BH 11-5. From Jun, Thu and Sat, 2-5.* Facilities 🅿️ ⛶🍴 (outdoor) ♿ (partly accessible) toilets for disabled shop

LOWESTOFT

Pleasurewood Hills

Leisure Way, Corton NR32 5DZ

☎ 01502 586000 (admin) 📠 01502 567393
e-mail: info@pleasurewoodhills.com
web: www.pleasurewoodhills.com
dir: off A12 at Lowestoft

Set in 50 acres of coastal parkland, Pleasurewood Hills has all the ingredients for a great day out for all the family. Adrenalin-fuelled thrills and spills for the bravest adventurers, such as the newest attraction, Wipeout, which claims to be the most extreme rollercoaster in the East of England. Fun rides for all the family including some for younger children. Wonderful shows with sealions, parrots, acrobats and the breathtaking Magic Circus spectacular. When the action gets too much, take a leisurely ride on the alpine chairlift or jump aboard one of two railways that weave their way through the park.

Times Open Apr-Oct. Please telephone for details or visit website.* **Facilities** 🅿 ⊑ ⑩ licensed 🎪 (outdoor) ♿ toilets for disabled shop ⊗

NEWMARKET

National Horseracing Museum and Tours

99 High St CB8 8JH

☎ 01638 667333 📠 01638 665600
web: www.nhrm.co.uk
dir: located in centre of High St

This friendly award-winning museum tells the story of the people and horses involved in racing in Britain. Have a go on the horse simulator in the hands-on gallery and chat to retired jockeys and trainers about their experiences. Special mini bus tours visit the gallops, a stable and horses' swimming pool.

Times Open Etr-Oct, daily 11-5 (also BH Mons). 10am on race days.* **Fees** £6 (ch £3, concessions £5). Family (2ad+2ch) £13.* **Facilities** 🅿 ⊑ ⑩ licensed 🎪 (outdoor) ♿ toilets for disabled shop ⊗

STOWMARKET

Museum of East Anglian Life

IP14 1DL

☎ 01449 612229   📄 01449 672307

e-mail: enquiries@eastanglianlife.org.uk

web: www.eastanglianlife.org.uk

dir: in centre of Stowmarket, signed from A14 & B1115

This 70-acre, all-weather museum is set in an attractive river-valley site with 3km of woodland and riverside nature trails. There are reconstructed buildings, including a working water mill, a smithy and also a wind pump, and the Boby Building houses craft workshops. There are displays on Victorian domestic life, gypsies, farming and industry. These include working steam traction engines, the only surviving pair of Burrell ploughing engines of 1879, and a Suffolk Punch horse. The William Bone Building illustrates the history of Ransomes of Ipswich.

Times Open late March-end Oct.* **Fees** £6.50 (ch 4-16 £3.50, concessions £5.50). Family ticket (2ad+2/3ch) £17.50. 1ad family £11. Party 10+.* **Facilities** ℗ 🖵 🎋 (outdoor) toilets for disabled shop

SUFFOLK WILDLIFE PARK

Africa Alive!

Kessingland NR33 7TF

☎ 01502 740291   📄 01502 741104

e-mail: info@africa-alive.co.uk

web: www.africa-alive.co.uk

dir: 25min S of Gt. Yarmouth just S of Lowestoft off A12

Set in 80 acres of dramatic coastal parkland, visitors can explore the sights and sounds of Africa at Africa Alive! There are giraffes, rhinos, cheetah, hyenas and many more, including a bird's eye view of the new lion enclosure. There are lots of daily feeding talks and animal encounter sessions, a magnificent bird of prey display, and free journey round the park with live commentary.

Times Open all year, daily from 10. Closed 25-26 Dec.* **Facilities** 🅿 🖵 🍽 licensed 🎋 toilets for disabled shop ⊗

WEST STOW

West Stow Anglo Saxon Village

West Stow Country Park, Icklingham Rd
IP28 6HG
☎ 01284 728718 📠 01284 728277
e-mail: weststow@stedsbc.gov.uk
web: www.weststow.org
dir: off A1101, 7m NW of Bury St Edmunds.
Follow brown heritage signs

The village is a reconstruction of a pagan Anglo-Saxon settlement dated 420-650 AD. Seven buildings have been reconstructed on the site of the excavated settlement. There is a Visitors' Centre which includes a new archaeology exhibition, DVD area and a children's play area. A new Anglo-Saxon Centre houses the original objects found on the site. Located in the 125 acre West Stow Country Park with river, lake, woodland and heath, plus many trails and paths.

Times Open all year, daily 10-5. Last entry 4 (3.30 in Winter) except Xmas period.* Facilities **P** ℗ 🖵 🎇 (outdoor) ♿ (partly accessible) toilets for disabled shop ⊗

WESTLETON

RSPB Nature Reserve Minsmere

IP17 3BY
☎ 01728 648281 📠 01728 648770
e-mail: minsmere@rspb.org.uk
web: www.rspb.org.uk/reserves/minsmere
dir: signed from A12 at Yoxford & Blythburgh and from Westleton Village

Set on the beautiful Suffolk coast, Minsmere offers an enjoyable day out for all. Nature trails take you through a variety of habitats to the excellent birdwatching hides. Spring is a time for birdsong, including nightingales and booming bitterns. In summer, you can watch breeding avocets and marsh harriers. Autumn is excellent for migrants, and in winter, hundreds of ducks visit the reserve. Look out for otters and red deer. The visitor centre has a well-stocked shop and licensed tearoom, and you can find out more about the reserve. There is a programme of events throughout the year, including several for children and families. Self-guided activity booklets for families.

Times Open all year, daily (ex 25-26 Dec) 9-9 (or dusk if earlier). Visitor centre: 9-5 (9-4 Nov-Jan).* Facilities **P** ℗ 🖵 🎇 (outdoor) ♿ (partly accessible) (Visitor Centre, parts of nature trail and some hides are accessible) toilets for disabled shop ⊗

WOODBRIDGE

Sutton Hoo

IP12 3DJ

☎ 01394 389700 🖷 01394 389702
e-mail: suttonhoo@nationaltrust.org.uk
web: www.nationaltrust.org.uk/suttonhoo
dir: off B1083 Woodbridge to Bawdsey road.
Follow signs from A12 avoiding Woodbridge itself

Discovered in 1939, this is the site of one of the
most important archaeological finds in Britain's
history: the complete 7th-century ship burial
of an Anglo-Saxon king, which lay undisturbed
for 1300 years. Sutton Hoo displays reveal how
Anglo-Saxon nobles lived, went to war and
founded a new kingdom in East Anglia. The
centre-piece is a full sized replica of an Anglo-
Saxon warrior king's burial chamber.

Times Open all year: Jun, Wed-Sun, 10.30-5; Jul-
Aug, daily 10.30-5; Sep-Oct, Wed-Sun, 10.30-5;
Nov-Feb, Sat-Sun, 11-4. Open: BHs.* Fees Gift
Aid Admission prices £6.50, (ch £3.40). Family
tickets £16.45. Gift aid admission includes a
voluntary donation but visitors can choose to pay
the standard prices displayed at the property
and on the website.* Facilities ℗ ⦿ licensed
⊓ ♿ (partly accessible) (Grounds partly access,
slopes, burial mound tours not accessible to
w/chairs or PMV) toilets for disabled shop ⊗ ⛵

CHERTSEY

Thorpe Park

Staines Rd KT16 8PN

☎ 0870 444 4466 🖷 01932 566367
web: www.thorpepark.com
dir: M25 junct 11 or 13 and follow signs via A320
to Thorpe Park

For hardcore adrenaline junkies, Thorpe Park is
the must-do destination for insanely thrilling
rollercoaster fun. Unleash the daredevil within
and take on the loops, spins, vertical drops and
incredible speeds of the nation's thrill capital.

Times Open 15 Mar-9 Nov. Opening times vary
throughout, check in advance.* Facilities ℗ ⧉
⦿ licensed ⊓ ♿ toilets for disabled shop ⊗

143

FARNHAM

Birdworld & Underwaterworld

Holt Pound GU10 4LD
☎ 01420 22140 📠 01420 23715
e-mail: bookings@birdworld.co.uk
web: www.birdworld.co.uk
dir: 3m S of Farnham on A325

Birdworld is the largest bird collection in the country and includes toucans, pelicans, flamingoes, ostriches and many others. Underwater World is a tropical aquarium with brilliant lighting that shows off collections of marine and freshwater fish, as well as the swampy depths of the alligator exhibit. Visitors can also visit some beautiful gardens, the Jenny Wren farm and the Heron Theatre.

Times Open all year, daily, 10-6 (summer), 10-4.30 (winter). Closed 25-26 Dec.*
Fees £13.95 (ch 3-6 £10.95 & 7-15 £11.95, concessions £11.95). Family ticket (2ad+2ch) £45.* **Facilities** 🅿 Ⓟ ❍ licensed ⊓ (outdoor) ♿ toilets for disabled shop ⊗

WEYBRIDGE

Brooklands Museum

Brooklands Rd KT13 0QN
☎ 01932 857381 📠 01932 855465
e-mail: info@brooklandsmuseum.com
web: www.brooklandsmuseum.com
dir: M25 junct 10/11, museum off B374, follow brown signs

Brooklands racing circuit was the birthplace of British motorsport and aviation. From 1907 to 1987 it was a world-renowned centre of engineering excellence. The Museum features old banked track and the 1-in-4 Test Hill. Many of the original buildings have been restored including the Clubhouse, the Shell and BP Petrol Pagodas, and the Malcolm Campbell Sheds in the Motoring Village. Many motorcycles, cars and aircraft are on display. Ring for details of special events.

Times Open all year, daily & BHs 10-5 (4 in winter).* **Facilities** 🅿 ⊑ ⊓ (outdoor) ♿ (partly accessible) (no wheelchair access to aircraft) toilets for disabled shop ⊗

ALFRISTON

Drusillas Park

Alfriston Rd BN26 5QS

☎ 01323 874100   📠 01323 874101
e-mail: info@drusillas.co.uk
web: www.drusillas.co.uk
dir: off A27 near Alfriston 12m from Brighton &
7m from Eastbourne

Widely regarded as the best small zoo in the
country, Drusillas Park offers an opportunity
to get nose to nose with nature, with the help
of hundreds of exotic animals, from monkeys
and crocodiles to penguins and meerkats.
Animals are only half the fun there's a fun:
Go Bananas! Amazon Adventure and Go Wild!
are perfect for energetic kids, and Thomas the
Tank Engine offers a train service 362 days a
year. Don't miss the Zoolympics Trail and free
Spotter Books, Jungle Adventure Golf, Panning
for Gold, Explorers' Lagoon or close encounters
in Lemurland.

Times Open all year, daily 10-5 (winter 10-4).
Closed 24-26 Dec. Fees Family of 4: peak £53.20,
standard £49.20, off peak £41.20* Facilities 🅿
🖵 🍴 licensed 🏕 (indoor & outdoor) ♿ toilets
for disabled shop ⊗

BATTLE

1066 Battle of Hastings Abbey & Battlefield

TN33 0AD

☎ 01424 773792   📠 01424 775059
web: www.english-heritage.org.uk
dir: A21 onto A2100

Explore the site of the Battle of Hastings,
where on 14th October 1066, one of the most
famous events in English history took place.
Free interactive wand tour of the battlefield and
atmospheric abbey ruins.

Times Open all year, Apr-Sep, daily 10-6; Oct-
Mar, daily 10-4. Closed 24-26 Dec & 1 Jan.
Fees £6.70 (concessions £5.70, ch £3.40). Family
£16.80. Opening times and prices are subject
to change from March 2010, for further details
please phone 0870 333 118. Facilities 🅿 ♿
(partly accessible) (steps to enter all abbey
buildings) toilets for disabled shop ⊞

BATTLE

Yesterday's World

89-90 High St TN33 0AQ
☎ 01424 893938 & 774269
📠 01424 893316
e-mail: shop@yesterdaysworld.co.uk
web: www.yesterdaysworld.co.uk
dir: M25 junct 5, A21 onto A2100 towards Battle, opposite Battle Abbey Gatehouse

Go on a magical time-travel adventure from the reign of Queen Victoria to the psychedelic 1970s. Explore five floors of displays with over 100,000 artefacts, virtual and interactive exhibits, sounds and smells. See an English country garden, a children's play village, the 1930s Nippy's Tea Room, nostalgic gift shop and traditional English sweet shop.

Times Open all year, Winter, daily 9.30-5.30; Summer, daily 9.30-6. Closed 25-26 Dec & 1 Jan.* **Fees** £7 (ch £3.95, concessions £5). Family ticket (2ad+2ch - extra child £3) £20. Discount for groups of 15+.* **Facilities** ℗ ⌷ ⼕ (outdoor) ⼓ (partly accessible) toilets for disabled shop ⊗

BODIAM

Bodiam Castle

TN32 5UA
☎ 01580 830196 📠 01580 830398
e-mail: bodiamcastle@nationaltrust.org.uk
web: www.nationaltrust.org.uk/bodiamcastle
dir: 2m E of A21 Hurst Green

With its tall round drum towers at each corner, Bodiam is something of a fairytale castle. It was built in 1386 by Sir Edward Dalyngrigge, for comfort and defence. The ramparts rise dramatically above a broad moat and the great gatehouse contains the original portcullis - a very rare example of its kind.

Times Open all year, Jan-12 Feb, Sat-Sun 10.30-4; 13 Feb-Oct, daily 10.30-5.30; Nov-19 Dec, Wed-Sun 10.30-4 (last entry 30 mins before closing). **Fees** Gift Aid donation: £6.20 (ch £3.10). Family ticket £15.50. Group 15+ £5.10 (ch £2.55). Includes a voluntary donation of 10% or more. Visitors can however, choose to pay the standard admission which is displayed at the property and on NT website. **Facilities** ℗ ⌷ ⼓ (partly accessible) (ground floor level is fully accessible, spiral staircase to upper levels) toilets for disabled shop ⊗ ⿊

BURWASH

Bateman's

TN19 7DS

☎ 01435 882302 🗎 01435 882811
e-mail: batemans@nationaltrust.org.uk
web: www.nationaltrust.org.uk
dir: 0.5m SW off A265

Rudyard Kipling lived for over 34 years in this 17th-century manor house and it remains much the same as it was during his lifetime. His 1928 Rolls Royce Phantom is on display, and the watermill at the bottom of the garden grinds wheat into flour on Saturday afternoons and Wednesdays.

Times Open 13 Mar-Oct, Sat-Wed 11-5, also open Good Fri, (last admission 4.30). House closes at 5. Fees Gift Aid donation: £8.20 (ch £4.10). Family ticket £20.50. Party £6.45 (ch £3.15). Includes a voluntary donation of 10% or more. Visitors can however, choose to pay the standard admission which is displayed at the property and on NT website. Facilities 🅿 💻 🍴 licensed 🍴 (outdoor) ♿ (partly accessible) (access to first floor & water mill restricted) toilets for disabled shop ⊗ 🎖

EAST DEAN

Seven Sisters Sheep Centre

Gilberts Dr BN20 0AA

☎ 01323 423302 🗎 01323 423302
e-mail: sevensisters.sheepcentre@talk21.com
web: www.sheepcentre.co.uk
dir: 3m W of Eastbourne on A259. Turn left in village of East Dean to Birling Gap and sea, 0.5m on left

Possibly the largest collection of sheep in the world, where over 40 different breeds can be visited at this family run farm. See lambs being born, sheep sheared and milked, cheese making and spinning. Take in the agricultural heritage and history of sheep on the South Downs.

Times Open 3 Mar-7 May & 30 Jun-2 Sep, 2-5 (11-5 wknds/E Sussex school hols)* Facilities 🅿 🅿 💻 🍴 (indoor & outdoor) shop ⊗

EASTBOURNE

"How We Lived Then" Museum of Shops & Social History

20 Cornfield Ter BN21 4NS
☎ 01323 737143
e-mail: howwelivedthen@btconnect.com
web: www.how-we-lived-then.co.uk
dir: just off seafront, between town centre & theatres, signed

Over the last 50 years, Jan and Graham Upton have collected over 100,000 items which are now displayed on four floors of authentic old shops and room-settings, transporting visitors back to their grandparents' era. Other displays, such as seaside souvenirs, wartime rationing and Royal mementoes, help to capture 100 years of social history.

Times Open all year, daily, 10-5 (last entry 4.30). Winter times subject to change, telephone establishment.* Fees £4.50 (ch 5-15 £3.50, under 5's free, concession £4). Party 10+.*
Facilities ℗ ♿ (partly accessible) (ground floor access only) shop

FOREST ROW

Ashdown Forest Llama Park

Wych Cross RH18 5JN
☎ 01825 712040   ▤ 01825 713698
e-mail: info@llamapark.co.uk
web: www.llamapark.co.uk
dir: on A22 between Uckfield & East Grinstead, 250mtrs S of junct with A275

Ashdown Forest Llama Park is home to more than 100 llamas and alpacas and these beautiful and gentle woolly animals, native to the high Andes of South America, are very much at home in Sussex. There are also now three reindeer who, in December, are an important part of the Christmas celebrations and Santa's Grotto. The park has wonderful views over Ashdown Forest and there is a marked trail around the Park, a picnic area and adventure play area. In the information centre, learn about the fascinating world of llamas and alpacas and other fibre producing animals and plants. The park is holder of a Green Tourist Award.

Times Open all year, daily 10-5. Closed 25-26 Dec & 1 Jan* Facilities ℗ ⛾ ⑩ licensed ☍ (outdoor) ♿ (partly accessible) (Shop and coffee shop accessible, some gravel areas in park but limited access to wheelchair users) toilets for disabled shop ⊗

HALLAND

Bentley Wildfowl & Motor Museum

BN8 5AF

☎ 01825 840573   📠 01825 841322
e-mail: barrysutherland@pavilion.co.uk
web: www.bentley.org.uk
dir: 7m NE of Lewes, signposted off A22, A26 &
B2192

Hundreds of swans, geese and ducks from all
over the world can be seen on lakes and ponds
along with flamingoes and peacocks. There is
a fine array of Veteran, Edwardian and Vintage
vehicles, and the house has splendid antiques
and wildfowl paintings. The gardens specialise
in old fashioned roses. Other attractions include
woodland walks, a nature trail, education centre,
adventure playground and a miniature train.

Times Open 17 Mar-Oct, daily 10.30-4.30. House
open from noon, Apr-Nov, Feb & part of Mar,
wknds only. Estate closed Dec & Jan. House
closed all winter.* Facilities ♿ 🖵 🎌 toilets for
disabled shop 🚭

HASTINGS

Blue Reef Aquarium

Rock-a-nore Rd TN34 3DW

☎ 01424 718776   📠 01424 721483
e-mail: hastings@bluereefaquarium.co.uk
web: www.bluereefaquarium.co.uk
dir: Follow signs to end of Rock-a-nore Rd on
seafront

Undersea safari in Hastings. Come face to face
with seahorses, sharks, giant crabs, stingrays
and many of other aquatic creatures. At the
aquarium's heart is a giant ocean tank where
an underwater walkthrough tunnel offers close
encounters with giant wrasse, tropical sharks
and hundreds of colourful fish. Talks and feeding
displays take place throughout the day.

Times Open all year daily 10-5 (10-4 winter).
Closed 25 Dec. Fees £7.75 (ch £5.75,
concessions £6.75, disabled & carers £4.99).
Family ticket (2ad+2ch) £24, (2ad+3ch)
£27.50.* Facilities ♿ 🖵 ♿ (partly accessible)
(Steps to tunnel) toilets for disabled shop 🚭

HASTINGS

1066 Story in Hastings Castle

Castle Hill Rd, West Hill TN34 3RG
☎ 01424 781111 & 781112 (info line)
🖹 01424 781186
e-mail: bookings@discoverhastings.co.uk
web: www.hastings.gov.uk
dir: close to A259 seafront, 2m from B2093

The ruins of the Norman castle stand on the
cliffs, close to the site of William the Conqueror's
first motte-and-bailey castle in England. It was
excavated in 1825 and 1968, and old dungeons
were discovered in 1894. An unusual approach
to the castle can be made via the West Hill Cliff
Railway.

Times Open daily, 27 Mar-Sep 10-5; Oct-26 Mar
11-3.30. Closed 24-26 Dec.* Facilities ℗ 🍽
shop ⊗

HASTINGS

Smugglers Adventure

St Clements Caves, West Hill TN34 3HY
☎ 01424 422964
e-mail: smugglers@discoverhastings.co.uk
web: www.discoverhastings.co.uk
dir: follow brown signs on A259, coast road,
through Hastings. Use seafront car park, then
take West Cliff railway or follow signed footpath

Journey deep into the heart of Hastings historic
West Hill to discover the fascinating world of the
Smugglers Adventure in St Cements Caves. Join
notorious smuggler 'Hairy Jack' as he leads you
through acres of underground caverns, passages
and tunnels on a voyage back through time to the
heyday of smuggling. Several events throughout
the year.

Times Open all year daily, Apr-Sep 10-5; Oct-Mar
11-4.* Fees £7 (ch £5, concessions £6). Family
ticket (2ad+2ch) £21, (2ad+3ch) £25* Facilities
℗ ♿ (partly accessible) (40 steps to entrance &
exit the attraction) shop ⊗

SHEFFIELD PARK STATION

Bluebell Railway

Sheffield Park Station TN22 3QL
☎ 01825 720800 & & 722370
📠 01825 720804
e-mail: info@bluebell-railway.co.uk
web: www.bluebell-railway.co.uk
dir: 4.5m E of Haywards Heath, off A275, 10m S
of East Grinstead A22-A275

A volunteer-run heritage steam railway with nine miles of track running through pretty Sussex countryside. Please note that there is no parking at Kingscote Station. If you wish to board the train here, catch the bus (service 473) which connects Kingscote and East Grinstead.

Times Open all year, Sat & Sun, daily Apr-Oct & during school hols. Santa Specials run Dec. For timetable and information regarding trains contact above.* Facilities 🅿 🅿 ⊑ 🛒 (indoor) ♿ (partly accessible) toilets for disabled shop

BIGNOR

Bignor Roman Villa & Museum

RH20 1PH
☎ 01798 869259   📠 01798 869259
e-mail: enquiries@bignorromanvilla.co.uk
web: www.bignorromanvilla.co.uk
dir: 6m S of Pulborough & 6m N of Arundel on A29, signed. 8m S of Petworth on A285, signed

Rediscovered in 1811, this Roman house was built on a grand scale. It is one of the largest known, and has spectacular mosaics. The heating system can also be seen, and various finds from excavations are on show. The longest mosaic in Britain (82ft) is on display here in its original position.

Times Open Mar-Apr, Tue-Sun & BH 10-5; May daily 10-5; Jun-Sep daily 10-6, Oct daily 10-5* Fees £5.50 (ch under 16 £2.50, pen £4). Family £14. Party 10+ 20% discount. Guided tours by arrangement.* Facilities 🅿 ⊑ 🛒 (outdoor) ♿ (partly accessible) (most areas accessible) shop 🚫

151

FISHBOURNE

Fishbourne Roman Palace

Salthill Rd PO19 3QR
☎ 01243 785859 📄 01243 539266
e-mail: adminfish@sussexpast.co.uk
web: www.sussexpast.co.uk
dir: off A27 onto A259 into Fishbourne. Turn right into Salthill Rd & right into Roman Way

The remains of the Roman Palace at Fishbourne were discovered in 1960. Here you can see Britain's largest collection of in-situ Roman floor mosaics. More everyday Roman objects found during the excavations are displayed in the museum gallery. An audio-visual presentation uses computer-generated images to interpret the site. Outside the garden has been replanted to its original plan, using plants that may have grown there when the palace was inhabited. The Collections Discovery Centre displays more artefacts from both Fishbourne and Chichester district. Join a 'behind the scenes' tour for an opportunity to handle some of these.

Times Open all year, daily Feb-15 Dec. Feb, Nov-mid Dec 10-4; Mar-Jul & Sep-Oct 10-5; Aug 10-6. Winter wknds 10-4.* Facilities 🅿 🚻 🍴 (outdoor) ♿ toilets for disabled shop ⊗

SINGLETON

Weald & Downland Open Air Museum

PO18 0EU
☎ 01243 811348 📄 01243 811475
e-mail: office@wealddown.co.uk
web: www.wealddown.co.uk
dir: 6m N of Chichester on A286

A showcase of English architectural heritage, where historic buildings have been rescued from destruction and rebuilt in a parkland setting. Vividly demonstrating the evolution of building techniques and use of local materials, these fascinating buildings bring to life the homes, farms and rural industries of the south east of the past 500 years. See also working Shire horses, cattle and traditional breeds of farm animals.

Times Open daily all year, during BST, 10.30-6 & 10.30-4 the rest of year. Winter opening days vary, see website for details. Fees £8.95 (ch £4.70, pen £7.95). Family ticket (2ad+3ch) £24.25.* Facilities 🅿 🚻 🍴 (indoor & outdoor) ♿ (partly accessible) (some areas of museum not suitable for disabled visitiors, but most key areas and exhibits are accessible) toilets for disabled shop

WISBOROUGH GREEN

Fishers Farm Park

Newpound Ln RH14 0EG

☎ 01403 700063   📄 01403 700823

e-mail: info@fishersfarmpark.co.uk

web: www.fishersfarmpark.co.uk

dir: follow brown & white tourist boards on all roads approaching Wisborough Green

All weather, all year farm and adventure park, providing a mixture of farmyard and dynamic adventure play. Please contact for details of special events.

Times Open all year, daily, 10-5. Closed 26-26 Dec. Fees Please phone for details. Facilities 🅿 🅟 🖵 †◎† licensed 🛱 (outdoor) ♿ (partly accessible) (woodland walkway inaccessible to wheelchairs) toilets for disabled shop ⊗

JARROW

Bede's World

Church Bank NE32 3DY

☎ 0191 489 2106   📄 0191 428 2361

e-mail: visitor.info@bedesworld.co.uk

web: www.bedesworld.co.uk

dir: off A185 near S end of Tyne tunnel

Bede's World is an ambitious museum based around the extraordinary life and work of the Venerable Bede (AD673-735) early Medieval Europe's greatest scholar and England's first historian. Attractions include an 'Age of Bede' exhibition in the museum, which displays finds excavated from the site of St Paul's monastery. Alongside the museum, Bede's World has developed Gyrwe, an Anglo-Saxon demonstration farm, which brings together the animals, timber buildings, crops and vegetables that would have featured in the Northumbrian Landscape of Bede's Day.

Times Open all year, Apr-Oct, Mon-Sat 10-5.30, Sun noon-5.30; Nov-Mar, Mon-Sat 10-4.30 & Sun 12-4.30. Please contact for Xmas/New Year opening times.* Facilities 🅿 🅟 🖵 †◎† licensed 🛱 (outdoor) toilets for disabled shop ⊗

NEWCASTLE UPON TYNE

Discovery Museum **FREE**

Blandford Square NE1 4JA
☎ 0191 232 6789 📄 0191 230 2614
e-mail: discovery@twmuseums.org.uk
web: www.twmuseums.org.uk/discovery
dir: off A6115/A6125. 5 mins walk from
Newcastle Central Station

Newcastle Discovery Museum offers something
for everyone. There are displays covering fashion,
military history, maritime splendours and
scientific curiosities. Local history is covered in
the fascinating Great City story. There is a gallery
housing Turbinia, once the world's fastest ship.

Times Open all year, Mon-Sat 10-5; Sun 2-5.
(Closed 25-26 Dec & 1 Jan). Facilities 🅿 Ⓟ 🍴
♿ toilets for disabled shop ⊗

NEWCASTLE UPON TYNE

Hancock Museum

Barras Bridge NE2 4PT
☎ 0191 222 7418 📄 0191 261 7537
e-mail: hancock@twmuseums.org.uk
web: www.twmuseums.org.uk/hancock
dir: follow exit signs for city centre A167, off A1

Newcastle's premier Natural History museum
unravels the natural world, through sensational
galleries and close encounters with resident
reptiles and insects. For more than 100 years the
Hancock Museum has provided visitors with a
glimpse of the animal kingdom and the powerful
and often destructive forces of nature. From the
dinosaurs to live animals, the Hancock is home to
creatures past and present and the odd Egyptian
mummy or two.

Times Open all year, Mon-Sat, 10-5, Sun 2-5.
Closed 25-26 Dec & 1 Jan.* Facilities 🅿 Ⓟ 🍴
🪑 toilets for disabled shop ⊗

NEWCASTLE UPON TYNE

Life Science Centre

Times Square NE1 4EP
☎ 0191 243 8210 📄 0191 243 8201
e-mail: info@life.org.uk
web: www.life.org.uk
dir: A1M, A69, A184, A1058 & A167, follow signs
to Centre for Life or Central Station

Life is an exciting place where science comes
alive in a fun and funky environment. Aiming
to inspire curiosity and encourage visitors to
uncover new things about life, whatever age. If
you are curious about the world around you, there
is something for all the family at Life. Step inside
for a hands-on, minds-on, hearts-on experience
and see what Life has to offer.

Times Open all year Mon-Sat 10-6, Sun 11-6 .
Closed 25-26 Dec & 1 Jan. (Last entry subject
to seasonal demand).* Fees £8 (ch 5-16 £5.85,
concessions £6.95). Family ticket (1ad&3ch)
£24.20 (2ad&2ch) £24.20.* Facilities ❷ ⓟ ⏛
🍴 licensed ☍ (indoor) ♿ toilets for disabled
shop ⊗

SOUTH SHIELDS

Arbeia Roman Fort & Museum

Baring St NE33 2BB
☎ 0191 456 1369 📄 0191 427 6862
web: www.twmuseums.org.uk
dir: 5 mins' walk from town centre

In South Shields town are the extensive remains
of Arbeia, a Roman fort in use from the 2nd to
4th century. It was the supply base for the Roman
army's campaign against Scotland. On site there
are full size reconstructions of a fort gateway,
a barrack block and part of the commanding
officer's house. Archaeological evacuations are in
progress throughout the summer.

Times Open all year, Apr-Oct, Mon-Sat 10-5.30,
Sun 1-5; Nov-Mar, Mon-Sat 10-3.30. Closed
25-26 Dec & 1 Jan* Fees Fort & Museum free
of charge ex for 'Timequest' Archaeological
Interpretation Gallery £1.50 (ch & concessions
80p).* Facilities ⓟ ☍ (outdoor) ♿ (partly
accessible) toilets for disabled shop

SUNDERLAND

National Glass Centre **FREE**

Liberty Way SR6 0GL
☎ 0191 515 5555 🖷 0191 515 5556
e-mail: info@nationalglasscentre.com
web: www.nationalglasscentre.com
dir: A19 onto A1231, signposted from all major roads

The National Glass Centre offers galleries showing an international programme of exhibitions. Home to the largest art glass making facility for kiln forming, a unique venue and a hub for activity inspired by glass. Artists' studios, glass production facilities and much more and located in an innovative glass and steel building on the banks of the River Wear. Explore with a behind-the-scenes tours.

Times Open all year, daily 10-5 (last admission to glass tour 4.30). Closed 25 Dec & 1 Jan. **Facilities** Ⓟ ☕ 🍽 licensed ♿ toilets for disabled shop ⊗

TYNEMOUTH

Blue Reef Aquarium

Grand Pde NE30 4JF
☎ 0191 258 1031 🖷 0191 257 2116
e-mail: tynemouth@bluereefaquarium.co.uk
web: www.bluereefaquarium.co.uk
dir: follow A19, taking A1058 (coast road), signed Tynemouth. Situated on seafront

From its position overlooking one of the North East's prettiest beaches, Blue Reef is home to a dazzling variety of creatures. Enjoy close encounters with seals, seahorses, sharks, stingrays, giant octopus, frogs, otters and hundreds of other aquatic lifeforms. Explore a dazzling coral reef and journey through the spectacular tropical ocean display in a transparent underwater tunnel. Informative, entertaining talks and feeding displays throughout the day.

Times Open all year, daily from 10. Closed 25 Dec.* **Fees** £7.75 (ch £5.75, concessions £6.75). Family (2ad+2ch) £24 (2ad+3ch) £27.50.* **Facilities** Ⓟ Ⓟ ☕ 🪑 (outdoor) ♿ toilets for disabled shop ⊗

WALLSEND

Segedunum Roman Fort, Baths & Museum

Buddle St NE28 6HR

☎ 0191 236 9347   ▤ 0191 295 5858
e-mail: segedunum@twmuseums.org.uk
web: www.twmuseums.org.uk/sege
dir: A187 from Tyne Tunnel, signposted

Hadrian's Wall was built by the Roman Emperor Hadrian in 122AD, Segedunum was built as part of the Wall, serving as a garrison for 600 soldiers until the collapse of Roman rule around 410AD. This major historical venture shows what life would have been like then, using artefacts, audio-visuals, reconstructed buildings and a 34m high viewing tower. Plenty of special events including craft activities and re-enactments from Roman cavalry and soldiers. Contact for details.

Times Open all year, Apr-Oct 10-5; Nov-Mar, 10-3. Fees £4.25 (ch, pen & concessions £2.50). (ch 16 and under free) Facilities ❷ ❷ ▭ ☶ (outdoor) ♿ toilets for disabled shop ⊗

WHITBURN

Souter Lighthouse & The Leas

Coast Rd SR6 7NH

☎ 0191 529 3161 & 01670 773966
▤ 0191 529 0902
e-mail: souter@nationaltrust.org.uk
web: www.nationaltrust.org.uk
dir: on A183 coast road, 2m S of South Shields, 3m N of Sunderland

When it opened in 1871, Souter was the most advanced lighthouse in the world, and warned shipping off the notorious rocks in the river approaches of the Tyne and the Wear. Painted red and white and standing at 150ft high, it is a dramatic building and hands-on displays and volunteers help bring it to life. Visitors can explore the whole building with its engine room and lighthouse keeper's cottage. You can take part in activities concerning shipwrecks and the workings of the lighthouse. Climb to the top of the lighthouse, or walk along the Leas, a 2.5 mile stretch of spectacular coastline.

Times Open 13 Mar-Oct daily (ex Fri but open Good Fri) 11-5. Fees £4.85 (ch £3.15) Family ticket £12.65. Group 10+ £4.* Facilities ❷ ❷ ﺮ licensed ☶ toilets for disabled shop ⊗ ⚘

GAYDON

Heritage Motor Centre

Banbury Rd CV35 0BJ

☎ 01926 641188 🖷 01926 641555

e-mail: enquiries@heritage-motor-centre.co.uk

web: www.heritage-motor-centre.co.uk

dir: M40 junct 12 and take B4100. Attraction signed

The Heritage Motor Centre is home to the world's largest collection of historic British cars. The museum boasts exciting and interactive exhibitions which uncover the story of the British motor industry from the 1890s to the present day. Fun for all the family with children's activity packs, special school holiday and lecture programs, plus free guided tours twice a day, onsite café and gift shop and a selection of outdoor activities including children's play area, picnic site, 4x4 Experience and Go-Karts.

Times Open all year, daily 10-5. (Closed over Xmas, check website or call 01926 641188 for details) **Fees** £9 (ch 5-16 £7, under 5 free, & concessions £8). Family ticket £28. (Additional charges apply to outdoor activities). Group & education rates available.* **Facilities** 🅿 ⏛ 🎋 (outdoor) ♿ toilets for disabled shop ⊗

KENILWORTH

Kenilworth Castle

CV8 1NE

☎ 01926 852078 🖷 01926 851514

web: www.english-heritage.org.uk

Explore the largest and most extensive castle ruin in England, with a past rich in famous names and events. Its massive red sandstone towers, keep and wall glow brightly in the sunlight. Discover the history of Kenilworth through the interactive model in Leicester's Barn.

Times Open all year, Mar-1 Nov, daily 10-5; 2 Nov-Feb, daily 10-4. Closed 24-26 Dec & 1 Jan. **Fees** £7 (concessions £6, ch £3.50). Family ticket £17.50. Prices and opening times are subject to change in March 2010. Please check web site or call 0870 333 1181 for the most up to date prices and opening times when planning your visit. **Facilities** 🅿 ⏛ 🎋 ♿ (partly accessible) (uneven surfaces, steep slopes, steps) toilets for disabled shop ♯

KENILWORTH

Stoneleigh Abbey

CV8 2LF
☎ 01926 858535 & 858585
📠 01926 850724
e-mail: enquire@stoneleighabbey.org
web: www.stoneleighabbey.org
dir: entrance off B4115 close to junct of A46 and A452

Stoneleigh Abbey is one of the finest country house estates in the Midlands and has been the subject of considerable restoration work. The abbey, founded in the reign of Henry II, is now managed by a charitable trust. Visitors will experience a wealth of architectural styles spanning more than 800 years. The magnificent state rooms and chapel, the medieval Gatehouse and the Regency stables are some of the major areas to be admired.

Times Open Good Fri-Oct, Tue-Thu, Sun & BHs for guided tours at 11, 1 & 3. Grounds open 10-5. **Fees** Grounds only, £3. Guided tour of house, £6.50 (1ch 5-12 free, additional ch £3) pen £5.50. **Facilities** Ⓟ ☕ ♿ (partly accessible) (access over exterior gravel paths will require assistance & lift access to state rooms) toilets for disabled shop ⊗

MIDDLETON

Ash End House Children's Farm

Middleton Ln B78 2BL
☎ 0121 329 3240 📠 0121 329 3240
e-mail: contact@thechildrensfarm.co.uk
web: www.childrensfarm.co.uk
dir: signed from A4091

Ideal for young children, this is a small family-owned farm with many friendly animals to feed and stroke, including some rare breeds. Café, new farm shop stocking local produce, play areas, picnic barns and lots of undercover activities. A recent addition is the New Farm Education Classroom to complement Food and Farming Year and an improved Toddlers Barn.

Times Open all year, daily 10-5 or dusk in winter. Closed 25 Dec until 2nd weekend in Jan* **Facilities** Ⓟ ☕ ⛩ (indoor & outdoor) ♿ toilets for disabled shop ⊗

STRATFORD-UPON-AVON

Stratford Butterfly Farm

Tramway Walk, Swan's Nest Ln CV37 7LS
☎ 01789 299288 📠 01789 415878
e-mail: sales@butterflyfarm.co.uk
web: www.butterflyfarm.co.uk
dir: south bank of River Avon opposite RSC

The UK's largest live butterfly and insect exhibit.
Hundreds of the world's most spectacular
and colourful butterflies, in the unique setting
of a lush tropical landscape, with splashing
waterfalls and fish-filled pools. See also the
strange and fascinating Insect City, a bustling
metropolis of ants, stick insects, beetles and
other remarkable insects. See the dangerous and
deadly in Arachnoland!

Times Open all year, daily 10-6 (winter 10-
dusk). Closed 25 Dec.* Fees £5.75 (ch £4.75,
concessions £5.25). Family £16.75.* Facilities
Ⓟ 🍴 (outdoor) ♿ shop ⊗

WARWICK

Warwick Castle

CV34 4QU
☎ 0870 442 2000 📠 0870 442 2394
e-mail: customer.information@warwick-castle.
com
web: www.warwick-castle.com
dir: 2m from M40 junct 15

From the days of William the Conqueror to
the reign of Queen Victoria, Warwick Castle
has provided a backdrop for many turbulent
times. Today it offers family entertainment
with a medieval theme. Attractions include the
world's largest siege engine, thrilling jousting
tournaments, birds of prey, daredevil knights,
and entire castleful of colourful characters. The
newest addition is the immersive and interactive
"Dream of Battle".

Times Open all year, daily 10-6 (5pm Nov-Mar).
Closed 25 Dec.* Facilities Ⓟ Ⓟ 🖵 🍴
licensed 🍴 toilets for disabled shop ⊗

BIRMINGHAM

Museum of the Jewellery Quarter **FREE**

75-80 Vyse St, Hockley B18 6HA
☎ 0121 554 3598 📠 0121 554 9700
e-mail: bmag-enquiries@birmingham.gov.uk
web: www.bmag.org.uk
dir: off A41 into Vyse St, museum on left after 1st side street

The Museum tells the story of jewellery making in Birmingham from its origins in the Middle Ages right through to the present day. Discover the skill of the jeweller's craft and enjoy a unique tour of an original jewellery factory frozen in time. For over eighty years the family firm of Smith and Pepper produced jewellery from the factory. This perfectly preserved 'time capsule' workshop has changed little since the beginning of the 20th century. The Jewellery Quarter is still very much at the forefront of jewellery manufacture in Britain and the Museum showcases the work of the city's most exciting new designers.

Times Open all year* Facilities ℗ ♿ toilets for disabled shop ⊗

BIRMINGHAM

Thinktank at Millennium Point

Millennium Point, Curzon St B4 7XG
☎ 0121 202 2222 📠 0121 202 2280
e-mail: findout@thinktank.ac
web: www.thinktank.ac

Thinktank offers a fun-packed day out for all the family. From steam engines to intestines this exciting museum has over 200 amazing artefacts and interactive exhibits on science and discovery. A state-of-the-art planetarium means you can tour the night sky and fly through the galaxy without stepping outside. There is an ever-changing programme of demonstrations, workshops and events. Contact for details.

Times Open daily 10-5 (last entry 4). Closed 24-26 Dec. Fees £9 (ch £7.15, concessions £7.15). Family ticket £27.40 (2ad+2ch).*
Facilities ℗ ℗ ⊑ ⊓ (indoor) toilets for disabled shop ⊗

BOURNVILLE

Cadbury World

Linden Rd B30 2LU
☎ 0845 450 3599 📄 0121 451 1366
e-mail: cadbury.world@csplc.com
web: www.cadburyworld.co.uk
dir: 1m S of A38 Bristol Rd, on A4040 Ring Rd.
Follow brown signs from M5 junct 2 and junct 4

Get involved in the chocolate making process,
and to find out how the chocolate is used to make
famous confectionery. Visitors can learn about
the early struggles and triumphs of the Cadbury
business, and follow the history of Cadbury
television advertising. Two recently added
attractions are: Essence, where visitors can
create their own unique product by combining
liquid chocolate with different tastes, and
Purple Planet, where you can chase a creme egg,
grow cocoa beans, and see yourself moulded
in chocolate. A new visitor centre explores the
innovative values of the Cadbury Brothers that
make Bournville the place it is.

Times Opening times vary throughout the
year please contact the information line 0845
450 3599.* Fees £13.45 (ch 4-15yrs £10.10,
concessions £10.30).* Facilities ⓟ ⌷ ⦿
licensed ⧢ (outdoor) ⚲ (partly accessible)
(limited access to landing area) toilets for
disabled shop ⊗

COVENTRY

Coventry Transport Museum FREE

Millennium Place, Hales St CV1 1JD
☎ 024 7623 4270 📄 024 7623 4284
e-mail: enquiries@transport-museum.com
web: www.transport-museum.com
dir: just off junct 1, Coventry ring road, Tower St
in city centre

Coventry is the traditional home of the British
motor industry, and the museum's world-
renowned collection displays over 150 years of its
history. You can design your own car, feel what
its like to break the sound barrier at 763mph
and even travel into the future. The Festival of
Motoring takes place over the fist weekend in
September and features vintage, veteran and
classic vehicles with family activities and stunt
show riders culminating in a car and motorcycle
rally around the region.

Times Open all year, daily 10-5. Closed 24-26
Dec & 1 Jan Facilities ⓟ ⌷⚲ toilets for
disabled shop ⊗

DUDLEY

Black Country Living Museum

Tipton Rd DY1 4SQ
☎ 0121 557 9643 & 520 8054
🖹 0121 557 4242
e-mail: info@bclm.co.uk
web: www.bclm.co.uk
dir: on A4037, near Showcase cinema

Meet the costumed characters and find out
what life was like around 1900. Ride on a
tramcar, explore the underground mine,
venture into the limestone caverns or visit the
fairground (additional charge). There are also
demonstrations of chainmaking, glass engraving
and sweet-making. Watch a silent movie,
taste fish and chips cooked on a 1930s range,
and finish your visit with a glass of real ale or
dandelion and burdock in the inn. Lots of varied
events throughout the year, contact for details.

Times Open all year, Mar-Oct, Mon-Sun 10-5;
Nov-Feb, Wed-Sun 10-4. (Telephone for Xmas
closing)* Fees £12.95 (ch & student with NUS
card £6.95, pen £10.50). Family (1ad+1ch)
£18 & (2ad+3ch) £34.95* Facilities 🅿 �
⦿ licensed ⅀ (indoor & outdoor) ⅁ (partly
accessible) (access to most buildings requires
use of temporary ramp. Staff will assist visitors
with restricted mobility) toilets for disabled
shop ⊗

DUDLEY

Dudley Zoological Gardens

2 The Broadway DY1 4QB
☎ 01384 215313   🖹 01384 456048
e-mail: marketing@dudleyzoo.org.uk
web: www.dudleyzoo.org.uk
dir: M5 junct 2 towards Wolverhampton/Dudley,
signed

From lions and tigers to snakes and spiders,
enjoy animal encounters and feeds. Get closer to
some furry, and some not so furry creatures, and
have fun on the fair rides, land train, and the
adventure playground. Step back in time and see
history come to life in the castle.

Times Open all year, Etr-mid Sep, daily 10-4; mid
Sep-Etr, daily 10-3. Closed 25 Dec.* Fees £11.90
(ch 3 £7.70 under 3's free, concessions £8.70).*
Facilities 🅿 🅿 ⦿ ⦿ licensed ⅀ (outdoor)
⅁ (partly accessible) (not all accessible for
wheelchairs due to hilly site) toilets for disabled
shop ⊗

SOLIHULL

National Motorcycle Museum

Coventry Rd, Bickenhill B92 0EJ
☎ 01675 443311   📄 0121 711 3153
web: www.nationalmotorcyclemuseum.co.uk
dir: M42 junct 6, off A45 near NEC

The National Motorcycle Museum is recognised
as the finest and largest motorcycle museum
in the world, with machines always being
added to the collection. It is a place where
legends live on and it is a tribute to and a living
record of this once great British industry that
dominated world markets for some sixty years.
The museum records for posterity the engineering
achievements of the last century.

Times Open all year, daily 10-6. Closed 24-26
Dec. **Fees** £6.95 (ch 12 & pen £4.95). Party 20+
£5.95. **Facilities** 🅿 🍴 licensed ♿ toilets for
disabled shop ⊗

STOURBRIDGE

The Falconry Centre

Hurrans Garden Centre, Kidderminster Road
South, Hagley DY9 0JB
☎ 01562 700014   📄 01562 700014
e-mail: info@thefalconrycentre.co.uk
web: www.thefalconrycentre.co.uk
dir: off A456

The centre houses some 70 birds of prey
including owls, hawks and falcons and is also a
rehabilitation centre for sick and injured birds of
prey. Spectacular flying displays are put on daily
from midday. There are picnic areas, special fun
days and training courses available.

Times Open all year, daily 10-5 & Sun 11-5.
Closed 25, 26 Dec & Etr Sun.* **Facilities** 🅿 ☕
🪑 toilets for disabled shop ⊗

ALUM BAY

The Needles Old Battery & New Battery

West High Down PO30 0JH
☎ 01983 754772   ▤ 01983 756978
e-mail: isleofwight@nationaltrust.org.uk
web: www.nationaltrust.org.uk/isleofwight
dir: at Needles Headland, W of Freshwater Bay and Alum Bay, B3322

The threat of a French invasion prompted the construction in 1862 of this spectacularly sited fort, which now contains exhibitions on the Battery's involvement in both World Wars. Two of the original gun barrels are displayed in the parade ground and a 60-yard tunnel leads to a searchlight emplacement perched above the Needles Rocks giving magnificent views of the Dorset coastline beyond. Opening times vary, phone for details.

Times Old battery open: 13 Mar-Oct, daily 10.30-5 (last admission 4.30). New battery 13 Mar-Oct, Sat-Sun & Tue 11-4. (both properties close in high winds). Fees Old battery with Gift Aid: £4.85 (ch £2.45). Family ticket £12.10. New battery free.* Facilities ℗ ⊑ & (partly accessible) (Access to the tunnel at Old Battery via spiral staircase. Uneven surfaces & steep paths. Access to New battery via steps to exhibition room). toilets for disabled shop ⚐

ALUM BAY

The Needles Park

PO39 0JD
☎ 0871 720 0022   ▤ 01983 755260
e-mail: info@theneedles.co.uk
web: www.theneedles.co.uk
dir: signed on B3322

Overlooking the Needles on the western edge of the island, the park has attractions for all the family: included in the wide range of facilities is the spectacular chair lift to the beach to view the famous coloured sand cliffs, Needles Rocks and lighthouse. Other popular attractions are Alum Bay Glass and the Isle of Wight Sweet Manufactory. Kids will enjoy the Junior Driver roadway, the Jurassic golf course and the Spins and Needles tea cup ride. Please contact for special events.

Times Open Etr-Oct, daily from 10am. (Some attractions available in winter). Fees No admission charged for entrance to Park, pay to park your car. Pay as you go attractions or Supersaver Attraction discount tickets. Facilities ℗ ⊑ ⑪ licensed ㅈ (outdoor) & (partly accessible) (Some slopes) toilets for disabled shop

BLACKGANG

Blackgang Chine Fantasy Park

PO38 2HN

☎ 01983 730330 📠 01983 731267

e-mail: info@blackgangchine.com

web: www.blackgangchine.com

dir: follow signs from Ventnor for Whitnell & Niton. From Niton follow signs for Blackgang

Opened as scenic gardens in 1843 covering some 40 acres, the park has imaginative play areas, water gardens, maze and coastal gardens. Set on the steep wooded slopes of the chine are the themed areas Smugglerland, Nurseryland, Dinosaurland, Fantasyland and Frontierland. St Catherine's Quay has a maritime exhibition showing the history of local and maritime affairs. Newer attractions include Cliffhanger: the roller coaster, and Pirate's Lair, an adventure play area. Recent themes include 'Chocolate Heaven', and a helicopter film cinema 'Wight Experience'.

Times Open late Mar-end Oct daily, 10-5; school summer hols open until 6. **Fees** Combined ticket (as from 15 May) to chine, sawmill & quay £9.50. Saver ticket (4 people) £35.* **Facilities** 🅿 ⛟ 🍴 (outdoor) ♿ (partly accessible) (park on cliff edge, sloping paths) toilets for disabled shop

PORCHFIELD

Colemans Animal Farm

Colemans Ln PO30 4LX

☎ 01983 522831

e-mail: chris@colemansfarmpark.co.uk

web: www.colemansfarmpark.co.uk

dir: A3054 Newport to Yarmouth road, follow brown tourist signs

Ideal for young children, this extensive petting farm has donkeys, goats, rabbits, guinea pigs, pigs, Highland Ankole cattle, llamas, Shetland ponies, chickens, ducks and geese. There is also a straw fun barn with slides and swings, an adventure playground, a Tractor Fun Park, and an Old Barn Café for adults who need to relax. Visitors can cuddle, stroke and feed the animals at special times throughout the day. Other special events run all day.

Times Open mid Mar-end Oct, Tue-Sun, 10-4.30 (last admission recommended 3.30). (Closed Mon, ex during school and BHs). Open for pre-booked events out of season.* **Fees** £7 (ch £6, concessions £5).* **Facilities** 🅿 ⛟ 🍴 (indoor & outdoor) ♿ (partly accessible) (90% accessible) toilets for disabled shop

SANDOWN

Dinosaur Isle

Culver Pde PO36 8QA

☎ 01983 404344 🖹 01983 407502

e-mail: dinosaur@iow.gov.uk

web: www.dinosaurisle.com

dir: In Sandown follow brown tourist signs to Dinosaur Isle, situated on B3395 on seafront

Britain's first purpose-built dinosaur attraction where, in a building reminiscent of a Pterosaur flying across the Cretaceous skies, you can walk back through fossilised time. In recreated landscape meet life-sized models of the island's five famous dinosaurs - Neovenator, Eotyrannus, Iguandon, Hypsilophodon and Polacanthus. Look out for the flying Pterodactyls and skeletons as they are found, watch volunteers preparing the latest finds or try the many hands-on activities. A guided fossil hunt (which must be pre-booked) has proven a popular addition.

Times Open all year daily, Apr-Sep 10-6; Oct 10-5; Nov-Mar 10-4. (Closed 24-26 Dec & 1 Jan). Please phone to confirm opening 5 Jan-6 Feb. (Last admission 1hr before closing.) Fees £5 (ch 3-15 £3, concessions £4). Family (2ad+2ch) £14.50* Facilities ❶ ℗ 🍴 (outdoor) ♿ toilets for disabled shop ⊗

LACOCK

Lacock Abbey, Fox Talbot Museum & Village

SN15 2LG

☎ 01249 730227 (abbey) & 730459

🖹 01249 730501

e-mail: lacockabbey@nationaltrust.org.uk

web: www.nationaltrust.org.uk

dir: 3m S of Chippenham, E of A350, car park signed

Lacock Abbey is the former home of William Henry Fox Talbot, who invented the photographic negative process. The oldest negative in existence is of a photograph of Lacock Abbey. As well as the museum there are newly-restored botanic gardens and greenhouse and a well-preserved country village. The Abbey has also been used as a film location, and can be seen in Harry Potter, Pride and Prejudice, Cranford, The Other Boleyn Girl and Wolfman.

Times Cloisters & Grounds, Mar-2 Nov, daily 11-5.30. Closed Good Fri. Abbey, 15 Mar-2 Nov, daily, ex Tue, 1-5.30. Closed Good Fri. Museum 23 Feb-2 Nov, daily 11-5.30; 8 Nov-21 Dec, Sat & Sun 11-4; 3-31 Jan, Sat & Sun 11-4* Facilities ❶ 🍴 (outdoor) toilets for disabled shop ⊗ ⌘

LONGLEAT

Longleat

The Estate Office BA12 7NW
☎ 01985 844400 🖷 01985 844885
e-mail: enquiries@longleat.co.uk
web: www.longleat.co.uk
dir: turn off A36 Bath-Salisbury road onto A362 Warminster-Frome road

Nestling within magnificent 'Capability' Brown landscaped grounds in the heart of Wiltshire, Longleat House, built by Sir John Thynne and completed in 1580, has remained the home of the same family ever since. Many treasures are contained within the house and the murals in the family apartments in the West Wing were painted by Alexander Thynne, the present Marquess, and are fascinating and remarkable additions to the collection. Apart from the ancestral home, Longleat is also renowned for its safari park. Here, visitors have the rare opportunity to see hundreds of animals in natural woodland and parkland settings. Among the most magnificent sights are the famous pride of lions, wolves, rhesus monkeys and zebra.

Times Open daily 14-22 Feb, wknds only 28 Feb-29 Mar; daily 4 Apr-1 Nov. Longleat House open daily (ex 25 Dec).* Facilities ❷ ☖ ⑩ licensed ☰ (outdoor) ♿ (partly accessible) toilets for disabled shop

STONEHENGE

Stonehenge

SP4 7DE
☎ 0870 333 1181 & 01722 343834
🖷 01722 343831
web: www.english-heritage.org.uk
dir: 2m W of Amesbury on junct A303 and A344/A360

Britain's greatest prehistoric monument and a World Heritage Site. What visitors see today are the substantial remains of the last in a series of monuments erected between around 3000 and 1600BC.

Times Open all year, 16 Mar-May & Sep-15 Oct, daily 9.30-6; Jun-Aug, daily 9-7; 16 Oct-15 Mar, daily 9.30-4; 26 Dec & 1 Jan, 10-4. Closed 24-25 Dec. (opening times may vary around Summer Solstice 20-22 Jun). Fees £6.60 (concessions £5.60, ch £3.30). Family ticket £16.50. NT members free. Prices and opening times are subject to change in March 2010. Please check web site or call 0870 333 1181 for the most up to date prices and opening times when planning your visit. Facilities ❷ ☖ shop ⊗ ⊞

SWINDON

STEAM - Museum of the Great Western Railway

Kemble Dr SN2 2TA
☎ 01793 466646 🖷 01793 466615
e-mail: steampostbox@swindon.gov.uk
web: www.steam-museum.org.uk
dir: from M4 junct 16 & A420 follow brown signs to 'Outlet Centre' & Museum

This fascinating day out tells the story of the men and women who built, operated and travelled on the Great Western Railway. Hands-on displays, world-famous locomotives, archive film footage and the testimonies of ex-railway workers bring the story to life. A reconstructed station platform, posters and holiday memorabilia recreate the glamour and excitement of the golden age of steam. Good value group packages, special events, exhibitions and shop.

Times Open daily 10-5. Closed 25-26 Dec & 1 Jan* Facilities Ⓟ toilets for disabled shop ⊗

TEFFONT MAGNA

Farmer Giles Farmstead

SP3 5QY
☎ 01722 716338 🖷 01722 716147
e-mail: farmergiles@farmergiles.co.uk
web: www.farmergiles.co.uk
dir: 11m W of Stonehenge, off A303 to Teffont. Follow brown signs

Forty acres of Wiltshire downland with farm animals to feed, ponds, inside and outside play areas, exhibitions, tractor rides, and gift shop. Working farm with hands-on rare breed animal feeding, cuddling and grooming. Pony rides, tractor rides, vast indoor and outdoor play areas and exhibitions.

Times Open mid Mar-mid Nov, daily 10-6 (last entry 4pm), wknds in winters & school hols, 10-dusk. Party bookings all year. Closed 25 & 26 Dec. Fees £5.50 (ch £4.50, under 2's free & pen £5) Family ticket £18.* Facilities Ⓟ Ⓟ ⦿I licensed ⊓ (indoor & outdoor) ♿ toilets for disabled shop ⊗

WESTBURY

Brokerswood Country Park

Brokerswood BA13 4EH
☎ 01373 822238 & & 823880
🖷 01373 858474
e-mail: info@brokerswood.co.uk
web: www.brokerswood.co.uk
dir: off A36 at Bell Inn, Standerwick. Follow brown signs from A350

Brokerswood Country Park's nature walk leads through 80 acres of woodlands, with a lake and wildfowl. Facilities include a woodland visitor centre (covering wildlife and forestry), two children's adventure playgrounds (Etr-Oct school holidays & wknds only) and the woodland railway, over a third of a mile long.

Times Open all year; Park open daily 10-5. Closed 24-26 Dec & 1 Jan. Ring for museum opening hours.* **Fees** £3.50 (ch 3-16 £2.50, concessions £2.50)* **Facilities** 🅿 ⛻ 🎋 (outdoor) ♿ (partly accessible) (ramp access to cafe) toilets for disabled shop

BEWDLEY

West Midland Safari & Leisure Park

Spring Grove DY12 1LF
☎ 01299 402114 🖷 01299 404519
e-mail: info@wmsp.co.uk
web: www.wmsp.co.uk
dir: on A456 between Kidderminster & Bewdley

Located in the heart of rural Worcestershire, this 200-acre site is the home to a drive-through safari and an amazing range of exotic animals. Animal attractions include Leopard Valley, Twilight Cave, Creepy Crawlies, the Reptile House, Sealion Theatre, and Seaquarium exhibit. There are also a variety of rides, amusements and live shows suitable for all members of the family.

Times Open daily mid Feb-early Nov. Times may change. Seasonal wknd opening early Nov-mid Feb. Check website for up to date opening times and information.* **Fees** £11.50 (ch 3-15yrs £10.50, ch under 3 free, concessions £10.50). Amusement rides extra.* **Facilities** 🅿 ⛻ 🍽 licensed 🎋 (outdoor) ♿ shop ⊗

KIDDERMINSTER

Worcestershire County Museum

Hartlebury Castle, Hartlebury DY11 7XZ
☎ 01299 250416 📠 01299 251890
e-mail: museum@worcestershire.gov.uk
web: www.worcestershire.gov.uk/museum
dir: 4m S of Kidderminster clearly signed from
A449

Housed in the north wing of Hartlebury Castle,
the County Museum contains a delightful
display of crafts and industries. There are
unique collections of toys and costume, displays
on domestic life, period room settings and
horse-drawn vehicles. Visitors can also see a
reconstructed forge, a schoolroom, scullery and
nursery. Family events at least one weekend
each month. Children's craft activities Tue-Fri
in school holidays. Phone for details of special
events.

Times Open 5 Jan-23 Dec, Tue-Fri 10-5; Sat,
Sun & BHs 11-5. Closed Good Fri. Fees £4 (ch &
concession £2). Family ticket (2ad+2ch) £10.*
Facilities 🅿 🅿 ⬜ 🍴 (outdoor) ♿ toilets for
disabled shop ⊗

GOOLE

The Yorkshire Waterways Museum

Dutch River Side DN14 5TB
☎ 01405 768730 📠 01405 769868
e-mail: info@waterwaysmuseum.org.uk
web: www.waterwaysmuseum.org.uk
dir: M62 junct 36, enter Goole, turn right at next
3 sets of lights onto Dutch River Side. 0.75m and
follow brown signs

Discover the story of the Aire & Calder Navigation
and the growth of the 'company town' of Goole
and its busy port. Find out how to sail and, in
the interactive gallery, see how wooden boats
were built. Enjoy the unique 'Tom Pudding' story,
brought to life through the vessels on the canal
and the boat hoist in South Dock. Rediscover
the Humber keels and sloops, and Goole's
shipbuilding history through the objects, photos
and memories of Goole people.

Times Open all year Mon-Fri 9-4, Sat-Sun 10-4.
(Closed Xmas & New Year).* Fees Free entry
to museum. Boat trip £4 (ch under 12 £3).*
Facilities 🅿 ⬜ 🍴 (outdoor) ♿ toilets for
disabled shop ⊗

KINGSTON UPON HULL

'Streetlife' - Hull Museum of Transport **FREE**

High St HU1 1PS
☎ 01482 613902 📠 01482 613710
e-mail: museums@hullcc.gov.uk
web: www.hullcc.gov.uk
dir: A63 from M62, follow signs for Old Town

This purpose-built museum uses a 'hands-on' approach to trace 200 years of transport history. With a vehicle collection of national importance, state-of-the-art animatronic displays and authentic scenarios, you can see Hull's Old Town brought vividly to life. The mail coach ride uses the very latest in computer technology to recreate a Victorian journey by four-in-hand.

Times Open all year, Mon-Sat 10-5, Sun 1.30-4.30. Closed 24-25 Dec & Good Fri*
Facilities ℗ 🚻♿ toilets for disabled shop ⊗

KINGSTON UPON HULL

The Deep

HU1 4DP
☎ 01482 381000 📠 01482 381018
e-mail: info@thedeep.co.uk
web: www.thedeep.co.uk
dir: follow signs from city centre

The Deep is a conservation and educational charity which runs one of the deepest and most spectacular aquariums in the world. It is a unique blend of stunning marine life, the latest interactives and audio-visual presentations which together tell the dramatic story of the world's oceans. Highlights include 40 sharks and 3500 fish, Europe's deepest viewing tunnel and a glass lift ride through a 10m deep tank. Includes 3D movie. The Deep has an annual programme of events all available online.

Times Open all year, daily 10-6. Closed 24-25 Dec (last entry 5). Fees £8.75 (ch under 16 £6.75). Family ticket (2ad+2ch) £28, (2ad+3ch) £33.25.* Facilities ❶℗ ⊑🍴 licensed 🚻 (indoor & outdoor) ♿ toilets for disabled shop ⊗

ELVINGTON

Yorkshire Air Museum & Allied Air Forces Memorial

Halifax Way YO41 4AU
☎ 01904 608595   🖶 01904 608246
e-mail: museum@yorkshireairmuseum.co.uk
web: www.yorkshireairmuseum.co.uk
dir: from York take A1079 then immediate right onto B1228, museum is signposted on right

This award-winning museum and memorial is based around the largest authentic former WWII Bomber Command Station open to the public. There is a restored tower, an air gunners museum, archives, an Airborne Forces display, Squadron memorial rooms, and much more. Among the exhibits are replicas of the pioneering Cayley Glider and Wright Flyer, along with the Halifax Bomber and modern jets like the Harrier GR3, Tornado GR1 and GR4. A new exhibition 'Against The Odds' tells the story of the RAF Bomber Command.

Times Open all year, daily, 10-5 (summer); 10-3.30 (winter). Closed 25-26 Dec.* Fees £7 (ch £4 & pen £6). Prices under review Facilities ⓟ ⌴ †◎† licensed ⊼ (outdoor) ♿ toilets for disabled shop

HAWES

Dales Countryside Museum & National Park Centre

Station Yard DL8 3NT
☎ 01969 666210   🖶 01969 666239
e-mail: hawes@yorkshiredales.org.uk
web: www.yorkshiredales.org.uk
dir: off A684 in Old Station Yard

Fascinating museum telling the story of the people and landscape of the Yorkshire Dales. Static steam loco and carriages with displays. Added features include hands-on interactive displays for children, temporary exhibitions and special events. Free family exhibition every summer with activities for visitors of all ages!

Times Open all year daily 10-5. Closed 24-26 Dec 1 Jan & Jan following Xmas hol period. Fees Museum: £3 (ch free, concessions £2). National park centre, temporary exhibitions free.* Facilities ⓟ ⓟ ⊼ (outdoor) ♿ toilets for disabled shop ⊗

KIRBY MISPERTON

Flamingo Land Theme Park & Zoo

The Rectory YO17 6UX
☎ 01653 668287 📠 01653 668280
e-mail: info@flamingoland.co.uk
web: www.flamingoland.co.uk
dir: turn off A64 onto A169, Pickering to Whitby
road

Set in 375 acres of North Yorkshire countryside
with over 100 rides and attractions there's
something for everyone at Flamingo Land. Enjoy
the thrills and spills of 12 white knuckle rides
or enjoy a stroll through the extensive zoo where
you'll find tigers, giraffes, hippos and rhinos. The
theme park also boasts 6 great family shows.

Times Open daily, 30 Mar-28 Oct.* Fees £22 (ch
under 3 free, concessions £11). Family ticket (4
people) £82.* Facilities 🅿 🅟 ⬚ 🍴 licensed
🇦 (outdoor) toilets for disabled shop

KIRKHAM

Kirkham Priory

Whitwell-on-the-Hill YO6 7JS
☎ 01653 618768
web: www.english-heritage.org.uk
dir: 5m SW of Malton on minor road off A64

Discover the ruins of this Augustinian priory,
which includes a magnificent carved gatehouse,
set in a peaceful and secluded valley by the River
Derwent.

Times Open Apr-Jul & Sep, Thu-Mon 10-5; Aug,
daily 10-5. Fees £3 (cconcessions £2.60, ch
£1.50). Prices and opening times are subject to
change in March 2010. Please check web site or
call 0870 333 1181 for the most up to date prices
and opening times when planning your visit.
Facilities 🅿 ⬚ (partly accessible) (steep steps
cloister to refectory) ⌗

KNARESBOROUGH

Knaresborough Castle & Museum

Castle Yard HG5 8AS
☎ 01423 556188 🖷 01423 556130
e-mail: museums@harrogate.gov.uk
web: www.harrogate.gov.uk/museums
dir: off High St towards Market Square, right at
police station into Castle Yard

Towering high above the town of Knaresborough,
the remains of this 14th-century castle look down
over the gorge of the River Nidd. This imposing
fortress was once the hiding place of Thomas
Becket's murderers and a summer home for the
Black Prince. Visit the King's Tower, the secret
underground tunnel and the dungeon. Discover
Knaresborough's history in the museum and
find out about 'Life in a Castle' in the hands-on
gallery. Play the new computer game "Time Gate:
The Prisoner of Knaresborough Castle". Special
events include a Medieval Day annually on the
third Sunday in June.

Times Open Good Fri-4 Oct, daily 10.30-5. Guided
tours regularly available* Fees £2.80 (ch £1.50,
concessions £1.80). Family ticket (2ad+3ch)
£7.50 Party 10+. Annual season tickets available
for Knaresborough Castle & Museum & The Royal
Pump Room Museum.* Facilities ❷ ℗ ♿
(partly accessible) (ground floor of King's Tower
accessible) toilets for disabled shop ⊗

LAWKLAND

Yorkshire Dales Falconry & Wildlife Conservation Centre

Crows Nest LA2 8AS
☎ 01729 822832 & 825164 (info line)
🖷 01729 825160
e-mail: mail@falconryandwildlife.com
web: www.falconryandwildlife.com
dir: on A65 follow brown signs

The first privately owned falconry centre in the
north of England. The main aim of the centre is
to educate and promote awareness that many
of the world's birds of prey are threatened
with extinction. Successful captive breeding
and educational programmes will help to
safeguard these creatures. Regular free flying
demonstrations throughout the day and falconry
courses throughout the week.

Times Open all year summer 10-6; winter
10-4. Closed 25-26 Dec & 1 Jan.* Fees £5.90
(ch £3.90, pen £4.80). Family ticket £18.50
(2ad+2ch). Group 20+ £4.90 (ch £3.50). 1 Ad
free with 10 ch.* Facilities ❷ ⊑ 闬 (indoor &
outdoor) ♿ toilets for disabled shop ⊗

MIDDLESBROUGH

Captain Cook Birthplace Museum **FREE**

Stewart Park, Marton TS7 8AT
☎ 01642 311211 🖹 01642 515659
e-mail: captcookmuseum@middlesbrough.gov.uk
web: www.captcook-ne.co.uk
dir: 3m S on A172

Opened to mark the 250th anniversary of the birth of the voyager in 1728, this museum illustrates the early life of James Cook and his discoveries with permanent and temporary exhibitions. Located in spacious and rolling parkland, the site also offers outside attractions for the visitor. The museum has a special resource centre which has fresh approaches to presentation with computers, films, special effects, interactives and educational aids.

Times Open all year: Mar-Oct, Tue-Sun, 10-5.30. Nov-Feb 9-4.00. (Last entry 45 mins before closure). Closed Mon & some BH, 24-26 Dec, 1 Jan & 1st full week Jan.* Facilities 🅿 🅟 ⊡ 🍽 licensed 🎍 (outdoor) ♿ toilets for disabled shop ⊗

NORTH STAINLEY

Lightwater Valley Theme Park

HG4 3HT
☎ 0871 720 0011 🖹 0871 721 0011
e-mail: leisure@lightwatervalley.co.uk
web: www.lightwatervalley.co.uk
dir: 3m N of Ripon on A6108

Set in 175 acres of beautiful North Yorkshire parkland, Lightwater Valley offers an exciting choice of activities. The thrilling theme park line-up comprises some amazing rides, including Europe's longest rollercoaster - The Ultimate. If you prefer to take things at a more leisurely pace, enjoy a gentle stroll around the picturesque lake, play crazy golf or just climb aboard the Lightwater Express for a round-the-park train ride. The Birds of Prey Centre with its purpose-built raptor complex offers the opportunity to learn how the birds are trained and handled, as well as being treated to flying shows every day.

Times Open 31 Mar-15 Apr, wknds only; 21 Apr-27 May inc BH Mon; daily from 26 May-2 Sep, wknds only, 8 Sep-21 Oct, daily 22-28 Oct. Gates open at 10, closes 4.30, depending on time of year.* Fees £17.95 over 1.3mtrs, £15.45 under 1.3mtrs, free under 1m (concessions £8.95). Family (2ad+2ch or 1ad+3ch under 16) £62.* Facilities 🅿 ⊡ 🍽 licensed 🎍 (outdoor) ♿ (partly accessible) toilets for disabled shop ⊗

PICKERING

North Yorkshire Moors Railway

Pickering Station YO18 7AJ
☎ 01751 472508 📠 01751 476970
e-mail: admin@nymr.pickering.fsnet.co.uk
web: www.northyorkshiremoorsrailway.com
dir: from A169 take road towards Kirkbymoorside, right at traffic lights, station 400yds on left

Operating through the heart of the North York Moors National Park between Pickering and Grosmont, steam trains cover a distance of 18 miles. The locomotive sheds at Grosmont are open to the public. Events throughout the year include Day Out with Thomas, Steam Gala, Santa Specials.

Times Open 29 Mar-Oct, daily; Dec, Santa specials and Xmas to New Year running. Further information available from Pickering Station.*
Facilities ❷ ⓟ ⊡ 🍽 licensed ☎ (outdoor) toilets for disabled shop

RIPLEY

Ripley Castle

HG3 3AY
☎ 01423 770152 📠 01423 771745
e-mail: enquiries@ripleycastle.co.uk
web: www.ripleycastle.co.uk
dir: off A61, Harrogate to Ripon road

Ripley Castle has been home to the Ingilby family for 26 generations and stands at the heart of an estate with deer park, lakes and Victorian walled gardens. The Castle has a rich history and a fine collection of Royalist armour housed in the 1555 tower. There are also tropical hot houses, a children's play trail, tearooms, woodland walks, pleasure grounds and the National Hyacinth Collection in spring.

Times Open Nov-8 Mar, Tue, Thu, Sat & Sun 10.30-3; Apr-Oct, daily 10.30-3; Dec-Feb wkends only, also BH and school hols. Groups all year by prior arrangement. Gardens open daily 9-5.*
Fees Castle & Gardens £8 (ch £5, pen £7). Gardens only £5.50 (ch £3.50, concessions £5). Party £5.* Facilities ❷ ⊡ 🍽 licensed ♿ (partly accessible) (two of the rooms in the castle on view are upstairs) toilets for disabled shop ⊗

THIRSK

Falconry UK - Birds of Prey Centre

Sion Hill Hall, Kirby Wiske YO7 4EU
☎ 01845 587522
e-mail: mail@falconrycentre.co.uk
web: www.falconrycentre.co.uk
dir: follow brown tourist signs, situated on A167
between Northallerton and Topcliffe

Set up to ensure that birds of prey would survive
to provide the public with a rare opportunity to
see and enjoy these beautiful birds. Enjoy the
excitement of falconry with over 70 birds and
30 species. Three different flying displays with
public participation where possible. After each
display, handling birds brought out for public
to hold.

Times Open Mar-Oct daily, 10.30-5. 3 Daily flying
displays (different birds in each display) at
11.30, 1.30, 3.30. Fees £6.50 (ch £4.50, under
3 free, pen £5.50). Family ticket £19 (2ad+2ch)
Facilities ❷ ℗ ⌴ ㅈ (outdoor) ♿ toilets for
disabled shop ⊗

WHITBY

Whitby Abbey

YO22 4JT
☎ 01947 603568 📄 01947 825561
web: www.english-heritage.org.uk
dir: on clifftop E of Whitby town centre

Uncover the full story of these atmospheric
ruins in their impressive clifftop location above
the picturesque fishing town with associations
ranging from Victorian jewellery and whaling, to
Count Dracula.

Times Open all year, Apr-Sep, daily 10-6; Oct-
Mar, Thu-Mon 10-4. Closed 24-26 Dec & 1 Jan.
Fees £5.50 (concessions £4.70, ch £2.80). Family
ticket £13.80. Prices and opening times are
subject to change in March 2010. Please check
web site or call 0870 333 1181 for the most up
to date prices and opening times when planning
your visit. Facilities ❷ ⌴ ㅈ shop ⌗

YORK

Jorvik Viking Centre

Coppergate YO1 9WT

☎ 01904 615505   📄 01904 627097

e-mail: jorvik@yorkat.co.uk

web: www.jorvik-viking-centre.com

dir: follow A19 or A64 to York. Jorvik in Coppergate shopping area (city centre) signed

Explore York's Viking history on the very site where archaeologists discovered remains of the city of Jorvik. See over 800 of the items discovered on site, learn what life was like here more than 1000 years ago, and journey through a reconstruction of actual Viking streets. 'Are You A Viking?' uses scientific evidence to discover if you have Viking ancestors. 'Unearthed' tells how the people of ancient York lived and died, as revealed by real bone material. Special events throughout the year.

Times Open all year, summer, daily 10-5; winter, daily 10-4. Closed 24-26 Dec. Opening times subject to change. Fees £8.50 (ch 5-15 £6, under 5 free, concessions £7) Family of 4 £26 & family of 5 £29. Telephone bookings on 01904 615505 (£1 booking fee per person at peak times).* Facilities ℗ ⬚ ♿ (partly accessible) (wheelchair users are advised to pre-book) toilets for disabled shop ⊗

YORK

National Railway Museum

Leeman Rd YO26 4XJ

☎ 01904 621261   📄 01904 611112

e-mail: nrm@nrm.org.uk

web: www.nrm.org.uk

dir: behind rail station. Signed from all major roads and city centre

The National Railway Museum is the world's largest railway museum. From record breakers to history makers the museum is home to a vast collection of locomotives, carriages and wagons, including The Royal Trains, a replica of Stephenson's Rocket, the Japanese Bullet Train and the elegant Duchess. With three enormous galleries, interactive exhibits and daily events, the National Railway Museum mixes education with fun. This attraction is also free. NB: There is a charge for certain special events.

Times Open all year 10-6. Closed 24-26 Dec. Fees Admission is free but there may be charges for special events and rides. Facilities ℗ ℗ ⬚ ⑩ licensed ⊼ (outdoor) ♿ toilets for disabled shop ⊗

YORK

York Castle Museum

The Eye of York YO1 1RY
☎ 01904 687687
e-mail: castle.museum@ymt.org.uk
web: www.yorkcastlemuseum.org.uk
dir: city centre, next to Clifford's Tower

Fascinating exhibits that bring memories to life, imaginatively displayed through reconstructions of period rooms and Victorian indoor streets, complete with cobbles and a Hansom cab. The museum was one of the first folk museums to display a huge range of everyday objects in an authentic scene. The Victorian street includes a pawnbroker, a tallow candle factory and a haberdasher's. An extensive collection of many other items ranging from musical instruments to costumes. The museum also has one of Britain's finest collections of Militaria. A special exhibition called 'Seeing it Through' explores the life of York citizens during the Second World War. Please contact the museum for details of exhibitions and events.

Times Open all year, daily 9.30-5 Fees £7.50 (ch £4 under 5's free, concessions £6.50). Family tickets available* Facilities ℗ ⊔ & (partly accessible) (main galleries accessible, no access up stairs) toilets for disabled shop ⊗

YORK

Yorkshire Museum

Museum Gardens YO1 7FR
☎ 01904 551800 📄 01904 551802
e-mail: yorkshire.museum@york.gov.uk
web: http://www.york.gov.uk
dir: park & ride service from 4 sites near A64/A19/A1079 & A166, also 3 car parks within short walk

The Yorkshire Museum is set in 10 acres of botanical gardens in the heart of the historic City of York, and displays some of the finest Roman, Anglo-Saxon, Viking and Medieval treasures ever discovered in Britain. The Middleham jewel, a fine example of English Gothic jewellery, is on display, and in the Roman Gallery, visitors can see a marble head of Constantine the Great. The Anglo-Saxon Gallery houses the delicate silver-gilt Ormside bowl and the Gilling sword.

Times Open all year, daily 10-5.* Facilities ℗ ⏠ toilets for disabled shop ⊗

ROTHERHAM

Magna Science Adventure Centre

Sheffield Rd, Templeborough S60 1DX
☎ 01709 720002 📄 01709 820092
e-mail: aholdsworth@magnatrust.co.uk
web: www.visitmagna.co.uk
dir: M1 junct 33/34, follow Templeborough sign
off rdbt, then brown heritage signs

Magna is the UK's first Science Adventure
Centre, an exciting exploration of Earth, Air, Fire
and Water. A chance for visitors to create their
own adventure through hands-on interactive
challenges. Visit the four Adventure Pavilions,
live show and outdoor playgrounds Sci-Tek and
Aqua-Tek.

Times Open all year, daily (Check website for
Mondays), 10-5. Closed 24-26 Dec. **Fees** £9.95
(ch under 4's free, ch & concessions £8.95).
Family ticket (2ad+1ch) £25 **Facilities** 🅿 🅟 ⬚
🍽 licensed ﹅ (indoor & outdoor) ♿ toilets for
disabled shop ⊗

BRADFORD

Bradford Industrial Museum and Horses at Work **FREE**

Moorside Mills, Moorside Rd, Eccleshill
BD2 3HP
☎ 01274 435900 📄 01274 636362
web: www.bradfordmuseums.org
dir: off A658

Moorside Mills is an original spinning mill, now
part of a museum that brings vividly to life the
story of Bradford's woollen industry. There is the
machinery that once converted raw wool into
cloth, and the mill yard rings with the sound of
iron on stone as shire horses pull trams, haul
buses and give rides. Daily demonstrations and
changing exhibitions.

Times Open all year, Tue-Sat 10-5, Sun 12-5.
Closed Mon ex BH, Good Fri & 25-26 Dec*
Facilities 🅟 ⬚ toilets for disabled shop ⊗

181

HALIFAX

Eureka! The National Children's Museum

Discovery Rd HX1 2NE
☎ 01422 330069 🖷 01422 330275
e-mail: info@eureka.org.uk
web: www.eureka.org.uk
dir: M62 junct 24 follow brown heritage signs to Halifax centre - A629

With over 400 'must touch' exhibits, interactive activities and challenges, visitors are invited to embark upon a journey of discovery through six main gallery spaces. They can find out how their bodies and senses work, discover the realities of daily life, travel from the familiar 'backyard' to amazing and faraway places and experiment with creating their own sounds and music.

Times Open all year, daily 10-5. Closed 24-26 Dec* **Fees** £7.25 (ch 1-2 £2.25, ch under 1 free) Family Saver ticket £31. Special group rates available.* **Facilities** Ⓟ Ⓟ ☕ ⛩ (indoor & outdoor) ♿ toilets for disabled shop ⊗

HAWORTH

Brontë Parsonage Museum

Church St BD22 8DR
☎ 01535 642323 🖷 01535 647131
e-mail: bronte@bronte.org.uk
web: www.bronte.info
dir: A629 & A6033 follow signs for Haworth, take Rawdon Rd, pass 2 car parks, next left, then right

Haworth Parsonage was the lifelong family home of the Brontës. An intensely close-knit family, the Brontës saw the parsonage as the heart of their world and the moorland setting provided them with inspiration for their writing. The house contains much personal memorabilia, including the furniture Charlotte bought with the proceeds of her literary success, Branwell's portraits of local worthies, Emily's writing desk and Anne's books and drawings. The museum is currently holding a two year exhibition focusing on Branwell Brontë, who as a child was considered the greatest genius of the family. Branwell declined into alcoholism while his sisters went on to write great novels.

Times Open all year, Apr-Sep, daily 10-5.30; Oct-Mar, daily 11-5 (final admission 30 min before closing). Closed 24-27 Dec & 2-31 Jan. **Fees** £6 (ch 5-16 £3, concessions £4.50). Family ticket £15.* **Facilities** Ⓟ Ⓟ ♿ (partly accessible) (please contact the museum for info) shop ⊗

LEEDS

Abbey House Museum

Abbey Walk, Abbey Rd, Kirkstall LS5 3EH
☎ 0113 230 5492   🖷 0113 230 5499
e-mail: abbey.house@leeds.gov.uk
web: www.leeds.gov.uk
dir: 3m W of city centre on A65

Displays at this museum include an interactive childhood gallery, a look at Kirkstall Abbey, and an exploration of life in Victorian Leeds. Three reconstructed streets allow the visitor to immerse themselves in the sights and sounds of the late 19th century, from the glamourous art furnishers shop to the impoverished widow washerwoman.

Times Open all year Tue-Fri 10-5, Sat noon-5, Sun 10-5. Closed Mon ex BH Mon (open 10-5)*
Facilities 🅿 🅟 ⛴ 🍽 licensed 🍴 (outdoor) toilets for disabled shop ⊗

LEEDS

Leeds Industrial Museum at Armley Mills

Canal Rd, Armley LS12 2QF
☎ 0113 263 7861
web: www.leeds.gov.uk/armleymills
dir: 2m W of city centre, off A65

Once the world's largest woollen mill, Armley Mills evokes memories of the 18th-century woollen industry, showing the progress of wool from the sheep to knitted clothing. The museum has its own 1930s cinema illustrating the history of cinema projection, including the first moving pictures taken in Leeds. The Museum is set in some lovely scenery, between the Leeds & Liverpool Canal and the River Aire. There are demonstrations of static engines and steam locomotives, a printing gallery and a journey through the working world of textiles and fashion.

Times Open all year, Tue-Sat 10-5, Sun 1-5. Last entry 4. Closed Mon ex BHs.* Facilities 🅿 🍴 (indoor & outdoor) ♿ (partly accessible) toilets for disabled shop ⊗

LEEDS

Royal Armouries Museum FREE

Armouries Dr LS10 1LT

☎ 0113 220 1999 & 0990 106 666

📄 0113 220 1955

e-mail: enquiries@armouries.org.uk

web: www.royalarmouries.org

dir: off A61 close to Leeds centre, follow brown heritage signs.

The museum is an impressive contemporary home for the renowned national collection of arms and armour. The collection is divided between five galleries: War, Tournament, Self-Defence, Hunting and Oriental. The Hall of Steel features a 100ft-high mass of 3000 pieces of arms and armour. Visitors are encouraged to take part in and handle some of the collections. Live demonstrations and interpretations take place throughout the year.

Times Open all year, daily, from 10-5. Closed 24-25 Dec* Facilities 🅿 ⬛ 🍴 licensed ⊓ (indoor) toilets for disabled shop ⊗

MIDDLESTOWN

National Coal Mining Museum for England FREE

Caphouse Colliery, New Rd WF4 4RH

☎ 01924 848806 📄 01924 844567

e-mail: info@ncm.org.uk

web: www.ncm.org.uk

dir: on A642 between Huddersfield & Wakefield

A unique opportunity to go 140 metres underground down one of Britain's oldest working mines. Take a step back in time with one of the museum's experienced local miners who will guide parties around the underground workings, where models and machinery depict methods and conditions of mining from the early 1800s to present day. Other attractions include the Hope Pit, pithead baths, Victorian steam winder, nature trail and adventure playground and meet the last ever working pit ponies. You are strongly advised to wear sensible footwear and warm clothing.

Times Open all year, daily 10-5. Closed 24-26 Dec & 1 Jan.* Facilities 🅿 ⬛ 🍴 licensed ⊓ (outdoor) ♿ toilets for disabled shop ⊗

ST PETER PORT

Guernsey Museum & Art Gallery

Candie Gardens GY1 1UG
☎ 01481 726518 📄 01481 715177
e-mail: admin@museums.gov.gg
web: www.museums.gov.gg
dir: On the outskirts of St Peter Port set in the
Victorian 'Candie gardens'

The museum, designed around a Victorian
bandstand, tells the story of Guernsey and its
people. There is an audio-visual theatre and an
art gallery, and special exhibitions are arranged
throughout the year. It is surrounded by beautiful
gardens with superb views over St Peter Port
harbour. In 2010 a summer exhibition on arts
and crafts made by Guernsey people deported
during WW2.

Times Open Feb-Dec, daily 10-5 (winter 10-4)
Fees £4.50 (ch over 7 & students £1, pen £3.75).
Season ticket available. Facilities ℗ 🖵 &
toilets for disabled shop ⊗

ST PETER

The Living Legend

Rue de Petit Aleval JE3 7ET
☎ 01534 485496 📄 01534 485855
e-mail: info@jerseyslivinglegend.co.je
web: www.jerseyslivinglegend.co.je
dir: from St Helier, along main esplanade & right
to Bel Royal. Left and follow road to attraction,
signed from German Underground Hospital

Pass through the granite archways into the
landscaped gardens and the world of the
Jersey Experience where Jersey's exciting past
is recreated in a three dimensional spectacle
featuring Stephen Tompkinson, Tony Robinson
and other well-known names. Learn of the heroes
and villains, the folklore and the story of the
island's links with the UK and its struggles with
Europe. Other attractions include an adventure
playground, street entertainment, the Jersey
Craft and Shopping Village, a range of shops
and the Jersey Kitchen Restaurant. Two 18-hole
adventure golf courses are suitable for all ages.
Jersey Karting is a formula one style experience. A
unique track featuring adult and cadet karts.

Times Open Apr-Oct, daily; Mar & Nov, Sat-Wed;
9-5.* Facilities ℗ 🖵 🍴 licensed & (partly
accessible) (Adventure Golf has lots of steps and
uneven surfaces) toilets for disabled shop ⊗

TRINITY

Durrell Wildlife Conservation Trust

Les Augres Manor, La Profunde Rue JE3 5BP
☎ 01534 860000   📄 01534 860001
e-mail: info@durrell.org
web: www.durrell.org
dir: From St Hellier follow A8 to Trinity until B31.
Turn right & follow B31, signed

Gerald Durrell's unique sanctuary and breeding
centre for many of the world's rarest animals.
Visitors can see these remarkable creatures,
some so rare that they can only be found here, in
modern, spacious enclosures in the gardens of
the 16th-century manor house. Major attractions
are the magical Aye-Ayes from Madagascar and
the world-famous family of Lowland gorillas.
There is a comprehensive programme of keeper
talks, animal displays and activities.

Times Open all year, daily 9.30-6 (summer);
9.30-5 (winter). Closed 25 Dec.* Fees £12.90
(ch £9.40, pen £10.50). Family ticket £39.95.*
Facilities 🅿 ☐ 🍴 licensed 🚻 (outdoor) ♿
(partly accessible) (some indoor areas cannot
accommodate wheelchairs/scooters) toilets for
disabled shop ⊗

BALLAUGH

Curraghs Wild Life Park

IM7 5EA
☎ 01624 897323   📄 01624 897327
e-mail: curraghswlp@gov.im
web: www.gov.im/wildlife
dir: on main road halfway between Kirk Michael
& Ramsey

This park has been developed adjacent to the
reserve area of the Ballaugh Curraghs and a
large variety of animals and birds can be seen. A
walk-through enclosure lets visitors explore the
world of wildlife, including local habitats along
the Curraghs Nature Trail. The miniature railway
runs on Sundays.

Times Open all year Etr-Oct, daily 10-6. (Last
admission 5). Oct-Etr, Sat-Sun 10-4.* Fees £7
(ch £3.50, under 3's free, pen £5). Family
ticket (2ad+2ch) £17.50.* Facilities 🅿 ☐ 🚻
(outdoor) ♿ (partly accessible) (some paths in
winter not accessible to wheelchairs) toilets for
disabled shop ⊗

CASTLETOWN

Castle Rushen

The Quay IM9 1LD
☎ 01624 648000   📄 01624 648001
e-mail: enquiries@mnh.gov.im
web: www.storyofmann.com
dir: centre of Castletown

One of the world's best preserved medieval castles, Castle Rushen is a limestone fortress rising out of the heart of the old capital of the Island, Castletown. Once the fortress of the Kings and Lords of Mann, Castle Rushen is brought alive with rich decorations, and the sounds and smells of a bygone era.

Times Open daily, Etr-Oct, 10-5.* Fees £5 (ch £2.50) Family £12. Group from £4.50 each.* Facilities ℗ shop ⊗

CASTLETOWN

Old Grammar School **FREE**

IM9 1LE
☎ 01624 648000   📄 01624 648001
e-mail: enquiries@mnh.gov.im
web: www.storyofmann.com
dir: centre of Castletown, opposite the castle

Built around 1200AD, the former capital's first church, St Mary's, has had a significant role in Manx education. It was a school from 1570 to 1930 and evokes memories of Victorian school life.

Times Open daily, Etr-late Oct, 10-5.* Facilities ℗ ℗ ⊼ (outdoor) ♿ (partly accessible) (restricted access narrow door, 3 steps) shop ⊗

CREGNEASH

The National Folk Museum at Cregneash

☎ 01624 648000 📄 01624 648001
e-mail: enquiries@mnh.gov.im
web: www.storyofmann.com
dir: 2m from Port Erin/Port St Mary, signed

The Cregneash story begins in Cummal Beg - the village information centre which shows what life was really like in a Manx crofting village during the early 19th century. As you stroll around this attractive village, set in beautiful countryside, call into Harry Kelly's cottage, a Turner's shed, a Weaver's house, and the Smithy. The Manx Four-horned Loghtan Sheep can be seen grazing along with other animals from the village farm.

Times Open Etr-Oct, daily 10-5.* **Fees** £3.50 (ch £1.70) Family £8.50. Group rates from £2.80*
Facilities 🅿 ⬚ 🙶 (outdoor) shop ⊗

DOUGLAS

Manx Museum **FREE**

IM1 3LY
☎ 01624 648000 📄 01624 648001
e-mail: enquiries@mnh.gov.im
web: www.storyofmann.com
dir: signed in Douglas

The Island's treasure house provides an exciting introduction to the "Story of Mann" where a specially produced film portrayal of Manx history complements the award-winning displays. Galleries depict natural history, archaeology and the social development of the Island. There are also examples of famous Manx artists in the National Art Gallery, together with the Island's National archive and reference library. Events and exhibitions throughout the year, please visit website for details.

Times Open all year, Mon-Sat, 10-5. Closed 25-26 Dec & 1 Jan.* **Facilities** 🅿 🅟 ⬚ 🍴 licensed 🙶 (outdoor) ⅙ toilets for disabled shop ⊗

ABERDEEN

Aberdeen Maritime Museum **FREE**

Shiprow AB11 5BY
☎ 01224 337700   📠 01224 213066
e-mail: info@aagm.co.uk
web: www.aberdeencity.gov.uk
dir: located in city centre

The award-winning Maritime Museum brings the history of the North Sea to life. Featuring displays and exhibitions on the offshore oil industry, shipbuilding, fishing and clipper ships.

Times Open all year, Tue-Sat, 10-5, Sun 2-5.*
Facilities ℗ 🖵 🍴 licensed ♿ (partly accessible) (2 rooms in Provost Ross's house not accessible due to stairs) toilets for disabled shop ⊗

ABERDEEN

The Gordon Highlanders Museum

St Luke's, Viewfield Rd AB15 7XH
☎ 01224 311200   📠 01224 319323
e-mail: museum@gordonhighlanders.com
web: www.gordonhighlanders.com

Presenting a large collection of artefacts, paintings, films and reconstructions, the Gordon Highlanders Museum is the perfect day out for anyone interested in Scottish military history, and is also the former home of 19th century artist, Sir George Reid. The exhibition includes interactive maps, original film footage, scaled reproductions, life-size models, touch screens, uniforms, medals and an armoury. The grounds also contain a tea-room, shop and gardens. See the website for details of changing exhibitions and events.

Times Open Apr-Oct, Tue-Sat 10-4.30, Sun 12.30-4.30. (Closed Mon). Nov, Feb & Mar Thu-Sat 10-4. Open by appointment only at other times.* **Facilities** 🅟 ℗ 🖵 ♿ toilets for disabled shop ⊗

BALMORAL

Balmoral Castle Grounds & Exhibition

AB35 5TB

☎ 013397 42534 📠 013397 42034
e-mail: info@balmoralcastle.com
web: www.balmoralcastle.com
dir: on A93 between Ballater & Braemar

Queen Victoria and Prince Albert first rented Balmoral Castle in 1848, and Prince Albert bought the property four years later. He commissioned William Smith to build a new castle, which was completed by 1856 and is still the Royal Family's Highland residence. Explore the exhibitions, grounds, gardens and trails as well as the magnificent Castle Ballroom.

Times Open Apr-Jul, daily 10-5 (last admission 4.30)* Fees £7 (ch £3, concessions £6). Family (2ad+4ch) £15.* Facilities ❷ ⬛ 🏠 (outdoor) ♿ toilets for disabled shop

MACDUFF

Macduff Marine Aquarium

11 High Shore AB44 1SL

☎ 01261 833369 📠 01261 831052
e-mail: macduff.aquarium@aberdeenshire.gov.uk
web: www.macduff-aquarium.org.uk
dir: off A947 and A98 to Macduff, aquarium signed

Exciting displays feature local sealife. The central exhibit, unique in Britain, holds a living kelp reef. Divers feed the fish in this tank. Other displays include an estuary exhibit, splash tank, rock pools, deep reef tank and ray pool. Young visitors especially enjoy the touch pools. There are talks, video presentations and feeding shows throughout the week.

Times Open all year, daily 10-5 (last admission 4.15). Closed 25-26 Dec & 31 Dec-2 Jan* Facilities ❷ Ⓟ 🏠 (outdoor) ♿ toilets for disabled shop ⊗

MARYCULTER

Storybook Glen

AB12 5FT

☎ 01224 732941 🖹 01224 732941

web: www.storybookglenaberdeen.co.uk

dir: 5m W of Aberdeen on B9077

This is a child's fantasy land, where favourite nursery rhyme and fairytale characters are brought to life. Grown-ups can enjoy the nostalgia and also the 20 acres of Deeside country, full of flowers, plants, trees and waterfalls.

Times Open all year, Mar-Oct, daily 10-6; Nov-Feb, 10-4.* Fees £5.40 (ch £3.85, concessions £4.05).* Facilities Ⓟ ☕ 🍽 licensed ⛩ (outdoor) ♿ toilets for disabled shop ⊗

MINTLAW

Aberdeenshire Farming Museum **FREE**

Aden Country Park AB42 5FQ

☎ 01771 624590 🖹 01771 623558

e-mail: museums@aberdeenshire.gov.uk

web: www.aberdeenshire.gov.uk/museums

dir: 1m W of Mintlaw on A950

Housed in 19th-century farm buildings, once part of the estate which now makes up the Aden Country Park. Two centuries of farming history and innovation are illustrated, and the story of the estate is also told. The reconstructed farm of Hareshowe shows how a family in the north-east farmed during the 1950s - access by guided tour only.

Times Open May-Sep, daily 11-4.30; Apr & Oct, wknds only noon-4.30. (Last admission 30 mins before closing). Park open all year, Apr-Sep 7-10; winter 7-7.* Facilities Ⓟ ⓟ ☕ ⛩ (outdoor) ♿ (partly accessible) (1st floor not accessible) toilets for disabled shop ⊗

OYNE

Archaeolink Prehistory Park

Berryhill AB52 6QP
☎ 01464 851500 📄 01464 851544
e-mail: info@archaeolink.co.uk
web: www.archaeolink.co.uk
dir: 1m off A96 on B9002

A stunning audio-visual show, a Myths and Legends Gallery and a whole range of interpretation techniques help visitors to explore what it was like to live 6000 years ago. In addition there are landscaped walkways, and outdoor activity areas including an Iron Age farm, Roman marching camp and Stone Age settlement in the 40-acre park. Enjoy daily hands-on activities for all ages, guided tours with costumed guides or relax in the coffee shop. Special weekend events held regularly.

Times Open Apr-Oct, daily 10-5 **Fees** £5.75 (ch £3.70, concessions £4.90) Family from £12.15* **Facilities** 🅿 🅟 ⬛ 🍴 licensed 🪑 (outdoor) toilets for disabled shop ⊗

BRECHIN

Pictavia Visitor Centre

Brechin Castle Centre, Haughmuir DD9 6RL
☎ 01356 626241 📄 01307 467357
e-mail: ecdev@angus.gov.uk
web: www.pictavia.org.uk
dir: off A90 at Brechin

Find about more about the ancient pagan nation of the Picts, who lived in Scotland nearly 2000 years ago. Visitors can learn about Pictish culture, art and religion through film, interactive displays and music. There are also nature and farm trails, a pets' corner, and an adventure playground in the adjacent country park (operated by Brechin Castle Centre). For details please check website.

Times Open all year, Mar-Oct, Mon-Sat 9-5, Sun 10-5; Nov-Feb, Sat 9-5, Sun 10-5. **Fees** £3.25 (ch & concessions £2.25, ch under 5 free). Family ticket £10. Group rates available for large parties & educational groups. **Facilities** 🅿 ⬛ 🍴 licensed 🪑 (outdoor) ♿ toilets for disabled shop ⊗

KIRRIEMUIR

J M Barrie's Birthplace

9 Brechin Rd DD8 4BX
☎ 0844 493 2142 📄 0844 493 2142
e-mail: information@nts.org.uk
web: www.nts.org.uk
dir: on A90/A926 in Kirriemuir, 6m NW of Forfar

The creator of Peter Pan, Sir James Barrie, was
born in Kirriemuir in 1860. The upper floors of No
9 Brechin Road are furnished as they may have
been when Barrie lived there, and the adjacent
house, No 11, houses an exhibition about him.
The wash-house outside was his first 'theatre'
and gave him the idea for Wendy's house in
Peter Pan.

Times 4 Apr-28 Jun, Sat-Wed 12-5; 29 Jun-30
Aug, daily 11-5; 31 Aug-1 Nov, Sat-Wed 12-5.*
Fees £5.50 (concessions £4.50). Family £15,(1
Parent £10).* Facilities ℗ ⚏ 🅿 ♿ (partly
accessible) (steps to reception room, wheelchair
access restricted to museum & wash house)
shop ⊗ 🍽

BARCALDINE

Scottish Sea Life Sanctuary

PA37 1SE
☎ 01631 720386 📄 01631 720529
e-mail: obansealife@merlinentertainments.biz
web: www.sealsanctuary.co.uk
dir: 10m N of Oban on A828 towards Fort William

Set in one of Scotland's most picturesque
locations, the Scottish Sea Life Sanctuary
provides dramatic views of native undersea life
including stingrays, seals, octopus and catfish.
There are daily talks and feeding demonstrations
and during the summer young seals can be
viewed prior to their release back into the wild.
Recent additions include Otter Creek - a large
naturally landscaped enclosure with deep diving
pool with underwater viewing and cascading
streams through other pools, and 'Into the Deep',
a themed interactive area displaying living
creatures from the deep. There is a restaurant,
gift shop, children's play park and a nature trail.

Times Open daily at 10am. Please call for last
admissions.* Fees Please telephone 01631
720386 for prices or book online.* Facilities ℗
⚏ 🅿 (outdoor) ♿ toilets for disabled shop ⊗

LOCHAWE

Cruachan Power Station

Visitor Centre, Dalmally PA33 1AN
☎ 01866 822618 📠 01866 822509
e-mail: visit.cruachan@scottishpower.com
web: www.visitcruachan.co.uk
dir: A85 18m E of Oban

A vast cavern hidden deep inside Ben Cruachan, which contains a 400,000-kilowatt hydro-electric power station, driven by water drawn from a high-level reservoir up the mountain. A guided tour takes you inside the mountain and reveals the generators in their underground cavern.

Times Open Etr-Nov, daily 9.30-5 (last tour 4.15). (Winter hours available on request).* Fees £5 (ch 6-16 £2, concessions £4.50).* Facilities 🅿 ⛾ ⊓ toilets for disabled shop ⊗

CREETOWN

Creetown Gem Rock Museum

Chain Rd DG8 7HJ
☎ 01671 820357 & 820554
📠 01671 820554
e-mail: enquiries@gemrock.net
web: www.gemrock.net
dir: follow signs from A75 at Creetown bypass

The Gem Rock is the leading independent museum of its kind in the UK, and is renowned worldwide. Crystals, gemstones, minerals, jewellery and fossils, the Gem Rock displays some of the most breathtaking examples of nature's wonders. See the audio-visual 'Fire in the Stones', the latest attraction 'Olga', a 50,000 year old cave bear skeleton, explore the Crystal Cave, relax in the Prospector's Study, and sample the home-baked Scottish cakes in the café.

Times Open daily, Feb-Mar 10-4; Apr-Sep 9.30-5.30, Oct-22 Dec 10-4. Closed 23 Dec-Jan. Fees £3.75 (ch £2.25, under 5 free, concessions £3.25). Family ticket (2ad+3ch) £9.75. Facilities 🅿 ⓟ ⛾ ⊓ (outdoor) ♿ toilets for disabled shop ⊗

KIRKCUDBRIGHT

Galloway Wildlife Conservation Park

Lochfergus Plantation DG6 4XX
☎ 01557 331645 📠 01557 331645
e-mail: info@gallowaywildlife.co.uk
web: www.gallowaywildlife.co.uk
dir: follow brown signs from A75, 1m from Kirkcudbright on B727

Galloway is the wild animal conservation centre for southern Scotland, set in 27 acres of mixed woodland. A varied zoological collection of over 150 animals from all over the world. Close animal encounters and bird of prey displays are some of the features giving an insight into wildlife conservation.

Times Open Feb-Nov, daily 10-6 (last admission 5).* Facilities ❷ ⛽ 🍴 (outdoor) ♿ (partly accessible) (due to the rising terrain, the nature trail is not accessible) toilets for disabled shop 🚫

NEW ABBEY

National Museum of Costume Scotland

Shambellie House DG2 8HQ
☎ 0131 247 4030
e-mail: info@nms.ac.uk
web: www.nms.ac.uk/costume
dir: 7m S of Dumfries, on A710

Become a dedicated follower of fashion. Shambellie House, a 19th-century country home in wooded grounds, is the perfect setting for discovering 100 years of costume, from the 1850s through to the 1950s. Put yourself in the shoes of those who wore the trends of the time. The museum holds special events and activities throughout the year.

Times Open Apr-Oct, daily, 10-5. Fees £3.50 (ch under 12 & members free, concessions £2.50). Facilities ❷ ⛽ 🍴 (outdoor) ♿ (partly accessible) (ramp & wheelchair lift provide access to ground floor of museum, tearoom & toilets) shop 🚫

THORNHILL

Drumlanrig Castle, Gardens & Country Park

DG3 4AQ

☎ 01848 331555 📄 01848 331682
e-mail: enquiries@drumlanrig.com
web: www.drumlanrig.com
dir: 4m N of Thornhill off A76

This unusual pink sandstone castle was built in the late 17th century in Renaissance style. It contains a outstanding collection of fine art. There is also French furniture, as well as silver and relics of Bonnie Prince Charlie. The old stable block has a craft centre with resident craft workers, and the grounds offer an extensive garden plant centre, mountain bike hire and woodland walks. The Scottish cycle museum and shop have been recently renovated. For details of special events phone 01848 331555.

Times Castle open 2 Apr-Aug, daily 11-4 (last tour). **Fees** £8 (ch £4.50 & pen £6.50). Grounds only £4. Party 20+ £6 each. **Facilities** 🅿 ℗ ⑩ licensed 🎋 (outdoor) ♿ (partly accessible) (some areas of garden not easily accessible to wheelchair users) toilets for disabled shop ⊗

WANLOCKHEAD

Hidden Treasures Museum of Lead Mining

ML12 6UT

☎ 01659 74387 📄 01659 74481
e-mail: miningmuseum@hotmail.com
web: www.leadminingmuseum.co.uk
dir: signed from M74 and A76

Wanlockhead is Scotland's highest village, set in the beautiful Lowther Hills. Visitors can see miners' cottages, and the miners' library as well as the 18th-century lead mine. Visitors can also pan for gold.

Times Open Apr-Nov, daily 11-4.30; Jul-Aug & BHs 10-5.* **Fees** £6.25 (ch & concessions £4.50). Family tickets available.* **Facilities** 🅿 ℗ ⑩ ⑩ licensed 🎋 (outdoor) ♿ toilets for disabled shop ⊗

DUNDEE

Camperdown Country Park

Coupar Angus Rd DD2 4TF
☎ 01382 431818 ▤ 01382 431810
e-mail: leisure.communities@dundeecity.gov.uk
web: www.camperdownpark.com
dir: A90 to Dundee then onto A923 (Coupar-Angus road), left at 1st rdbt to attraction

Camperdown is Dundee's largest park, covers an area of over 400 acres and is home to some 190 species of tree. There is a good range of facilities, including an 18-hole golf course, a putting green, boating pond, children's play area, footpaths and woodland trails, and Camperdown Wildlife Centre. There is also a year-round calendar of special events, contact for details.

Times Open Park: all year. Wildlife Centre: daily Mar-Sep, 10-4.30 (last admission 3.45), Oct-Feb, daily 10-3.30 (last admission 2.45).* **Fees** Park - free admission. Wildlife Centre charged, £3.40 (ch £2.75 under 3 £1, concessions £2.75), family (2ad+3ch) £9.80, accompanied group £3.90pp, unaccompanied group £2.75pp.* **Facilities** ℗ ⬚ ⴹ (outdoor) ⴲ toilets for disabled shop ⊗

DUNDEE

Discovery Point & RRS Discovery

Discovery Quay DD1 4XA
☎ 01382 309060 ▤ 01382 225891
e-mail: info@dundeeheritage.co.uk
web: www.rrsdiscovery.com
dir: follow brown heritage signs for Historic Ships

Discovery Point is the home of RRS Discovery, Captain Scott's famous Antarctic ship. Spectacular lighting, graphics and special effects re-create key moments in the Discovery story. The restored bridge gives a captain's view over the ship and the River Tay. Learn what happened to the ship after the expedition, during the First World War and the Russian Revolution, and find out about her involvement in the first survey of whales' migratory patterns.

Times Open all year, Apr-Oct, Mon-Sat 10-6. Sun 11-6; Nov-Mar, Mon-Sat 10-5, Sun 11-5.* **Fees** £7.50 (ch £4.50, concessions £5.75). Family ticket £20.* **Facilities** ℗ ℗ ⬚ ⓧ licensed ⴹ (outdoor) ⴲ (partly accessible) (access to exhibition on top deck, no access to lower deck, but virtual tour available) toilets for disabled shop ⊗

DUNDEE

Mills Observatory

Balgay Park, Glamis Rd DD2 2UB
☎ 01382 435967 🖷 01382 435962
e-mail: mills.observatory@dundeecity.gov.uk
web: www.dundeecity.gov.uk/mills
dir: 1m W of city centre, in Balgay Park, on
Balgay Hill. Vehicle entrance at Glamis Rd gate
to Balgay Park

Mills Observatory is Britain's only full-time
public observatory. See breathtaking views of
the stars and planets through the impressive
Victorian refracting telescope. The telescope with
state-of-the-art 'go to' technology, allows you
to 'hop' from one object to another more quickly
than ever before! During October to March, the
Planetarium Shows provide the chance to learn
about constellations, planets and other jewels of
the night sky. There are also displays on the solar
system and space exploration.

Times Open all year, Apr-Sep, Tue-Fri 11-5, Sat
& Sun 12.30-4; Oct-Mar, Mon-Fri 4pm-10pm,
Sat & Sun 12.30-4. Closed 25-26 Dec & 1-3
Jan.* Fees Free entry, small charge for public
Planetarium shows and groups* Facilities ❷ ℗
🎪 (outdoor) ♿ (partly accessible) (ground floor
accessible) toilets for disabled shop ⊗

GALSTON

Loudoun Castle Theme Park

KA4 8PE
☎ 01563 822296 🖷 01563 822408
e-mail: loudouncastle@btinternet.com
web: www.loudouncastle.co.uk
dir: signed from A74(M), from A77 and from A71

Loudoun Castle Theme Park is a great day out
for the whole family. Theme park rides, live
entertainment and McDougals Farm are just a
taster of what's on offer.

Times Open Etr-end of Sep. Please phone for
further details.* Facilities ❷ ⊑ 🍽 licensed 🎪
(indoor & outdoor) toilets for disabled shop ⊗

198

ABERLADY

Myreton Motor Museum

EH32 0PZ

☎ 01875 870288 & 07947 066666

🖶 01368 860199

e-mail: myreton.motor.museum@aberlady.org

dir: 1.5m from A198, 2m from A1

The museum has on show a large collection, from 1899, of cars, bicycles, motor cycles and commercials. There is also a large collection of period advertising, posters and enamel signs.

Times Open all year, Mar-Oct daily 10.30-4.30, Nov-Feb, wknds only 11-3.* Fees £7 (ch £3, concessions £6). Facilities ♿ 🎪 (outdoor) ♿ 🚫

EAST FORTUNE

National Museum of Flight Scotland

East Fortune Airfield EH39 5LF

☎ 0131 247 4238

e-mail: info@nms.ac.uk

web: www.nms.ac.uk

dir: signed from A1 near Haddington. Onto B1347, past Athelstaneford, 20m E of Edinburgh

The National Museum of Flight is situated on 63 acres of one of Britain's best preserved wartime airfields. The museum has four hangars, with more than 50 aeroplanes, plus engines, rockets and memorabilia. Items on display include two Spitfires, a Vulcan bomber and Britain's oldest surviving aeroplane, built in 1896; recent exhibits also include a Phantom jet fighter, and a Harrier jump-jet. The Concorde Experience explores the story of this historic plane through the lives of those who worked or travelled on it.

Times Open all year, Apr-Oct, daily, 10-5. Nov-Mar, wknds only, 10-4. (Contact for details of seasonal variations in opening times.) Fees £8.50 (ch under 12 & NMS members free, concessions £6.50). Facilities ♿ 🍴 🎪 (outdoor) ♿ (partly accessible) (no wheelchair access to Concorde's passenger cabin, most display areas are on ground floor) toilets for disabled shop 🚫

NORTH BERWICK

Scottish Seabird Centre

The Harbour EH39 4SS
☎ 01620 890202 ▤ 01620 890222
e-mail: info@seabird.org
web: www.seabird.org
dir: A1 from Edinburgh, then A198 to North
Berwick. Brown heritage signs clearly marked
from A1

Escape to another world at this award-winning
wildlife visitor attraction. Breathtaking
panoramic views over the sea and sandy
beaches. See wildlife close up with amazing live
cameras - puffins spring-cleaning their burrows,
gannets with fluffy white chicks, seals sunning
themselves and occasional sightings of dolphins
and whales. The Discovery Centre has a Wildlife
cinema, Environment Zone, Kid' Playzone and
Migration Flyway. There's a packed programme of
festivals and events, see the website for details.

Times Open all year, Feb, Mar & Oct Mon-Fri
10-5, Sat-Sun 10-5.30. Apr-Sep 10-6 every
day. Nov-Jan Mon-Fri 10-4, Sat-Sun 10-5.30.*
Facilities ❶ ℗ ▽ ⏵ licensed 🍴 (outdoor) ♿
toilets for disabled shop ⊗

PRESTONPANS

Prestongrange Museum **FREE**

Prestongrange
☎ 0131 653 2904 ▤ 01620 828201
e-mail: elms@eastlothian.gov.uk
web: www.prestongrange.org
dir: on B1348 coast road between Prestonpans &
Musselburgh

The oldest documented coal mining site in
Scotland, with 800 years of history, this museum
shows a Cornish Beam Engine and on-site
evidence of associated industries such as
brickmaking and pottery. It is located next to a
16th-century customs port. Contact for details of
special events or see website.

Times Open Apr-Oct, daily, 11-4.30. **Facilities** ❶
▽ 🍴 (outdoor) ♿ (partly accessible) (grounds
partly accessible) toilets for disabled shop ⊗

EDINBURGH

Dynamic Earth

Holyrood Rd EH8 8AS

☎ 0131 550 7800 📄 0131 550 7801

e-mail: enquiries@dynamicearth.co.uk

web: www.dynamicearth.co.uk

dir: on edge of Holyrood Park, opposite Palace of Holyrood House

How the Earth works. Take a walk through Scotland's geological history. Travel back in time to follow the creation of Planet Earth. Be shaken by a volcano, feel the chill of polar ice and get caught in a tropical rainstorm. Please visit website for details of events running throughout the year.

Times Open all year, Apr-Oct daily & Nov-Mar Wed-Sun 10-5, (last entry 3.50); Jul-Aug daily, 10-6, (last entry 4.50).* Facilities 🅿 🅟 ⛳ 🍴 (indoor & outdoor) toilets for disabled shop ⊗

EDINBURGH

Edinburgh Castle

EH1 2NG

☎ 0131 225 9846

web: www.historic-scotland.gov.uk

This historic stronghold stands on the precipitous crag of Castle Rock. One of the oldest parts is the 11th-century chapel of the saintly Queen Margaret, but most of the present castle evolved later, during its stormy history of sieges and wars, and was altered again in Victorian times. The Scottish crown and other royal regalia are displayed in the Crown Room. Also notable is the Scottish National War Memorial.

Times Open all year, Apr-Sep, daily, 9.30-6; Oct-Mar 9.30-5; 1 Jan, 11-4.30. Closed 25-26 Dec.* Fees £10.30 (ch £4.50, concessions £8.50). Please phone or check website for further details.* Facilities 🅿 ⛳ 🍴 licensed toilets for disabled shop ⊗ 🚩

EDINBURGH

Edinburgh Zoo

134 Corstorphine Rd, Murrayfield EH12 6TS
☎ 0131 334 9171 📠 0131 314 0382
e-mail: info@rzss.org.uk
web: www.edinburghzoo.org.uk
dir: 3m W of city centre on A8 towards Glasgow

Scotland's largest wildlife attraction set in 82 acres of leafy hillside parkland, just ten minutes from the city centre. With over 1,000 animals ranging from the UK's only koalas to massive Indian rhinos, including many other threatened species. See the world's largest penguin pool or visit our chimpanzees in the world-class, Budongo Trail.

Times Open all year, daily Apr-Sep, 9-6; Oct & Mar, 9-5; Nov-Feb, 9-4.30.* Fees £12.60 (ch £8.50, concessions £10.80). Family ticket (2ad+2ch) £42.* Facilities 🅿 Ⓟ ⌨ 🍴 licensed ⅋ (indoor & outdoor) ⅓ (partly accessible) (Zoo is on a hillside, but there is a free hilltop safari to the top of the hill) toilets for disabled shop ⊗

EDINBURGH

Museum of Childhood **FREE**

42 High St, Royal Mile EH1 1TG
☎ 0131 529 4142 📠 0131 558 3103
e-mail: moc@edinburgh.gov.uk
web: www.cac.org.uk
dir: On the Royal Mile

One of the first museums of its kind, this was the brainchild of a local councillor, and first opened in 1955. It has a wonderful collection of toys, games and other belongings of children through the ages, to delight visitors both old and young. Ring for details of special events.

Times Open all year, Mon-Sat 10-5, Sun 12-5.* Facilities Ⓟ ⅓ (partly accessible) toilets for disabled shop ⊗

EDINBURGH

National Museum of Scotland **FREE**

Chambers St EH1 1JF
☎ 0131 225 7534
e-mail: info@nms.ac.uk
web: www.nms.ac.uk
dir: situated in Chambers St in Old Town. A few mins walk from Princes St and The Royal Mile

Scotland - past, present and future. The Museum's collections tell you the story of Scotland - land, people and culture. What influence has the world had on Scotland, and Scotland on the world? Your journey of discovery starts here. For generations the museum has collected key exhibits from all over Scotland and beyond. Viking brooches, Pictish stones, ancient chessmen and Queen Mary's clarsach. There's more! Connect with Dolly the sheep, design a robot, test drive a Formula One car or blast off into outer space. See website for special exhibitions and events. Part of the Victorian Royal museum building is closed for refurbishment and will re-open in 2011.

Times Open all year, daily 10-5. Facilities ⓟ ☐ ⊙ licensed ₼ toilets for disabled shop ⊗

EDINBURGH

Palace of Holyroodhouse

EH8 8DX
☎ 0131 556 5100   📄 020 7930 9625
e-mail: bookinginfo@royalcollection.org.uk
web: www.royalcollection.org.uk
dir: at east end of Royal Mile

The Palace grew from the guest house of the Abbey of Holyrood, said to have been founded by David I after a miraculous apparition. Mary, Queen of Scots had her court here from 1561 to 1567, and 'Bonnie' Prince Charlie held levees at the Palace during his occupation of Edinburgh. Today the Royal Apartments are used by HM The Queen for state ceremonies and official entertaining, and are finely decorated with works of art from the Royal Collection.

Times Open all year, daily, Apr-Oct 9.30-6 (last admission 5); Nov-Mar 9.30-4.30 (last admission 3.30). Closed Good Fri, 25-26 Dec and when The Queen is in residence.* Fees £10.50 (ch £6.50, concessions £9.50). Family ticket (2ad+3ch) £28. Provides unlimited admission for 12 months.
Facilities ⓟⓟ ☐₼ (partly accessible) (historic apartments accessible by spiral staircase) toilets for disabled shop ⊗

EDINBURGH

The Royal Yacht Britannia

Ocean Terminal, Leith EH6 6JJ

☎ 0131 555 5566   📠 0131 555 8835

e-mail: enquiries@tryb.co.uk

web: www.royalyachtbritannia.co.uk

dir: follow signs to North Edinburgh & Leith. Situated within Ocean Terminal

Visit the Royal Yacht Britannia, now in Edinburgh's historic port of Leith. The experience starts in the Visitor Centre where you can discover Britannia's fascinating story. Then step aboard for a self-led audio tour which takes you around five decks giving you a unique insight into what life was like for the Royal Family, officers and yachtsmen. Highlights include the State Apartments, Admiral's Cabin, Engine Room, Laundry and Sick Bay. Visit the new Royal Deck tearoom.

Times Open all year daily from 10 (Jul & Aug from 9.30). Last admission 4 (Apr-Jul, Sep-Oct), 4.30 (Aug) or 3.30 (Nov-Mar). Closed 25 Dec & 1 Jan. Fees £10.50 (ch 5-17 £6.25, concessions £9) Family ticket (2ad+3ch) £29.75. Facilities 🅿 ℗ 🖵 ♿ toilets for disabled shop ⊗

BIRKHILL

Birkhill Fireclay Mine

EH51 9AQ

☎ 01506 825855   & 822298

📠 01506 828766

e-mail: mine@srps.org.uk

web: www.srps.org.uk

dir: A706 from Linlithgow, A904 from Grangemouth, follow brown signs to Steam Railway & Fireclay Mine. Main access is by train from Bo'ness

Tour guides will meet you at Birkhill Station and lead you down into the ancient woodland of the beautiful Avon Gorge, and then into the caverns of the Birkhill Fireclay mine. See how the clay was worked, what it was used for and find the 300-million-year-old fossils in the roof of the mine.

Times Open wknds Apr-Oct, daily in Jul-Aug. Fees Mine & Train £9 (ch £5, concessions £7.50) Family ticket (2ad+2ch) £23. Mine only £3.10 (ch £2.10, concessions £2.60) Family ticket £8.25.* Facilities 🅿 ℗ ⼐ (outdoor) toilets for disabled

BO'NESS

Bo'ness & Kinneil Railway

Bo'ness Station, Union St EH51 9AQ
☎ 01506 825855 & 822298
🖹 01506 828766
e-mail: enquiries.railway@srps.org.uk
web: www.srps.org.uk
dir: A904 from all directions, signed

Historic railway buildings, including the station
and train shed, have been relocated from sites
all over Scotland. The Scottish Railway Exhibition
tells the story of the development of railways
and their impact on the people of Scotland.
Take a seven mile return trip by steam train to
the tranquil country station at Birkhill. Thomas
the Tank Engine weekends in May, August and
September, and Santa Specials in December.
Booking is essential for these special events.

Times Open wknds Apr-Oct, daily Jul-Aug.
Fees Return fare £9 (ch 5-15 £5, concessions
£7.50). Family ticket £23. (Ticket for return train
fare & tour of Birkhill Fireclay Mine).* Facilities
P ℗ ⏇ � (outdoor) ♿ toilets for disabled
shop

ANSTRUTHER

Scottish Fisheries Museum

St Ayles, Harbour Head KY10 3AB
☎ 01333 310628 🖹 01333 310628
e-mail: info@scotfishmuseum.org
web: www.scotfishmuseum.org
dir: A917 through St Monans & Pittenweem to
Anstruther

This award-winning national museum tells the
story of Scottish fishing and its people from the
earliest times to the present. With 10 galleries,
2 large boatyards, and a restored fisherman's
cottage, which contain many fine paintings and
photographs, boat models and 17 actual boats,
clothing and items of daily life to see, a visit to
the museum makes for an exceptional day out.
Contact the museum for details of events. 2009
is the 40th anniversary of the opening of the
museum, and there are events and celebrations
on throughout the year to mark this event.

Times Open all year, Apr-Sep, Mon-Sat 10-5.30,
Sun 11-5; Oct-Mar, Mon-Sat 10-4.30, Sun
12-4.30. Closed 25-26 Dec & 1-2 Jan. (Last
admission 1 hr before closing).* Fees £5 (ch
in school groups £1.50, accompanied ch free,
concessions £4).* Facilities ℗ ⏇♿ toilets for
disabled shop ⊗

CUPAR

The Scottish Deer Centre

Bow-of-Fife KY15 4NQ

☎ 01337 810391 📄 01337 810477

e-mail: info@tsdc.co.uk

web: www.tsdc.co.uk

dir: From South M90 junct 8 to A91 Cupar, from North M90 junct 9 to A912, join A91. Follow brown tourist sign

Guided tours take about 30 minutes and allow you to meet and feed deer. There are indoor and outdoor adventure play areas. Other features include daily falconry displays and a tree top walkway. European Wolves are fed every-day (except Friday) at 3pm.

Times Open all year, daily, Winter 10-4, Summer 10-5, 5.30 Jul-Aug. Fees £6.95 (ch 3-15 £4.95).* Facilities ❶ ⮂ ☕ 🍴 (indoor & outdoor) ♿ toilets for disabled shop ⊗

NORTH QUEENSFERRY

Deep Sea World

Forthside Ter KY11 1JR

☎ 01383 411880 📄 01383 410514

e-mail: info@deepseaworld.co.uk

web: www.deepseaworld.com/

dir: from N, M90 take exit for Inverkeithing. From S follow signs to Forth Rd Bridge, 1st exit left

The UK's longest underwater tunnel gives you a diver's eye view of an underwater world. Come face to face with Sand Tiger sharks, and watch divers hand-feed a wide array of sea life. Visit the Amazon Experience with ferocious piranhas and the amazing amphibian display featuring the world's most poisonous frog. Also featuring the Seal Sanctuary, dedicated to the rehabilitation and release of injured and orphaned seal pups. Please telephone or visit website for details of events running throughout the year.

Times Open all year, daily from 10. See website for seasonal closing times. Fees £11.75 (ch 3-15 £8, under 3 free, concessions £10). Family ticket discount available.* Facilities ❶ ⓟ ☕ 🍴 (outdoor) ♿ toilets for disabled shop ⊗

ST ANDREWS

St Andrews Aquarium

The Scores KY16 9AS
☎ 01334 474786 🖹 01334 475985
web: www.standrewsaquarium.co.uk
dir: signed in town centre

This continually expanding aquarium is home
to shrimps, sharks, eels, octopi, seals and
much much more. Special features include the
Seahorse Parade, and the Sea Mammal Research
Unit, which is committed to the care of sea
mammals and their environment.

Times Open all year, daily from 10. Please phone
for winter opening* Facilities ❷ ⓟ 🖵 🍴
licensed 🪑 toilets for disabled shop ⊗

GLASGOW

Glasgow Science Centre

50 Pacific Quay G51 1EA
☎ 0141 420 5000 🖹 0871 540 1006
e-mail: admin@glasgowsciencecentre.org
web: www.glasgowsciencecentre.org
dir: M8 junct 24 or M77 junct 21, follow brown
signs, across Clyde from SECC

The centre is home to many entertaining and
exciting attractions and contains hundreds
of interactive exhibits apart from over 2
acres of science floors. Highlights include the
Planetarium, Scotland's only IMAX cinema and
the 127 metre Glasgow Tower, a remarkable free-
standing structure that gives breathtaking views
of the city (check availability before visiting).
GSC presents the world of science and technology
in new and exciting ways.

Times Open all year, 29 Oct-30 Mar, 10-5 Tue-
Sun; 30 Mar-29 Oct daily 10-5.* Fees £8.25 (ch
& concessions £6.25). Tower, Planetarium, &
Imax Science Film £2.50 each.* Facilities ❷ ⓟ
🖵 🪑 (indoor & outdoor) ♿ toilets for disabled
shop ⊗

Holmwood House

61-63 Netherlee House, Cathcart G44 3YG
☎ 0844 493 2204   📠 0844 493 2204
e-mail: information@nts.org.uk
web: www.nts.org.uk
dir: off Clarkston Rd

Completed in 1858, Holmwood is considered to
be the finest domestic design by the architect
Alexander 'Greek' Thomson. Many rooms are richly
ornamented in wood, plaster and marble.

Times Open Apr-Oct, Thu-Mon 12-5.* Fees £5.50
(concessions £4.50). Family £15, (1 Parent
£10).* Facilities 🅿 ⬛ 🎪 ♿ (partly accessible)
(access to first floor via lift) shop ⊗ ♨

Hunterian Museum **FREE**

Gilbert Scott Building, The University of
Glasgow G12 8QQ
☎ 0141 330 4221   📠 0141 330 3617
e-mail: hunter@museum.gla.ac.uk
web: www.hunterian.gla.ac.uk
dir: on University of Glasgow campus in Hillhead
District, 2m W of city centre

Named after the 18th-century physician, Dr
William Hunter, who bequeathed his large and
important collections of coins, medals, fossils,
geological specimens and archaeological and
ethnographic items to the university. The exhibits
are shown in the main building of the university,
and temporary exhibitions are held.

Times Open all year, Mon-Sat 9.30-5. Closed
certain BHs phone for details.* Facilities 🅿
toilets for disabled shop ⊗

GLASGOW

Museum of Transport **FREE**

1 Bunhouse Rd G3 8DP
☎ 0141 287 2720   📄 0141 287 2692
e-mail: museums@csglasgow.org
web: www.glasgowmuseums.com
dir: 1.5m W of city centre

Visit the Museum of Transport and the first impression is of gleaming metalwork and bright paint. All around you there are cars, caravans, carriages and carts, fire engines, buses, steam locomotives, prams and trams. The museum uses its collections of vehicles and models to tell the story of transport by land and sea, with a unique Glasgow flavour. Visitors can even go window shopping along the recreated Kelvin Street of 1938. Upstairs 250 ship models tell the story of the great days of Clyde shipbuilding. The Museum of Transport has something for everyone.

Times Open all year, Mon-Thu & Sat 10-5, Fri & Sun 11-5 until Apr 2010 when museum closes due to collections moving to a new museum.
Facilities 🅿 🅿   🖵 ♿ toilets for disabled shop ⊗

GLASGOW

Scotland Street School Museum **FREE**

225 Scotland St G5 8QB
☎ 0141 287 0500   📄 0141 287 0515
e-mail: museums@csglasgow.org
web: www.glasgowmuseums.com

Designed by Charles Rennie Mackintosh between 1903 and 1906 for the School Board of Glasgow, and now a museum telling the story of education in Scotland from 1872 to the late 20th century. Also hosts temporary exhibitions.

Times Open all year daily 10-5, Fri & Sun 11-5. (closed 25,26,31 Dec & pm 1 & 2 Jan) **Facilities** 🅿 🖵 ♿ toilets for disabled shop ⊗

CARRBRIDGE

Landmark Forest Adventure Park

PH23 3AJ
☎ 01479 841613 & 0800 731 3446
🖨 01479 841384
e-mail: landmarkcentre@btconnect.com
web: www.landmark-centre.co.uk
dir: off A9 between Aviemore & Inverness

This innovative centre is designed to provide a fun and educational visit for all ages. Microworld takes a close-up look at the incredible microscopic world around us. There is a 70ft forest viewing tower and a treetop trail. There are also demonstrations of timber sawing, on a steam-powered sawmill and log hauling by a Clydesdale horse throughout the day. Attractions include a 3-track Watercoaster, a maze and a large covered adventure play area, mini electric cars and remote-controlled truck arena. New features include; 'RopeworX', the Tarzan Trail aerial highwire obstacle courses, and 'Skydive', a parachute jump simulator.

Times Open all year, daily, Apr-mid Jul 10-6; mid Jul-mid Aug 10-7; Sep-Oct 10-5.30; Nov-Mar 10-5. Closed 25 Dec, 1 Jan. Fees Apr-Oct £10.55 (ch & pen £8.25), Nov-Mar £3.50 (ch & pen £2.65). Facilities 🅿 🄿 ⛶ 🍽 licensed ♿ (partly accessible) (all areas accessible, some attractions not suitable) toilets for disabled shop

DRUMNADROCHIT

Official Loch Ness Exhibition Centre, Loch Ness 2000

IV3 6TU
☎ 01456 450573 & 450218
🖨 01456 450770
web: www.lochness.com
dir: on A82, 12m S Inverness

This award-winning centre has a fascinating and popular multi-media presentation lasting 30 minutes. Seven themed areas cover the story of the Loch Ness Monster, from the pre-history of Scotland, through the cultural roots of the legend in Highland folklore, and into the 50-year controversy which surrounds it. The centre uses the latest technology in computer animation, lasers and multi-media projection systems.

Times Open all year; Nov-end Jan, 10-3.30, Xmas hols 10-5, Feb-end May & Oct 9.30-5, Jun & Sep, 9-6, Jul & Aug 9-6.30* Facilities 🅿 🄿 ⛶ 🍽 licensed 🪑 (outdoor) ♿ toilets for disabled shop ⊗

HELMSDALE

Timespan

Dunrobin St KW8 6JX
☎ 01431 821327   📠 01431 821058
e-mail: enquiries@timespan.org.uk
web: www.timespan.org.uk
dir: off A9 in centre of village, by Telford Bridge

Located in a historic fishing village, this museum relates to the social and natural history of the area, and the art gallery has changing exhibitions of contemporary art and works by local artists. The garden has over 100 varieties of herbs and plants. There is a gift shop, and a café with beautiful views of the Telford Bridge.

Times Open Etr-end Oct, Mon-Sat 10-5, Sun 12-5.* Fees £4 (ch £2, concessions £3). Family ticket £10.* Facilities ❷ ℗ ☐ ♿ toilets for disabled shop ⊗

KINCRAIG

Highland Wildlife Park

PH21 1NL
☎ 01540 651270   📠 01540 651236
e-mail: info@highlandwildlifepark.org
web: www.highlandwildlifepark.org
dir: on B9152, 7m S of Aviemore

As you drive through the main reserve, you can see awe-inspiring European bison grazing alongside wild horses, red deer and highland cattle plus a wide variety of other species. Then in the walk-round forest, woodland and moorland habitats prepare for close encounters with animals such as wolves, capercaillie, arctic foxes, wildcats, pine martens, otters and owls. Visit the snow monkeys in their beautiful lochside enclosure and the red pandas usually found climbing high up in the trees.

Times Open all year, weather permitting. Apr-Oct, 10-5 (last entry 4); Nov-Mar 10-4. (Last entry 3).* Fees £11.50 (ch £8.75, concessions £9.50). Family ticket (2ad+2ch) £37; (2ad+3ch) £42.* Facilities ❷ ☐ ♨ (outdoor) ♿ (partly accessible) (some steep inclines & rocky roads can restrict wheelchair access) toilets for disabled shop ⊗

NEWTONMORE

Highland Folk Museum **FREE**

Aultlarie Croft PH20 1AY
☎ 01540 673551 📄 01540 673693
e-mail: highland.folk@highland.gov.uk
web: www.highlandfolk.com
dir: on A86, follow signs off A9

An early 18th-century farming township with turf
houses has been reconstructed at this award-
winning museum. A 1930s school houses old
world maps, little wooden desks and a teacher
rules! Other attractions include a working croft
and tailor's workshop. Squirrels thrive in the
pinewoods and there is an extensive play area at
reception. A vintage bus runs throughout the site.

Times Open daily Etr-Aug, 10.30-5.30; Sep-Oct,
11-4.30. Facilities 🅿 ⌷ 🛱 (outdoor) toilets for
disabled shop ⊗

STRATHPEFFER

Highland Museum of Childhood

The Old Station IV14 9DH
☎ 01997 421031
e-mail: info@highlandmuseumofchildhood.
org.uk
web: www.highlandmuseumofchildhood.org.uk
dir: 5m W of Dingwall on A834

Located in a renovated Victorian railway
station of 1885, the museum tells the story of
childhood in the Highlands amongst the crofters
and townsfolk; a way of life recorded in oral
testimony, displays and evocative photographs.
An award-winning video, A Century of Highland
Childhood is shown. There are also doll and toy
collections.

Times Open Apr-Oct, daily 10-5, (Sun 2-5). Other
times by arrangement. Fees £2.50 (ch £1.50,
concessions £2). Family ticket (2ad+4ch) £6.
Facilities ❶ 🅿 ⌷ 🛱 (outdoor) ♿ shop ⊗

WICK

Wick Heritage Museum

18-27 Bank Row KW1 5EY
☎ 01955 605393   ▤ 01955 605393
e-mail: museum@wickheritage.org
web: www.wickheritage.org
dir: close to the harbour

The heritage centre is near the harbour in a complex of eight houses, yards and outbuildings. The centre illustrates local history from Neolithic times to the herring fishing industry. In addition, there is a complete working 19th-century lighthouse, and the famous Johnston collection of photographs.

Times Open Apr-Oct, Mon-Sat 10-5, last admission 3.45. (Closed Sun).* Facilities ℗ ㅐ (outdoor) ♿ (partly accessible) toilets for disabled

DALKEITH

Edinburgh Butterfly & Insect World

Dobbies Garden World, Mellville Nursery, Lasswade EH18 1AZ
☎ 0131 663 4932   ▤ 0131 654 2774
e-mail: info@edinburgh-butterfly-world.co.uk
web: www.edinburgh-butterfly-world.co.uk
dir: 0.5m S of Edinburgh city bypass at Gilmerton exit or at Sherrifhall rdbt

Rich coloured butterflies from all over the world can be seen flying among exotic rainforest plants, trees and flowers. The tropical pools are filled with giant waterlilies, colourful fish and are surrounded by lush vegetation. There are daily animal handling sessions and opportunities to see the leaf-cutting ants, scorpions, poison frogs, snakes, tarantulas and other remarkable creatures. There is also a unique honeybee hive that can be visited in season.

Times Open all year, summer daily 9.30-5.30; winter daily 10-5. Closed 25-26 Dec & 1 Jan. Fees £6.50 (ch 3-15 £4.50, concessions £5.50). Family ticket from £21 (2ad+2ch). Party rates. Facilities ℗ ㅁ ﺅ licensed ㅐ (outdoor) ♿ toilets for disabled shop ⊗

NEWTONGRANGE

Scottish Mining Museum

Lady Victoria Colliery EH22 4QN
☎ 0131 663 7519   📄 0131 654 0952
e-mail: visitorservices@scottishminingmuseum.com
web: www.scottishminingmuseum.com
dir: 10m S of Edinburgh on A7, signed from bypass

Based at Scotland's National Coalmining Museum offering an outstanding visit to Britains' finest Victorian colliery. Guided tours with miners, magic helmets, exhibitions, theatres, interactive displays and a visit to the coal face. Home to Scotland's largest steam engine.

Times Open all year, daily Mar-Oct, 10-5. Nov-Feb, daily, 10-4.* Fees £6.50 (ch & concessions £4.50). Family ticket £19.95. Party 12+ (£5.50, ch £3.50)* Facilities 🅿 🅟 ⬛ ◻🍽 licensed 🗛 (outdoor) ♿ toilets for disabled shop ⊗

SPEY BAY

The WDCS Wildlife Centre FREE

IV32 7PJ
☎ 01343 829109   📄 01343 829065
e-mail: enquiries@mfwc.co.uk
web: www.mfwc.co.uk
dir: off A96 onto B9014 at Fochabers, follow road approx 5m to village of Spey Bay. Turn left at Spey Bay Hotel and follow road for 500mtrs

The centre, owned and operated by the Whale and Dolphin Conservation Society, lies at the mouth of the River Spey and is housed in a former salmon fishing station, built in 1768. There is a free exhibition about the Moray Firth dolphins and the wildlife of Spey Bay. Visitors can browse through a well-stocked gift shop and enjoy refreshments in the cosy tea room.

Times Open Apr-Oct 10.30-5. Check for winter opening times* Facilities 🅿 🅟 ⬛ 🗛 (outdoor) toilets for disabled shop ⊗

COATBRIDGE

Summerlee Industrial Museum **FREE**

Heritage Way, West Canal St ML5 1QD
☎ 01236 638460 📠 01236 638454
e-mail: museums@northlan.gov.uk
web: www.visitlanarkshire.com/summerlee
dir: follow main routes towards town centre, adjacent to Coatbridge central station

A 20-acre museum of social and industrial history centering on the remains of the Summerlee Ironworks which were put into blast in the 1830s. The exhibition hall features displays of social and industrial history including working machinery, hands-on activities and recreated workshop interiors. Outside, Summerlee operates the only working tram in Scotland, a coal mine and reconstructed miners' rows with interiors dating from 1840.

Times Open summer 10-5, winter 10-4. **Facilities** 🅿 ⓟ 🖵 ⌇ (outdoor) ♿ (partly accessible) (coal mine tour not accessible, miner's cottages narrow doors and single step) toilets for disabled shop ⊗

MOTHERWELL

Motherwell Heritage Centre **FREE**

High Rd ML1 3HU
☎ 01698 251000 📠 01698 268867
e-mail: museums@northlan.gov.uk
web: www.nlcmuseums.bravehost.com
dir: A723 for town centre. Left at top of hill, after pedestrian crossing and just before railway bridge

This award-winning audio-visual experience, 'Technopolis', traces the history of the area from Roman times to the rise of 19th-century industry and the post-industrial era. There is also a fine viewing tower, an exhibition gallery and family history research facilities. A mixed programme of community events and touring exhibitions occur throughout the year.

Times Open all year Wed-Sat 10-5 (Thu 10-7), Sun 12-5. Also open BHs. Local studies library closed Sun* **Facilities** 🅿 ⓟ ♿ toilets for disabled shop ⊗

PITLOCHRY

Scottish Hydro Electric Visitor Centre, Dam & Fish Pass **FREE**

PH16 5ND

☎ 01796 473152 🖷 01796 473152

dir: off A9, 24m N of Perth

The visitor centre features an exhibition showing how electricity is brought from the power station to the customer, and there is access to the turbine viewing gallery. The salmon ladder viewing chamber allows you to see the fish as they travel upstream to their spawning ground.

Times Open Apr-Oct, Mon-Fri 10-5. Wknd opening Jul, Aug & BHs Facilities ❷ ℗ ♿ (partly accessible) (access to shop only) toilets for disabled shop ⊗

SCONE

Scone Palace

PH2 6BD

☎ 01738 552300 🖷 01738 552588

e-mail: visits@scone-palace.co.uk

web: www.scone-palace.co.uk

dir: 2m NE of Perth on A93

Visit Scone Palace, the crowning place of Scottish Kings and the home of the Earls of Mansfield. The Palace dates from 1803 but incorporates 16th century and earlier buildings, and is a unique treasury of furniture, fine art and other objets d'art. As well as beautiful gardens the grounds are home to the Murray Star Maze, the Pinetum, an adventure playground, livestock, Highland cattle and champion trees.

Times Open Apr-Oct, daily 9.30-5.30, Sat last admission 4. Fees Palace & Grounds £8.50 (ch £5.30, concessions £7.30). Family ticket £24. Grounds only £4.80 (ch £3.20, concessions £4.20). Group £7.30 (ch £4.80 concessions £6.30)* Facilities ❷ ⊑ ⓣⓞⓘ licensed ⋈ (outdoor) ♿ toilets for disabled shop ⊗

ALLOWAY

Burns National Heritage Park

Murdoch's Lone KA7 4PQ

☎ 01292 443700   🖃 01292 441750

e-mail: info@burnsheritagepark.com

web: www.burnsheritagepark.com

dir: 2m S of Ayr

The birthplace of Robert Burns, Scotland's National Poet set in the gardens and countryside of Alloway. An introduction to the life of Robert Burns, with an audio-visual presentation - a multi-screen 3D experience describing the Tale of Tam O'Shanter. This attraction consists of the museum, Burn's Cottage, visitor centre, tranquil landscaped gardens and historical monuments. Please telephone for further details.

Times Open all year, Apr-Sep 10-5.30, Oct-Mar 10-5. Closed 25-26 Dec & 1-2 Jan* Facilities 🅿 ℗ ☐ 🍴 licensed ♿ (partly accessible) (access limited in some parts of property) toilets for disabled shop ⊗

BLANTYRE

David Livingstone Centre

165 Station Rd G72 9BT

☎ 0844 493 2207   🖃 0844 493 2206

e-mail: information@nts.org.uk

web: www.nts.org.uk

dir: M74 junct 5 onto A725, then A724, follow signs for Blantyre, right at lights. Centre is at foot of hill

Share the adventurous life of Scotland's greatest explorer, from his childhood in the Blantyre Mills to his explorations in the heart of Africa, dramatically illustrated in the historic tenement where he was born. Various events are planned throughout the season.

Times Open Apr-24 Dec, Mon-Sat 10-5, Sun 12.30-5.* Fees £5.50 (concessions £4.50) Family £15 (1 Parent £10).* Facilities 🅿 ℗ ☐ �🇦 ♿ toilets for disabled shop ⊗ 🐾

EAST KILBRIDE

National Museum of Rural Life Scotland

Wester Kittochside, Philipshill Rd, (off Stewartfield Way) G76 9HR

☎ 0131 225 7534

e-mail: info@nms.ac.uk

web: www.nms.ac.uk/rural

dir: From Glasgow take A749 to East Kilbride. From Edinburgh follow M8 to Glasgow, turn off junct 6 onto A725 to East Kilbride. Kittochside is signed before East Kilbride

Get a healthy dose of fresh air. Take in the sights, sounds and smells as you explore this 170-acre farm. Discover what life was like for country people in the past and how this has shaped Scotland's countryside today. Would you cope with life on a 1950s farm? Try milking 'Clover' by hand, hitch a ride on the farm explorer, meet Mairi the horse and the sheep, cows and hens. See the website for details of a wide range of special events and exhibitions.

Times Open daily 10-5. (Closed 25-26 Dec & 1 Jan). Fees £5.50 (ch under 12 free, concessions £4.50) NMS and NTS members free. Charge for some events.* Facilities 🅿 ℗ ⬚ 🎪 (outdoor) ♿ (partly accessible) (wheelchair users have access to ground floor of farmhouse only, some steep paths) toilets for disabled shop ⊗

NEW LANARK

New Lanark Visitor Centre

Mill 3, New Lanark Mills ML11 9DB

☎ 01555 661345   🖷 01555 665738

e-mail: trust@newlanark.org

web: www.newlanark.org

dir: 1m S of Lanark. Signed from all major routes. Founded in 1785, New Lanark became well known in the early 19th century as a model community managed by enlightened industrialist and educational reformer Robert Owen. Surrounded by woodland and situated close to the Falls of Clyde, this unique world heritage site explores the philosophies of Robert Owen, using theatre, interactive displays, and the 'Millennium Experience', a magical ride through history. (Accommodation is available at the New Lanark Mill Hotel, and there's also a Youth Hostel.) The village is also home to the Scottish Wildlife Trust's Falls of Clyde Reserve. A wide variety of exciting, fun and educational events take place every year.

Times Open all year daily. Jun-Aug 10.30-5; Sep-May 11-5. Closed 25 Dec & 1 Jan. Fees £6.95 (ch, concessions £5.95). Family ticket (2ad+2ch) £21.95. Family ticket (2ad+4ch) £27.95.* Facilities 🅿 ⬚ 🍴 licensed 🎪 (outdoor) ♿ toilets for disabled shop ⊗

BLAIR DRUMMOND

Blair Drummond Safari & Leisure Park

FK9 4UR

☎ 01786 841456 & 841396

📄 01786 841491

e-mail: enquiries@blairdrummond.com

web: www.blairdrummond.com

dir: M9 junct 10, 4m on A84 towards Callander

Drive through the wild animal reserves where zebras, North American bison, antelope, lions, tigers, white rhino and camels can be seen at close range. Other attractions include the sea lion show, a ride on the boat safari through the waterfowl sanctuary and around Chimpanzee Island, an adventure playground, giant astraglide, and pedal boats. There are also African elephants, giraffes and ostriches.

Times Open 19 Mar-3 Oct, daily 10-5.30. (Last admission 4.30)* Facilities 🅿 ⌨ 🍴 licensed 🪑 (outdoor) toilets for disabled shop ⊗

STIRLING

Stirling Castle

Upper Castle Hill FK8 1EJ

☎ 01786 450000

web: www.historic-scotland.gov.uk

Sitting on top of a 250ft rock, Stirling Castle has a strategic position on the Firth of Forth. As a result it has been the scene of many events in Scotland's history. James II was born at the castle in 1430. Mary, Queen of Scots spent some years there, and it was James IV's childhood home. Among its finest features are the splendid Renaissance palace built by James V, and the Chapel Royal, rebuilt by James VI.

Times Open all year, Apr-Sep, daily 9.30-6; Oct-Mar, daily 9.30-5. Closed 25-26.* Fees £9 (ch £4.50, concessions £7). Please phone or check website for further details.* Facilities 🅿 🍴 licensed 🪑 toilets for disabled shop ⊗ 🎒

BRODICK

Isle of Arran Heritage Museum

Rosaburn KA27 8DP

☎ 01770 302636

e-mail: tom.macleod@arranmuseum.co.uk

web: www.arranmuseum.co.uk

dir: right at Brodick Pier, approx 1m

The setting is an 18th-century croft farm, including a cottage restored to its pre-1920 state and a 'smiddy' where a blacksmith worked until the late 1960s. There are also several demonstrations of horse-shoeing, sheep-shearing and weaving and spinning throughout the season - please ring for details. There is a large archaeology and geology section with archive, where help with research is available. Also, a school room set in the 1940's and a new geology display which reflects the importance of Arran in geological terms.

Times Open Apr-Oct, daily 10.30-4.30. Fees £3 (ch £1.50, pen £2). Family £7. Facilities ❷ ☕ ☎ (outdoor) toilets for disabled shop ⊗

BRYNSIENCYN

Anglesey Sea Zoo

LL61 6TQ

☎ 01248 430411   🖹 01248 430213

e-mail: info@angleseyseazoo.co.uk

web: www.angleseyseazoo.co.uk

dir: 1st turning off Britannia Bridge onto Anglesey then follow Lobster signs along A4080 to zoo

Nestling by the Menai Straits, this all-weather undercover attraction contains a shipwreck bristling with conger eels, a lobster hatchery, a seahorse nursery, crashing waves and the enchanting fish forest.

Times Open Feb half term-late Oct half term. Telephone for times.* Facilities ❷ ❷ ☕ ☎ licensed ☎ (outdoor) toilets for disabled shop ⊗

CAERPHILLY

Caerphilly Castle

CF8 1JL
☎ 029 2088 3143
web: www.cadw.wales.gov.uk
dir: on A469

The concentrically planned castle was begun in 1268 by Gilbert de Clare and completed in 1326. It is the largest in Wales, and has extensive land and water defences. A unique feature is the ruined tower - the victim of subsidence - which manages to out-lean even Pisa! The south dam platform, once a tournament-field, now displays replica medieval siege-engines.

Times Open all year, Apr-Oct, daily 9-5; Nov-Mar, Mon-Sat 9.30-4, Sun 11-4.* Fees £3.60 (ch 5-15, concessions £3.20, disabled visitors and assisting companion free). Family ticket (2ad+all ch/grandch under 16) £10.40. Group rates available. Prices quoted apply until 31 Mar 2010.* Facilities ℗ shop ⊗ ⟳

CARDIFF

Cardiff Castle

Castle St CF10 3RB
☎ 029 2087 8100   ▤ 029 2023 1417
e-mail: cardiffcastle@cardiff.gov.uk
web: www.cardiffcastle.com
dir: from M4, A48 & A470 follow signs to city centre

Cardiff Castle is situated in the heart of the city. Contained within its mighty walls is a history spanning nearly 2000 years, dating from the coming of the Romans to the Norman Conquest and beyond. Discover spectacular interiors on your guided tour, and enjoy magnificent views of the city from the top of the 12th-century Norman keep. The new Interpretation Centre includes a film presentation and a multimedia guide around the Castle grounds. Regular events throughout the year include a teddy bear's picnic, open air theatre, medieval and Roman re-enactments and much more.

Times Open all year, daily (ex 25-26 Dec & 1 Jan) including guided tours, Mar-Oct, 9.30-6 (last tour 5); Nov-Feb, 9.30-5.00 (last tour 4). Royal Regiment of Wales Museum closed Tue.* Facilities ℗ ⊑ ₺ (partly accessible) (Castle apartments and Norman Keep not accessible to wheelchair users, cobblestone path at entrance) toilets for disabled shop ⊗

CARDIFF

Millennium Stadium Tours

Millennium Stadium, Westgate St, Gate 3
CF10 1JA

☎ 029 2082 2228 ▤ 029 2082 2151
e-mail: mgibbons@wru.co.uk
web: millenniumstadium.com/tours
dir: A470 to city centre. Westgate St opposite
Castle far end. Turn by Angel Hotel on corner of
Westgate Street.

In the late 1990s this massive stadium was
completed as part of an effort to revitalise
Welsh fortunes. It replaced Cardiff Arms Park,
and now hosts major music events, exhibitions,
and international rugby and soccer matches. Its
capacity of around 75,000 and its retractable
roof make it unique in Europe. The home of Welsh
Rugby and Welsh Football.

Times Open all year, Mon-Sat, 10-5; Sun 10-4*
Facilities ⓟ ♿ toilets for disabled shop ⊗

CARDIFF

Techniquest

Stuart St CF10 5BW
☎ 029 2047 5475 ▤ 029 2048 2517
e-mail: info@techniquest.org
web: www.techniquest.org
dir: A4232 to Cardiff Bay

Located in the heart of the Cardiff Bay, there's
always something new to explore at this exciting
science discovery centre. Journey into space in
the planetarium, enjoy an interactive Science
Theatre Show or experience one of the 120
hands-on exhibits. Please visit website for details
of events running throughout the year.

Times Open all year, school days 9.30-4.30; all
other times 10-5. Closed Xmas. Fees £7 (ch &
concessions £5). Family ticket (2ad+3ch) £23.
Friends season ticket available. Discounts for
groups Facilities ⓟ ⊒♿ toilets for disabled
shop ⊗

ST FAGANS

St Fagans: National History Museum

CF5 6XB

☎ 029 2057 3500 📄 029 2057 3490
web: www.museumwales.ac.uk
dir: 4m W of Cardiff on A4232. From M4 exit at junct 33 and follow brown signs

A stroll around the indoor galleries and 100 acres of beautiful grounds will give you a fascinating insight into how people in Wales have lived, worked and spent their leisure hours since Celtic times. You can see people practising the traditional means of earning a living, the animals they kept and at certain times of year, the ways in which they celebrated the seasons.

Times Open all year daily, 10-5. (Closed 24-26 Dec). Fees Free. Charge may apply to some events. Facilities 🅿 ▯ ◉ licensed 🍴 (outdoor) ♿ (partly accessible) (wheelchair access possible to most parts) toilets for disabled shop ⊗

DRE-FACH FELINDRE

National Woollen Museum

SA44 5UP

☎ 01559 370929 📄 01559 371592
e-mail: post@museumwales.ac.uk
web: www.museumwales.ac.uk
dir: 16m W of Carmarthen off A484, 4m E of Newcastle Emlyn

The museum is housed in the former Cambrian Mills and has a comprehensive display tracing the evolution of the industry from its beginnings to the present day. Demonstrations of the fleece to fabric process are given on 19th-century textile machinery.

Times Open all year, Apr-Sep, daily 10-5; Oct-Mar, Tue-Sat 10-5. Phone for details of Xmas opening times. Fees Free admission but charge may be made for some events. Facilities 🅿 🅿 ▯ 🍴 (outdoor) ♿ toilets for disabled shop ⊗

LLANARTHNE

The National Botanic Garden of Wales

SA32 8HG

☎ 01558 668768 📠 01558 668933
e-mail: info@gardenofwales.org.uk
web: www.gardenofwales.org.uk
dir: 8m E of Carmarthen on A48, dedicated
intersection - signed

Set amongst 568 acres of parkland in the beautiful Towy Valley in West Wales. The Garden's centrepiece is the Great Glasshouse, an amazing tilted glass dome with a six-metre ravine. The Mediterranean landscape enables the visitor to experience the aftermath of an Australian bush fire, pause in an olive grove or wander through Fuchsia collections from Chile. The Tropical House features orchids, palms and other tropical plants. A 220 metre herbaceous board walk forms the spine of the garden and leads to the children's play area and the Old Stables Courtyard. Here the visitor can view art exhibitions, wander in the gift shop or enjoy a meal in the restaurant. Land train tours will take the visitor around the necklace of lakes, which surround the central garden.

Times Open all year, 24 Mar-26 Oct 10-6; 27 Oct-22 Mar 10-4.30* Facilities ❷ ⛝ ¶❍¶ licensed ⋔ (outdoor) toilets for disabled shop ⊗

PUMSAINT

Dolaucothi Gold Mines

SA19 8US

☎ 01558 650177 📠 01588 651919
e-mail: dolaucothi@nationaltrust.org.uk
web: www.nationaltrust.org.uk
dir: on A482, signed both directions

Here is an opportunity to spend a day exploring the gold mines and to wear a miner's helmet and lamp while touring the underground workings. It is the only Roman gold mine in the UK.

Times Open 13 Mar-Jun & Sep-Oct, daily 11-5, Jul-Aug 10-6. Fees £3.27 (ch £1.64) Family £8.18. With Gift Aid £3.60 (ch £1.80) Family £9. Guided underground tours £3.80 (ch £1.19) Family £9.50. Facilities ❷ ⛝ ⋔ (outdoor) ⅋ (partly accessible) (only one underground tour accessible, most other areas accessible) toilets for disabled shop ⅜

COLWYN BAY

Welsh Mountain Zoo

Old Highway LL28 5UY
☎ 01492 532938 📠 01492 530498
e-mail: info@welshmountainzoo.org
web: www.welshmountainzoo.org
dir: A55 junct 20 signed Rhos-on-Sea. Zoo signed

Set high above Colwyn Bay with panoramic views and breath-taking scenery, this caring conservation zoo is set among beautiful gardens. Among the animals are many rare and endangered species, and there are daily shows which include Penguins' Playtime, Chimp Encounter, Sealion Feeding and Birds of Prey.

Times Open all year, Mar-Oct, daily 9.30-6; Nov-Feb, daily 9.30-5. Closed 25 Dec. Fees £8.95 (ch & students £6.60, pen £7.80). Family ticket (2ad+2ch or 1ad+3ch) £28.25* Facilities ℗ ⊐ 🍴 licensed 🎋 (outdoor) ♿ (partly accessible) toilets for disabled shop ⊗

LLANDUDNO

Great Orme Bronze Age Copper Mines

Pyliau Rd, Great Orme LL30 2XG
☎ 01492 870447
e-mail: gomines@greatorme.freeserve.co.uk
web: www.greatormemines.info
dir: Follow 'copper mine' signs from Llandudno Promenade

Take a look at some original 4,000 year old Bronze Age artefacts and a selection of Bronze Age mining tools. After watching two short films take a helmet and make your way down to the mines. Walking through tunnels mined nearly 4,000 years ago look into some of the smaller tunnels and get a feel for the conditions our prehistoric ancestors faced in their search for valuable copper ores. Excavation on the surface will continue for decades and one of the team is usually available to answer visitors' questions as they walk around the site and view the prehistoric landscape being uncovered.

Times Open mid Mar-end Oct, daily 10-5.*
Fees £6 (ch £4, under 5's free). Family ticket (2ad+2ch) £16, extra child £3.* Facilities ℗ ℗ ⊐ 🎋 (outdoor) ♿ (partly accessible) (no wheelchair access to underground mine) toilets for disabled shop

CORWEN

Ewe-Phoria Sheepdog Centre

Glanrafon, Llangwm LL21 0PE

☎ 01490 460369

e-mail: info@adventure-mountain.co.uk

web: www.ewe-phoria.co.uk

dir: off A5 to Llangwm, follow signs

Ewe-Phoria is an Agri-Theatre and Sheepdog Centre that details the life and work of the shepherd on a traditional Welsh farm. The Agri-Theatre has unusual living displays of sheep with accompanying lectures on their history and breed, while outside sheepdog handlers put their dogs through their paces. Try your hand at quad biking and off-road rally karting on Adventure Mountain.

Times Open Etr-end Oct, Wed-Fri & Sun. Closed Sat & Mon ex BHs* **Facilities** ❷ ⛝ ❑ licensed ⏣ ♿ toilets for disabled shop ⊗

LLANGOLLEN

Horse Drawn Boats Centre

The Wharf, Wharf Hill LL20 8TA

☎ 01978 860702 & 01691 690322

📄 01978 860702

e-mail: bill@horsedrawnboats.co.uk

web: www.horsedrawnboats.co.uk

dir: A5 onto Llangollen High St, across river bridge to T-junct. Wharf opposite, up the hill

Take a horse drawn boat trip along the beautiful Vale of Llangollen. There is also a narrow boat trip that crosses Pontcysyllte Aqueduct, the largest navigable aqueduct in the world. Full bar on board, commentary throughout. Tea room serving light meals & breakfast.

Times Open Etr-end Oct, daily, 9.30-5; Tea room Nov-Mar, wknds 10-4.30. **Fees** Horse Drawn Boat Trip from £5 (ch £2.50). Family £12.50 Aquaduct Trip £11 (ch £9).* **Facilities** ⓟ ⛝ ♿ (partly accessible) (no access to motor boat, access to tea room & Horse Drawn Boats) toilets for disabled shop ⊗

BEDDGELERT

Sygun Copper Mine

LL55 4NE

☎ 01766 890595 & 510101

🖹 01766 890595

e-mail: sygunmine@hotmail.com

web: www.syguncoppermine.co.uk

dir: 1m E of Beddgelert on A498

Spectacular audio-visual underground experience where visitors can explore the workings of this 19th-century coppermine and see the magnificent stalactite and stalagmite formations. Other activities include archery, panning for gold, metal detecting and coin making. Marvel at the fantastic coin collection from Julius Caesar to Queen Elizabeth II, and visit the Time-Line Museum with Bronze Age and Roman artefacts.

Times Open Mar-end Oct 9.30-5. Feb half term, 10-4* **Facilities** 🅿 Ⓟ ⬚ ⅋ (outdoor) ♿ (partly accessible) (gift shop, cafe & museum accessible for wheelchairs) shop

BLAENAU FFESTINIOG

Llechwedd Slate Caverns

LL41 3NB

☎ 01766 830306 🖹 01766 831260

e-mail: quarrytours@aol.com

web: www.llechwedd-slate-caverns.co.uk

dir: beside A470, 1m from Blaenau Ffestiniog

The Miners' Tramway travels deep into the mountainside with tour guides who introduce you to the tools of the trade and working conditions underground. There is also an audio-visual tour through ten spectacular caverns. Free surface attractions include various exhibitions, museums, and the Victorian village with shops, bank, Miners Arms pub, chemist and viewpoint.

Times Open all year, daily from 10. (Last tour Etr-Sep, 5.15, Sep-Etr, 4.15). Closed 25-26 Dec & 1 Jan. **Fees** Single Tour £9.45 (ch £7.15, sen £7.95). Both tours £15.20 (ch £11.60, pen £12.95). Group discounts, 10% family discount when taking both tours. **Facilities** 🅿 ⬚ ⅋◎⅋ licensed ⅋ (outdoor) ♿ (partly accessible) (access to underground mine tours via steps, some areas of loose slate chipping) toilets for disabled shop ⊗

CAERNARFON

Caernarfon Castle

LL55 2AY
☎ 01286 677617
web: www.cadw.wales.gov.uk

Edward I began building the castle and extensive town walls in 1283 after defeating the last independent ruler of Wales. Completed in 1328, it has unusual polygonal towers, notably the 10-sided Eagle Tower. There is a theory that these features were copied from the walls of Constantinople, to reflect a tradition that Constantine was born nearby. Edward I's son and heir was born and presented to the Welsh people here, setting a precedent that was followed in 1969, when Prince Charles was invested as Prince of Wales.

Times Open all year, Apr-Oct, daily 9-5; Nov-Mar, Mon-Sat 9.30-4, Sun 11-4.* **Fees** £4.95 (ch 5-15, pen & students £4.60, disabled visitors & assisting compainion free). Family ticket (2 ad & all ch/grandch under 16) £14.50. Group rates available. Prices quoted apply until 31 Mar 2010.* **Facilities** Ⓟ shop ⊗ ✦

CAERNARFON

Segontium Roman Museum **FREE**

Beddgelert Rd LL55 2LN
☎ 01286 675625   ▤ 01286 678416
e-mail: info@segontium.org.uk
web: www.segontium.org.uk
dir: on A4085 to Beddgelert approx 1m from Caernarfon

Segontium Roman Museum tells the story of the conquest and occupation of Wales by the Romans and displays the finds from the auxiliary fort of Segontium, one of the most famous in Britain. You can combine a visit to the museum with exploration of the site of the Roman Fort, which is in the care of Cadw: Welsh Historic Monuments. The exciting discoveries displayed at the museum vividly portray the daily life of the soldiers stationed in this most westerly outpost of the Roman Empire.

Times Open all year, Tue-Sun 12.30-4. Closed Mon except BH* **Facilities** Ⓟ shop ⊗

LLANBERIS

Snowdon Mountain Railway

LL55 4TY

☎ 01286 870223   📠 01286 872518
e-mail: info@snowdonrailway.co.uk
web: www.snowdonrailway.co.uk
dir: on A4086, Caernarfon to Capel Curig road.
7.5m from Caernarfon

The journey of just over four-and-a-half miles
takes passengers more than 3,000ft up to the
summit of Snowdon; breathtaking views include,
on a clear day, the Isle of Man and the Wicklow
Mountains in Ireland. The round trip to the
summit and back takes two and a half hours
including a half hour at the summit.

Times Open daily mid Mar-Oct, (weather
permitting).* Fees Return £23 (ch £16). Early
bird discount on 9am train, pre-booking only.
3/4 distance return £16 (ch £12). Facilities 🅿
Ⓟ ⊑ 🛱 (outdoor) ♿ (partly accessible) (some
carriages suitable for wheelchairs - must notify)
toilets for disabled shop 🚫

LLANBERIS

Welsh Slate Museum

Gilfach Ddu, Padarn Country Park LL55 4TY
☎ 01286 870630   📠 01286 871906
e-mail: slate@museumwales.ac.uk
web: www.museumwales.ac.uk
dir: 0.25m off A4086. Museum within Padarn
Country Park

Set among the towering quarries at Llanberis,
the Welsh Slate Museum is a living, working site
located in the original workshops of Dinorwig
Quarry, which once employed 15,000 men and
boys. You can see the foundry, smithy, workshops
and mess room which make up the old quarry,
and view original machinery, much of which is
still in working order.

Times Open all year, Etr-Oct, daily 10-5; Nov-
Etr, Sun-Fri 10-4. Fees Some events may incur
a charge. Facilities 🅿Ⓟ ⊑ 🛱 ♿ (partly
accessible) toilets for disabled shop 🚫

PORTHMADOG

Ffestiniog Railway

Harbour Station LL49 9NF
☎ 01766 516000 🖹 01766 516006
e-mail: enquiries@festrail.co.uk
web: www.festrail.co.uk
dir: SE end of town beside the harbour, on A487

One of the Great Little Train of Wales, this railway runs for 13.5 through Snowdonia. Originally built to carry slate from the quarries at Blaenau Ffestiniog to the harbour at Porthmadog, the little trains now carry passengers through the beautiful scenery of the national park. A licensed at-your-seat refreshment service is available on all main trains. Day rover tickets allow you to break your journey to make the most of your day. First class observation carriage on all trains.

Times Open daily late Mar-late Oct. Limited Winter service mid wk trains Nov & early Dec. Santa specials in Dec. Open Feb half term.
Fees Full distance return £17.95 (1 ch under 16 free, concessions £16.15). Other fares available.*
Facilities 🅿 🅿 ⬛ †�◎† licensed 🎋 (outdoor) ♿ (partly accessible) (most train services accessible, phone in advance, main station/platforms & restaurant accessible) toilets for disabled shop ⊗

PORTMEIRION

Portmeirion

LL48 6ER
☎ 01766 770000 🖹 01766 771331
e-mail: info@portmeirion-village.com
web: www.portmeirion-village.com
dir: off A487 at Minffordd

Welsh architect Sir Clough Williams Ellis built his fairy-tale, Italianate village on a rocky, tree-clad peninsula on the shores of Cardigan Bay. A bell-tower, castle and lighthouse mingle with a watch-tower, grottoes and cobbled squares among pastel-shaded picturesque cottages let as holiday accommodation. The 60-acre Gwyllt Gardens include miles of dense woodland paths and are famous for their fine displays of rhododendrons, azaleas, hydrangeas and sub-tropical flora. There is a mile of sandy beach and a playground for children. The village is probably best known as the major location for 1960s cult TV show, The Prisoner.

Times Open daily Oct-Mar, 9.30-5.30; Apr-Sep, 9.30-7.30. Fees £7.50 (ch £4, concessions £6). Family ticket (2ad+2ch) £19.* Facilities 🅿 ⬛ †◎† licensed 🎋 (outdoor) ♿ (partly accessible) (steep slopes and many steps make access difficult to some areas) toilets for disabled shop ⊗

GROSMONT

Grosmont Castle **FREE**

☎ 01981 240301
web: www.cadw.wales.gov.uk
dir: on B4347

Grosmont is one of the 'trilateral' castles of
Hubert de Burgh (see also Skenfrith and White
Castle). It stands on a mound with a dry moat,
and the considerable remains of its 13th-century
great hall can be seen. Three towers once
guarded the curtain wall, and the western one is
well preserved.

Times Open all year, access available at all
reasonable times, which will normally be 10-4
daily.* **Facilities** ⊗ ⟳

MONMOUTH

The Nelson Museum & Local History Centre **FREE**

New Market Hall, Priory St NP25 3XA
☎ 01600 710630
e-mail: nelsonmuseum@monmouthshire.gov.uk
dir: in town centre

One of the world's major collections of Admiral
Nelson-related items, including original letters,
glass, china, silver, medals, books, models,
prints and Nelson's fighting sword feature here.
The local history displays deal with Monmouth's
past as a fortress market town, and include a
section on the co-founder of the Rolls Royce
company, Charles Stewart Rolls, who was also
a pioneer balloonist, aviator and, of course,
motorist.

Times Open all year, Mar-Oct, Mon-Sat & BH 11-1
& 2-5, Sun 2-5; Nov-Feb, Mon-Sat 11-1 & 2-4,
Sun 2-4. **Facilities** ℗ ♿ (partly accessible)
(mezzanine display area accessible only by stairs
- 25% of whole museum display area) toilets for
disabled shop ⊗

SKENFRITH

Skenfrith Castle **FREE**

☎ 01443 336000
web: www.cadw.wales.gov.uk
dir: on B4521

This 13th-century castle has a round keep set inside an imposing towered curtain wall. Hubert de Burgh built it as one of three 'trilateral' castles to defend the Welsh Marches.

Times Open all year, access available at all reasonable times, which will normally be 10-4 daily. Key keeper arrangement.* **Facilities** ℗ ⊗ ✥ ❦

WHITE CASTLE

White Castle

NP7 8UD
☎ 01600 780380
web: www.cadw.wales.gov.uk
dir: 7m NE of Abergavenny, unclass road N of B4233

The impressive 12th to 13th-century moated stronghold was built by Hubert de Burgh to defend the Welsh Marches. Substantial remains of walls, towers and a gatehouse can be seen. This is the finest of a trio of castles, the others being at Skenfrith and Grosmont.

Times Open Apr-Oct, 10-5 daily. Open 10-4 daily and unstaffed with no admission charge at all other times.* **Fees** £2.60 (ch 5-15, concessions £2.25, disabled visitors & assisting companion free). Family ticket (2ad+all ch/grandch under 16) £7.45. Group rates available. Prices quoted apply until 31 Mar 2010.* **Facilities** ℗ ⊗ ⊕

CRYNANT

Cefn Coed Colliery Museum **FREE**

SA10 8SN

☎ 01639 750556   🖷 01639 750556
e-mail: colliery@btconnect.com
web: www.neath-porttalbot.gov.uk
dir: 1m S of Crynant, on A4109

The museum is on the site of a former working colliery, and tells the story of mining in the Dulais Valley. A steam-winding engine has been kept and is now operated by electricity, and there is also a simulated underground mining gallery, boilerhouse, compressor house, and exhibition area. Outdoor exhibits include a stationary colliery locomotive. Exhibitions relating to the coal mining industry are held on a regular basis. The museum is now home to the Dulais Valley Historical Model Railway Society who, with the help from the Heritage Lottery Fund have created an ever increasing layout depicting the Neath-Brecon railway through the valley.

Times Open Apr-Oct, daily 10.30-5; Nov-Mar, groups welcome by prior arrangement.* Facilities ℗ 🍴 (outdoor) ♿ (partly accessible) (access to exhibition areas, but not to underground gallery) toilets for disabled shop

CAERLEON

National Roman Legion Museum **FREE**

High St NP18 1AE

☎ 01633 423134   🖷 01633 422869
e-mail: roman@museumwales.ac.uk
web: www.museumwales.ac.uk
dir: close to Newport, 20 min from M4, follow signs from Cardiff & Bristol

The museum illustrates the history of Roman Caerleon and the daily life of its garrison. On display are arms, armour and equipment, with a collection of engraved gemstones, a labyrinth mosaic and finds from the legionary base at Usk. Please telephone for details of children's holiday activities.

Times Open all year: Mon-Sat 10-5, Sun 2-5.*
Facilities ℗ toilets for disabled shop ⊗

CRYMYCH

Castell Henllys Iron Age Fort

Pant-Glas, Meline SA41 3UT
☎ 01239 891319 📄 01239 891319
e-mail: celts@castellhenllys.com
web: www.castellhenllys.com
dir: off A487 between Cardigan and Newport

This Iron Age hill fort is set in the beautiful
Pembrokeshire Coast National Park. Excavations
began in 1981 and three roundhouses have
been reconstructed, another roundhouse has
been completed and is the largest on the site.
Celtic roundhouses have been constructed in the
original way using hazel wattle walls, oak rafters
and thatched conical roofs. A forge, smithy and
looms can be seen, with other attractions such
as trails and a herb garden. Please telephone for
details of special events.

Times Open all year, Etr-Oct, daily 10-5 (last
entry 4.30); Nov-Mar 11-3 (last entry 2.30).
Closed 24-31 Dec. **Fees** £3.90 (concessions
£2.75). Family £10.50.* **Facilities** 🅿 🏞
(outdoor) ♿ toilets for disabled shop

FISHGUARD

OceanLab

The Parrog, Goodwick SA64 0DE
☎ 01348 874737 📄 01348 872528
e-mail: fishguardharbour.tic@pembrokeshire.
gov.uk
web: www.ocean-lab.co.uk
dir: A40 to Fishguard, turn at by-pass, follow
signs for Stenaline ferry terminal, pass 2
garages, turn right at rdbt & follow signs to
attraction

Overlooking the Pembrokeshire coastline,
OceanLab is a multifunctional centre, which aims
to provide a fun-filled experience for the family.
There is also a hands-on ocean quest exhibition,
a soft play area and a cybercafé. An exhibition is
centred around 'Ollie the Octopus's Garden', with
hands-on displays and activities.

Times Open Apr-Oct, 9.30-5 (6 wk summer hols
9.30-6); Nov-Mar 10-4. **Fees** Free admission. £1
soft play under 5's, £2 cyber cafe for 30 mins.
Facilities 🅿 Ⓟ 🖥 🏞 (outdoor) ♿ toilets for
disabled shop ⊗

NARBERTH

Oakwood Park

Canaston Bridge SA67 8DE
☎ 01834 861889 📄 01834 891380
e-mail: info@oakwoodthemepark.co.uk
web: www.oakwoodthemepark.co.uk
dir: M4 W junct 49, take A48 to Carmarthen, signed

Oakwood Theme Park has over 30 rides and attractions. Thrill seekers can brave Speed, the UK's first roller-coaster with a beyond vertical drop, the award-winning wooden roller coaster Megafobia, the 50 metre high sky coaster Vertigo and shot 'n' drop tower coaster The Bounce, or cool off on Hydro, the steepest and wettest ride in Europe! There are also plenty of family rides and lots of fun to be had for smaller kids with a designated children's area available with smaller rides.

Times Open Etr-Oct, days & times vary please call for details* Fees £14.95 (under 2's free, ch 3-9 £13.50, pen £10 & disabled £11.50). Family ticket (4) £53, (6) £77. Party 20+ tickets available £12.95* Facilities ♿ 💻 ⭐ licensed ⊼ (outdoor) ♿ (partly accessible) (most areas of park are accessible apart from a few rides) toilets for disabled shop ⊗

PEMBROKE

Pembroke Castle

SA71 4LA
☎ 01646 681510 & & 684585
📄 01646 622260
e-mail: info@pembrokecastle.co.uk
web: www.pembrokecastle.co.uk
dir: W end of main street

This magnificent castle commands stunning views over the Milford estuary. Discover its rich medieval history, and that of Henry VII, the first Tudor king, through a variety of exhibitions. There are lively guided tours and events each Sunday in July and August. Before leaving, pop into the Brass Rubbing Centre and make your own special souvenir. To complete the day, wander round the tranquil millpond and medieval town walls, which surround other architectural gems from Tudor and Georgian times. Special Events: 1st week in Sep 'Pembroke Festival'. Please telephone for details.

Times Open all year, daily, Apr-Sep 9.30-6; Mar & Oct 10-5; Nov-Feb, 10-4. Closed 24-26 Dec & 1 Jan.* Facilities ℗ 💻 ⊼ (outdoor) toilets for disabled shop

ABERCRAF

Dan-Yr-Ogof The National Showcaves Centre for Wales

SA9 1GJ
☎ 01639 730284   📄 01639 730293
e-mail: info@showcaves.co.uk
web: www.showcaves.co.uk
dir: M4 junct 45, midway between Swansea & Brecon on A4067, follow brown tourist signs for Dan-Yr-Ogof

This award-winning attraction includes three separate caves, dinosaur park, Iron Age Farm, museum, shire horse centre and covered children's play area.

Times Open daily Apr-Oct, from 10.30 (last admission 3)* Facilities 🅿 ⛄ 🎋 (outdoor) toilets for disabled shop ⊗

MACHYNLLETH

Centre for Alternative Technology

SY20 9AZ
☎ 01654 705950
e-mail: info@cat.org.uk
web: www.cat.org.uk
dir: 3m N of Machynlleth, on A487

The Centre for Alternative Technology promotes practical ideas and information on sustainable technologies. The exhibition includes displays of wind, water and solar power, organic gardens, low-energy buildings, and a unique water-powered railway which ascends a 200ft cliff from the car park. Free children's activities and guided tours during the summer holidays.

Times Open all year (closed Dec 23-27 & 3-14 Jan), 10-5.30 or dusk in winter.* Fees Summer £8.40 (ch over 5 £4.20, concessions £7.40); Winter, £6.40 (ch over 5 £4.20, concessions £5.40). Discounts available for cyclists, walkers and users of public transport.* Facilities 🅿 🍴 licensed 🎋 (indoor & outdoor) ♿ toilets for disabled shop ⊗

MACHYNLLETH

King Arthur's Labyrinth

Corris SY20 9RF

☎ 01654 761584 📠 01654 761575
e-mail: info@kingarthurslabyrinth.co.uk
web: www.kingarthurslabyrinth.com
dir: on A487 between Machynlleth and Dolgellau

An underground storytelling adventure where visitors travel by boat deep inside the vast caverns of the labyrinth, and far back into the past. Tales of King Arthur and other legends are re-told as you explore the spectacular underground setting. Complete with colourful scenes, and sound and light effects, this is a fascinating attraction for all ages.

Times Open daily, 22 Mar-end Oct, 10-5.
Fees £6.50 (ch £4.65, concessions £5.85).*
Facilities ❷ ♨ ㈜ (outdoor) ♿ (partly accessible) (full access to reception, shop & units of craft centre. Labyrinth tour includes 0.5m walk through caverns) toilets for disabled shop ⊗

TREHAFOD

Rhondda Heritage Park

Lewis Merthyr Colliery, Coed Cae Rd CF37 7NP

☎ 01443 682036 📠 01443 687420
e-mail: info@rhonddaheritagepark.com
web: www.rhonddaheritagepark.com
dir: between Pontypridd & Porth, off A470, follow brown heritage signs from M4 junct 32

Based at the Lewis Merthyr Colliery, the Heritage Park is a fascinating 'living history' attraction. You can take the Cage Ride to 'Pit Bottom' and explore the underground workings of a 1950s pit, guided by men who were miners themselves. There are children's activities, an art gallery and a museum illustrating living conditions in the Rhondda Valley. Special events throughout the year, phone for details.

Times Open all year, daily 10-6. Closed Mon from Oct-Etr. (Last admission 4). Closed 25 Dec-early Jan.* Fees £5.60 (ch £4.30, pen £4.95). Family (4) ticket from £16.50, (6) £21.* Facilities ❷ ℗ ♨ ⒪ licensed ㈜ (indoor & outdoor) ♿ (partly accessible) toilets for disabled shop ⊗

PARKMILL

Gower Heritage Centre

Y Felin Ddwr SA3 2EH

☎ 01792 371206   📠 01792 371471

e-mail: info@gowerheritagecentre.co.uk

web: www.gowerheritagecentre.co.uk

dir: follow signs for South Gower on A4118 W from Swansea. W side of Parkmill village

Based around a 12th-century water-powered cornmill, the site also contains a number of craft workshops, two play areas, animals, a museum and a miller's cottage, all set in attractive countryside in an Area of Outstanding Natural Beauty.

Times Open all year, daily, Mar-Oct 10-5.30; Nov-Feb 10-4.30. Closed 25 Dec.* Facilities 🅿 🅿 ⬚ 🍽 licensed 🚻 toilets for disabled shop

BLAENAVON

Big Pit National Coal Museum **FREE**

NP4 9XP

☎ 01495 790311   📠 01495 792618

e-mail: post@museumwales.ac.uk

web: www.museumwales.ac.uk

dir: M4 junct 25/26, follow signs on A4042 & A4043 to Pontypool & Blaenavon. Signed off A465

The Real Underground Experience, Big Pit is the UK's leading mining museum. It is a real colliery and was the place of work for hundreds of men, woman and children for over 200 years. A daily struggle to extract the precious mineral that stoked furnaces and lit household fires across the world.

Times Open all year 9.30-5. Please call for underground guided tour availability* Facilities 🅿 ⬚ ♿ (partly accessible) toilets for disabled shop ⊗

BLAENAVON

Blaenavon Ironworks **FREE**

North St NP4 9RN
☎ 01495 792615
web: www.cadw.wales.gov.uk

The Blaenavon Ironworks were a milestone in the history of the Industrial Revolution. Constructed in 1788-99, they were the first purpose-built, multi-furnace ironworks in Wales. By 1796, Blaenavon was the second largest ironworks in Wales, eventually closing down in 1904.

Times Open all year, Apr-Oct, daily 10-5; Nov-Mar, Fri-Sat 9.30-4, Sun 11-4.* Facilities Ⓟ
⊗ ✛

BARRY

Welsh Hawking Centre

Weycock Rd CF62 3AA
☎ 01446 734687   📄 01446 739620
e-mail: norma@welsh-hawking.co.uk
dir: on A4226

There are over 200 birds of prey here, including eagles, hawks, owls, buzzards and falcons. They can be seen and photographed in the mews and some of the breeding aviaries. There are flying demonstrations at regular intervals during the day. A variety of tame, friendly animals, such as guinea pigs, horses and rabbits will delight younger visitors.

Times Open late Mar-late Sep, daily 10.30-5 (1hr before dusk in winter)* Facilities Ⓟ ⊑ ⊓ (outdoor) ♿ toilets for disabled shop ⊗

PENARTH

Cosmeston Lakes Country Park & Medieval Village

Lavernock Rd CF64 5UY
☎ 029 2070 1678   📠 029 2070 8686
e-mail: NColes@valeofglamorgan.gov.uk
web: www.valeofglamorgan.gov.uk
dir: on B4267 between Barry and Penarth

Deserted during the plagues and famines of the 14th century, the original village was rediscovered through archaeological excavations. The buildings have been faithfully reconstructed on the excavated remains, creating a living museum of medieval village life. Special events throughout the year include re-enactments and Living History.

Times Open all year, daily 11-5 in Summer, 11-4 in Winter. Closed 25 Dec. Country park open at all times.* Facilities 🅿 ⬛ 🍴 licensed ㅠ toilets for disabled shop

BALLYMENA

Ecos Visitor & Conference Centre **FREE**

Ecos Centre, Kernohams Ln, Broughshane Rd BT43 7QA
☎ 028 2566 4400   📠 028 2563 8984
e-mail: www.ballymena.gov.uk/ecos
web: www.ballymena.gov.uk/ecos
dir: follow signs from M2 bypass at Ballymena

Plenty of fun and adventure for all the family with duck feeding, toy tractors and sand pit. The centre hosts two interactive galleries, one on sustainability and one on biodiversity, and you can stroll through the willow tunnel and enjoy the play park.

Times Open Etr-Oct, Mon-Fri 9-5; Jun-Aug, Sat-Sun 12-5 (last admission 4). Facilities 🅿 ⬛ ㅠ (outdoor) ♿ toilets for disabled shop ⊗

CARRICK-A-REDE

Carrick-a-Rede Rope Bridge and Larrybane Visitor Centre

BT54 6LS
☎ 028 2076 9839 & 2073 1582 (office)
📄 028 2073 2963
e-mail: carrickarede@nationaltrust.org.uk
web: www.nationaltrust.org.uk
dir: E of Ballintoy on B15

On the North Antrim Coastal Path is one of Northern Ireland's best-loved attractions: Carrick-a-Rede Rope Bridge and the disused limestone quarry of Larrybane. The island of Carrick is known as 'the rock in the road', as it is an obstacle on the path of migrating salmon, and fishermen have taken advantage of this to net the fish here for over 300 years.

Times Open Bridge daily (weather permitting), 28 Feb-24 May & Sep-1 Nov 10-6, 25 May-Aug 10-7. (Last admission 45 mins before closing). Coastal path open all year.* Facilities 🅿 ⫐ 🛏 (outdoor) toilets for disabled 🐾

GIANT'S CAUSEWAY

Giant's Causeway Centre

44 Causeway Rd BT57 8SU
☎ 028 2073 1855   📄 028 2073 2537
e-mail: causewaytic@hotmail.com
web: www.northantrim.com
dir: 2m N of Bushmills on B146

This dramatic rock formation is undoubtedly one of the wonders of the natural world. The Centre provides an exhibition and audio-visual show, and Ulsterbus provides a minibus service to the stones and there are guided walks, and special facilities for the disabled.

Times Open all year, daily from 10 (closes 7 Jul & Aug). Closed 1 wk Xmas.* Facilities 🅿 ⫐ 🍴 licensed 🛏 toilets for disabled shop 🚫

ARMAGH

Armagh County Museum **FREE**

The Mall East BT61 9BE
☎ 028 3752 3070 🖷 028 3752 2631
e-mail: acm.info@nmni.com
web: www.magni.org.uk
dir: in city centre

Housed in a 19th-century schoolhouse, this museum contains an art gallery and library, as well as a collection of local folkcrafts and natural history. Special events are planned thoughout the year.

Times Open all year, Mon-Fri 10-5, Sat 10-1 & 2-5. Facilities ℗ ♿ toilets for disabled shop ⊗

ARMAGH

Armagh Planetarium

College Hill BT61 9DB
☎ 028 3752 3689 & 4725
🖷 028 3752 6187
e-mail: info@armaghplanet.com
web: www.armaghplanet.com
dir: on Armagh-Belfast road close to mall, city centre

The Planetarium is home to The Digital Theatre, a multi-media environment equipped with the latest Planetarim projector technology and state-of-the-art sound system. Also featured are the space displays in the Galileo Hall, Copernicus Hall, Tycho, Cassini and Kepler rooms and surrounding the Planetarium is the Astropark, a 25-acre area where you can walk through the Solar System and the Universe.

Times Open all year, Sat 11.30-5. Sun 11.30-5, Mon during term time; May-Jun & Sep-Dec wkdys 1-5, July-Aug wkdys 11.30-5.* Facilities ❶ ℗ ⊡ ⼊ (outdoor) ♿ toilets for disabled shop ⊗

BELFAST

Belfast Zoological Gardens

Antrim Rd BT36 7PN

☎ 028 9077 6277 📠 028 9037 0578

e-mail: info@belfastzoo.co.uk

web: www.belfastzoo.co.uk

dir: M2 junct 4 signed to Glengormley. Follow signs off rdbt to Zoo

The 50-acre zoo has a dramatic setting on the face of Cave Hill, enjoying spectacular views. Attractions include the primate house (gorillas and chimpanzees), penguin enclosure, free-flight aviary, African enclosure, and underwater viewing of sealions and penguins. There are also red pandas, lemurs and a group of very rare spectacled bears. Recent additions to the collection include capybara, crowned lemurs, tawny frogmouth and laughing kookaburra, tree kangaroo and giant anteater.

Times Open all year, Apr-Sep, daily 10-7 (last admission 5); Oct-Mar 10-4 (last admission 2.30). Closed 25-26 Dec.* Fees Summer: £8.30 (ch £4.40), Winter: £6.90 (ch £4.40, ch under 4, pen and disabled free).* Facilities 🅿 Ⓟ ⬚ 🍽 licensed ⛱ (outdoor) ♿ toilets for disabled shop ⊗

BELFAST

W5 at Odyssey

2 Queens Quay BT3 9QQ

☎ 028 9046 7700 📠 028 9046 7707

web: www.w5online.co.uk

W5 investigates Who? What? Where? When? Why?... and that pretty much sums up the intent behind Ireland's first purpose built discovery centre. Visitors of any age will want to get their hands on interactive science and technology displays that include the laser harp, the fog knife, microscopes, robots and computers. W5 is part of a massive Millennium Landmark Project in the heart of Belfast.

Times Open all year Mon-Sat 10-6, Sun 12-6. Closed 25-26 Dec & 12 Jul.* Facilities 🅿 Ⓟ 🍽 licensed ⛱ toilets for disabled shop ⊗

DOWNPATRICK

Down County Museum **FREE**

The Mall, BT30 6AH

☎ 028 4461 5218   🖹 028 4461 5590

e-mail: museum@downdc.gov.uk

web: www.downcountymuseum.com

dir: on entry to town follow brown signs to museum

The museum is located in the restored buildings of the 18th-century county gaol. In addition to restored cells that tell the stories of some of the prisoners, there are exhibitions on the history of County Down. Plus temporary exhibits, events, tea-room and shop.

Times Open all year, Mon-Fri 10-5, wknds 1-5*
Facilities ℗ ⌴ ⊼ (outdoor) toilets for disabled shop ⊗

HOLYWOOD

Ulster Folk and Transport Museum

Cultra BT18 0EU

☎ 028 9042 8428   🖹 01232 428728

e-mail: uftm.info@magni.org.uk

web: www.uftm.org.uk

dir: 12m outside Belfast on A2, past Holywood on main road to Bangor

Voted Northern Ireland's Best Visitor Attraction and Irish Museum of the Year, this attraction illustrates the way of life and traditions of Northern Ireland. The galleries of the Transport Museum display collections of horse drawn carts, cars, steam locomotives and the history of ship and aircraft building. Please telephone for details of special events running throughout the year.

Times Open all year Mar-Jun, Mon-Fri 10-5, Sat 10-6, Sun 11-6; Jul-Sep, Mon-Sat 10-6, Sun 11-6; Oct-Feb, Mon-Fri 10-4, Sat 10-5, Sun 11-5.* **Facilities** ❷ ℗ ⌴ ⊼ (outdoor) toilets for disabled shop

PORTAFERRY

Exploris Aquarium

The Rope Walk, Castle St BT22 1NZ
☎ 028 4272 8062   🖹 028 4272 8396
e-mail: info@exploris.org.uk
web: www.exploris.org.uk
dir: A20 or A2 or A25 to Strangford Ferry Service

Exploris Aquarium is Northern Ireland's only public aquarium and now includes a seal sanctuary. Situated in Portaferry on the shores of Strangford Lough it houses some of Europe's finest displays. The Open Sea Tank holds 250 tonnes of sea water. The complex includes a park with duck pond, picnic area, children's playground, caravan site, woodland and bowling green.

Times Open all year, Mon-Fri 10-6, Sat 11-6, Sun 1-6. (Sep-Mar closing 1 hr earlier).* **Facilities** 🅿 🅟 ⛲ 🎪 (outdoor) ♿ toilets for disabled shop ⊗

ENNISKILLEN

Marble Arch Caves Global Geopark

Marlbank Scenic Loop BT92 1EW
☎ 028 6634 8855   🖹 028 6634 8928
e-mail: mac@fermanagh.gov.uk
web: www.marblearchcaves.net
dir: off A4 Enniskillen to Sligo road. Left onto A32 and follow signs

One of Europe's finest cave systems, under Cuilcagh Mountain. Visitors are given a tour of a wonderland of stalagmites, stalactites and underground rivers and lakes, starting with a boat trip on the lower lake. The streams, which feed the caves, flow down into the mountain then emerge at Marble Arch, a 30ft detached limestone bridge. The geological, historical and economic benefits of Marble Arch Caves and Cuilcagh Mountain Park were recognised on an international scale when they were jointly awarded the title of European Geopark by UNESCO in 2001.

Times Open late Mar-Sep daily 10-4.30, Jul & Aug 10-5. **Fees** £8 (ch £5, pen & concessions £5.25). Family £18. Group rates available. **Facilities** 🅿 ⛲ 🎪 (outdoor) ♿ (partly accessible) (cave not accessible) toilets for disabled shop ⊗

LONDONDERRY

Tower Museum

Union Hall Place BT48 6LU
☎ 028 7137 2411   📄 028 7137 7633
e-mail: museums@derrycity.gov.uk
web: www.derrycity.gov.uk/museums
dir: behind city wall, facing Guildhall

Opened in 1992, the museum has won the
Irish and British Museum of the Year Awards.
It has two permanent exhibitions as well as
hosting temporary and travelling exhibitions
throughout the year. The multimedia 'Story of
Derry' exhibition has reopened following extensive
refurbishment. There is also an exhibition about
the Spanish Armada which includes artefacts
from a galleon shipwrecked in Kinnagoe Bay in
1588.

Times Open all year, Sep-Jun, Tue-Sat 10-5.
Jul-Aug, Mon-Sat 10-5, Sun 12-4. Please check
local press for opening details on BH.* Fees £4
(concessions £2.50)* Facilities ℗ ♿ toilets for
disabled ⊗

BALLYGAWLEY

U S Grant Ancestral Homestead

Dergenagh Rd BT70 1TW
☎ 028 8555 7133   📄 028 8555 7133
e-mail: killymaddy.reception@dungannon.gov.uk
web: www.dungannon.gov.uk
dir: off A4, 2m on Dergenagh road, signed

Ancestral homestead of Ulysses S Grant, 18th
President of the United States of America. The
homestead and farmyard have been restored to
the style and appearance of a mid-19th-century
Irish smallholding. There are many amenities
including a children's play area, purpose built
barbecue and picnic tables and butterfly garden.
Bike hire available (£1/hr).

Times Open all year daily 9-5. Fees Free
admission. Advisable to book in advance for
audio visual show.* Facilities ℗ ⊓ (outdoor)
♿ ⊗

OMAGH

Ulster American Folk Park

2 Mellon Rd, Castletown BT78 5QY
☎ 028 8224 3292   ▤ 028 8224 2241
e-mail: uafpinfo@nmni.com
web: www.nmni.com
dir: 5m NW Omagh on A5

An award winning outdoor museum of emigration which tells the story of millions of people who emigrated from these shores throughout the 18th and 19th centuries. The Old World and New World layout of the park illustrates the various aspects of emigrant life on both sides of the Atlantic. Traditional thatched buildings, American log houses and a full-scale replica emigrant ship plus the dockside gallery help to bring a bygone era back to life. Costumed demonstrators go about their everyday tasks including spinning, open hearth cookery, printing and textiles. The museum also includes an indoor Emigrants Exhibition and a centre for Migration Studies/library which is accessible to all visitors if they wish to find further information on the history of emigration and the place of their families in it.

Times Open all year Apr-Oct daily 10.30-6, Sun & BH 11-6.30; Nov-Mar Mon-Fri 10.30-5. (Last admission 1hr 30mins before closing).*
Facilities ℗ Ⓟ ⌨🍽 licensed ⴹ (outdoor) ♿ toilets for disabled shop ⊗

BUNRATTY

Bunratty Castle & Folk Park

☎ 061 360788   ▤ 061 361020
e-mail: reservations@shannonheritage.com
web: www.shannonheritage.com
dir: approx 11km from Shannon Airport just off the main dual carriageway (N18) between Limerick and Ennis. Follow the tourist sign from the N18

Magnificent Bunratty Castle was built around 1425. The restored castle contains mainly 15th and 16th century furnishings and tapestries. Within its grounds is Bunratty Folk Park where 19th-century Irish life is recreated. Rural farmhouses, a village street and Bunratty House with its formal Regency gardens are recreated and furnished, as they would have appeared at the time.

Times Open all year, Jan-May & Sep-Dec 9-5.30; Jun-Aug, Mon-Fri 9-5.30 (last admission 4.15) & Sat & Sun 9-6 (last admission 5.15). Last admission to the castle is 4pm year round. Closed Dec 24-26 Dec. Opening times may be subject to change* Fees Castle & Folk Park €15.75 (ch €9.45) Family tickets, senior, student tickets also available.* Facilities Ⓟ ⌨🍽 licensed ⴹ (outdoor) ♿ (partly accessible) (castle is not accessible to wheelchair users) toilets for disabled shop

BLARNEY

Blarney Castle & Rock Close

☎ 021 4385252 📄 021 4381518
e-mail: info@blarneycastle.ie
web: www.blarneycastle.ie
dir: 5m from Cork on main road towards Limerick

The site of the famous Blarney Stone, known the world over for the eloquence it is said to impart to those who kiss it. The stone is in the upper tower of the castle, and, held by your feet, you must lean backwards down the inside of the battlements in order to receive the 'gift of the gab'. There is also a large area of garden open to the public all year round, woodland walks, lake, fern garden, rock close (laid out in the 18th century) and stable yard.

Times Open Blarney Castle & Rock Close. Mon-Fri, May & Sep 10-4, Jun-Aug 9-7. Oct-Apr 9-sundown or 6. Sun, Summer 9.30-5.30, Winter 9.30-sundown. Closed 24-25 Dec.
Fees Blarney Castle & Rock Close €10 (ch 8-14 €3.50, concessions €8). Family ticket (2ad+2ch) €23.50* **Facilities** 🅿 Ⓟ ♿ (partly accessible) shop ⊗

CARRIGTWOHILL (CARRIGTOHILL)

Fota Wildlife Park

Fota Estate
☎ 021 4812678 📄 021 4812744
e-mail: info@fotawildlife.ie
web: www.fotawildlife.ie
dir: 16km E of Cork. From N25 (Cork to Waterford road) take Cobh road

Established with the primary aim of conservation, Fota has more than 90 species of exotic wildlife in open, natural surroundings. Many of the animals wander freely around the park. Giraffes, zebras, ostriches, antelope, cheetahs and a wide array of waterfowl are among the species here.

Times Open all year, 17 Mar-Oct, daily, 10-6 (Sun 11-6) (last admission 5); Nov-17 Mar 10-4.30 (Sun 11-4.30). (Last admission 3.30).* **Facilities** 🅿 ⛾ 🍴 (outdoor) ♿ toilets for disabled shop ⊗

CORK

Cork City Gaol

Convent Av, Sundays Well
☎ 021 4305022   📄 021 4307230
e-mail: corkgaol@indigo.ie
web: www.corkcitygaol.com
dir: 2km NW from Patrick St off Sundays Well Rd

A restored 19th-century prison building. Furnished cells, lifelike characters and sound effects combine to allow visitors to experience day-to-day life for prisoners and gaoler. There is an audio-visual presentation of the social history of Cork City. Individual sound tours are available in a number of languages. A permanent exhibition, the Radio Museum Experience, is located in the restored 1920s broadcasting studio, home to Cork's first radio station, 6CK. Unfortunately the 1st and 2nd floors are not accessible to wheelchair users.

Times Open all year Mar-Oct, daily 9.30-5; Nov-Feb, daily 10-4. Closed 23-28 Dec.* Facilities ℗ ℗ ⊑⊓ (outdoor) ♿ (partly accessible) (3 cells on the first floor inaccessible) toilets for disabled shop 🚫

KINSALE

Desmond Castle

Cork St
☎ 021 4774855
e-mail: desmondcastle@opw.ie
web: www.desmondcastle.ie
dir: R600 from Cork city to Kinsale. From post office, 1st left then right, opposite Regional Museum then left and right again, castle on left

Built by the Earl of Desmond around the beginning of the 16th century, this tower was originally a custom house, but has also served as an ordnance office, prison, workhouse, stable and meeting place for the Local Defence Force during World War II. In 1938 it was declared a National Monument and restored. The Castle now houses the International Museum of Wine.

Times Open early Apr-late Sep, daily 10-6. (Last admission 45mins before closing).* Fees €3, (ch & students €1, pen €2) Family €8.* Facilities ℗ 🚫

LETTERKENNY

Glenveagh National Park & Castle

Churchill
☎ 074 9137090 & 9137262
🖷 074 9137072
e-mail: claire.bromley@environ.ie
web: www.glenreaghnationalpark.ie
dir: left off N56 from Letterkenny

Over 40,000 acres of mountains, glens, lakes and woods. A Scottish-style castle is surrounded by one of the finest gardens in Ireland, contrasting with the rugged surroundings.

Times Open all year, daily 9.30-6 (winter times may change). Fees Park: free, Castle €3 (ch & students €1.50, pen €2). Family ticket €7, group 20+ €2. Buses €1 & €2* Facilities ❷ 🖵 🍴 licensed 🍽 (outdoor) ♿ (partly accessible) (no lift access to first floor) toilets for disabled ⊗

MALAHIDE

Malahide Castle

☎ 01 8462184 🖷 01 8462537
e-mail: malahidecastle@dublintourism.ie
web: www.malahidecastle.com
dir: from Dublin city centre follow signs for Malahide, then approaching village, main entrance to castle is signed to right off main road

One of Ireland's oldest castles, this romantic and beautiful structure, set in 250 acres of grounds, has changed very little in 800 years. Tours offer views of Irish period furniture and historical portrait collections. Additional paintings from the National Gallery depict figures from Irish life over the last few centuries.

Times Open Jan-Dec, Mon-Sat 10-5; Apr-Sep, Sun & PHs, 10-6; Oct-Mar, Sun & PHs 11-5* Facilities ❷ ⓟ 🖵 🍴 licensed 🍽 (outdoor) shop ⊗

DUBLIN

Dublinia & The Viking World

St Michael's Hill, Christ Church
☎ 01 6794611   📄 01 6797116
e-mail: info@dublinia.ie
web: www.dublinia.ie
dir: in city centre

The story of medieval Dublin. Housed in the former Synod Hall beside Christ Church Cathedral and developed by the Medieval Trust, Dublinia recreates the period from the arrival of Strongbow and the Anglo-Normans in 1170 to the closure of the monasteries by Henry VIII in 1540. Also included is the exhibition on the Viking World which tells the story of their way of life and turbulent voyages.

Times Open all year daily 10-5 (last admission 4.15) Fees €6.25 (ch €3.95, concessions €5). Family ticket (2ad+3ch) €17* Facilities ℗ 🍴 ♿ (partly accessible) (2 floors accessible, but bridge and tower are not) toilets for disabled shop ⊗

DUBLIN

Dublin Zoo

Phoenix Park
☎ 01 4748900   📄 01 6771660
e-mail: info@dublinzoo.ie
web: www.dublinzoo.ie
dir: 10mins bus ride from city centre

Dublin Zoo first opened to the public in 1830, making it one of the oldest zoos in the world and has consistently been Ireland's favourite attraction. The Kaziranga Forest Trail is the latest development within Dublin Zoo. Visitors wander along winding paths to glimpse a breeding herd of Asian elephants. Dublin Zoo is a modern zoo with conservation, education and study as its mission. The majority of the animals here have been born and bred in zoos and are part of global breeding programmes to ensure their continued survival.

Times Open all year, Mar-Oct, Mon-Sat 9.30-6, Sun 10.30-6; Nov-Feb, daily 10.30-dusk.* Facilities ℗ ℗ 🍴🍽 licensed 🍴 (outdoor) ♿ (partly accessible) toilets for disabled shop ⊗

DUBLIN

Natural History Museum FREE

Merrion St
☎ 01 6777444   📄 01 6777828
e-mail: education.nmi@indigo.ie
dir: in city centre

The Natural History Museum, which is part of
The National Museum of Ireland, is a zoological
museum containing diverse collections of world
wildlife. The Irish Room, on the ground floor, is
devoted largely to Irish mammals, sea creatures
and insects. It includes the extinct giant Irish
deer and the skeleton of a basking shark. The
World Collection, has as its centre piece, the
skeleton of a 60ft whale suspended from the roof.
Other displays include the Giant Panda and a
Pygmy Hippopotamus.

Times Open all year, Tue-Sat 10-5, Sun 2-5.
Closed Mon, 25 Dec & Good Fri* Facilities ⓟ 🚫

GALWAY

Galway Atlantaquaria

Salthill
☎ 091 585100   📄 091 584360
e-mail: atlantaquaria@eircom.net
web: www.nationalaquarium.ie
dir: follow signs for Salthill. Next to Tourist Office
at seafront rdbt

Concentrating on the native Irish marine
ecosystem, the Galway Atlantiquaria contains
some 170 species of fish and sealife, and
features both fresh and saltwater exhibits.

Times Open all year, Apr-Jun & Sep, daily 10-5;
Jul & Aug, daily ,10-6; Oct-Mar, Wed-Sun, 10-5.
Closed Mon & Tue.* Facilities ⓟ ⓟ 🞐 🍴
licensed toilets for disabled shop 🚫

ROUNDSTONE

Roundstone Music, Crafts & Fashion **FREE**

Craft Centre
☎ 095 35875 📄 095 35980
e-mail: bodhran@iol.ie
web: www.bodhran.com
dir: N59 from Galway to Clifden. After approx 50m turn left at Roundstone sign, 7m to village. Attraction at top of village

The Roundstone Music Craft and Fashion shop is located within the walls of an old Franciscan Monastery. Here you can see Ireland's oldest craft: the Bodhran being made, and regular talks and demonstrations are given. The first RiverDance stage drums were made here and are still on display in the Craftsman's Craftshop. There is an outdoor picnic area in a beautiful location alongside the bell tower by the water where the dolphins swim up to the wall in summer.

Times Open Apr-Oct 9.30-6, Jul-Sep 9-7, Winter 6 days 9.30-6.* Facilities 🅿 Ⓟ ⬚ 🚏 (indoor & outdoor) ♿ toilets for disabled shop ⊗

CASTLEISLAND

Crag Cave

☎ 066 7141244 📄 066 7142352
e-mail: info@cragcave.com
web: www.cragcave.com
dir: 1m N, signed off N21

Crag Cave is one of the longest surveyed cave systems in Ireland, with a total length of 3.81km. It is a spectacular world, where pale forests of stalagmites and stalactites, thousands of years old, throw eerie shadows around vast echoing caverns complemented by dramatic sound and lighting effects. Now features new indoor and outdoor soft play areas, which are priced seperately. Tours of the caves last about 30 minutes.

Times Open daily all year, 10-6. (Dec-Mar telephone for times).* Facilities 🅿 Ⓟ ⬚ 🍴 licensed 🚏 (outdoor) ♿ (partly accessible) toilets for disabled shop ⊗

TRALEE

Kerry County Museum

Ashe Memorial Hall, Denny St
☎ 066 7127777   🖨 066 7127444
e-mail: info@kerrymuseum.com
web: www.kerrymuseum.com
dir: in town centre, follow signs for museum & tourist information office

The museum tells the story of Kerry (and Ireland) from the Stone Age to the present day. Archaeological treasures are displayed in the Museum Gallery, while a stroll through the Medieval Experience reveals the streets of Tralee as they were in 1450, with all the sights, sounds and smells of a bustling community. Discover what people wore, what they ate and where they lived, and find out why the Earls of Desmond, who founded the town, also destroyed it.

Times Open all year, Jan-Mar, Tue-Fri 10-4.30; Apr-May, Tue-Sat 9.30-5.30; Jun-Aug, daily 9.30-5.30; Sep-Dec, Tue-Sat 9.30-5; BH wknds Sun & Mon 10-5.* Facilities 🅿 🅟 ☕ toilets for disabled shop ⊗

VALENCIA ISLAND

The Skellig Experience

☎ 066 9476306   🖨 066 9476351
e-mail: info@skelligexperience.com
web: www.skelligexperience.com
dir: Ring of Kerry road, signed after Cahersiveen then Valentia bridge, or ferry from Rena Rd Point

The Skellig Rocks are renowned for their scenery, sea bird colonies, lighthouses, Early Christian monastic architecture and rich underwater life. The two islands - Skellig Michael and Small Skellig - stand like fairytale castles in the Atlantic Ocean, rising to 218 metres and their steep cliffs plunging 50 metres below the sea. The Heritage Centre, (on Valentia Island, reached from the mainland via a bridge), tells the story of the Skellig Islands in an exciting multimedia exhibition. Cruises around Valentia Habour are also available.

Times Open May-Jun 10-6; Jul-Aug 10-7; Sep 10-6. Mar, Apr & Oct-Nov 10-5* Facilities 🅿 ☕ toilets for disabled shop ⊗

KILDARE

Irish National Stud, Gardens & Horse Museum

Irish National Stud, Tully
☎ 045 521617   🖹 045 522964
e-mail: japanesegardens@eircom.net
web: www.irish-national-stud.ie
dir: off M7, exit 13 then R415 towards Nurney & Kildare. Attraction well signed from rdbt

Situated in the grounds of the Irish National Stud, the gardens were established by Lord Wavertree between 1906 and 1910, and symbolise 'The Life of Man' in a Japanese-style landscape. You can also visit the Horse Museum which includes the skeleton of Arkle, an Irish racehorse that won a number of major races in the 1960s. The Commemorative Millennium Garden of St Fiachra has 4 acres of woodland and lakeside walks and features a Waterford Crystal garden and monastic cells of limestone.

Times Open 12 Feb-23 Dec, daily, 9.30-5.*
Facilities 🅿 ⛴ 🍽 licensed ⛱ (outdoor) ♿ (partly accessible) (all parts of stud, garden & house accessible. Japanese gardens partly accessible) toilets for disabled shop ⊗

FERRYCARRIG

The Irish National Heritage Park

☎ 053 9120733   🖹 053 9120911
e-mail: info@inhp.com
web: www.inhp.com
dir: 3m from Wexford, on N11

Sixteen historical sites set in a magnificent 35-acre mature forest explaining Ireland's history from the Stone and Bronze Ages, through the Celtic period and concluding with the Vikings and Normans. Among the exhibits are a reconstructed Mesolithic camp, a Viking boatyard with two full-size ships and a Norman motte and bailey. Please visit website for details of events running throughout the year.

Times Open all year, daily, Oct-Mar 9.30-5.30; Apr-Sep 9.30-6.30.* Facilities 🅿 ⛴ 🍽 licensed ⛱ (outdoor) ♿ toilets for disabled shop ⊗

The Irish Agricultural Museum

Johnstown Castle Estate
☎ 053 9184671 & 9171247
e-mail: info@irishagrimuseum.ie
web: www.irishagrimuseum.ie
dir: 4m SW of town, signed off N25

This museum is located in the old farm and
stable buildings of the Johnstown Castle Estate.
There are a vast range of artefacts relating to
a bygone era. Farming and rural life are the
main themes explored, with exhibits covering
rural transport, farming and the activities of
the farmyard and farmhouse; and includes a
large exhibition on the history of the potato and
the Great Famine (1845-49). Johnstown Castle
Garden is a delightful 50 acres of ornamental
grounds surrounding a Victorian castle. The
grounds contain a wide variety of trees and
shrubs, as well as two lakes and various follies.

Times Open all year: Museum Apr-Nov, Mon-Fri
9-5, Sat-Sun & BHs 11-5; Dec-Mar, Mon-Fri 9-5
(closed for lunch 12.30-1.30, wknds & BHs).
Grounds open daily 9-5. Fees Museum €6 (ch &
students €4, concessions & group €5). Facilities
🅿 Ⓟ ⬚ ⤴ (outdoor) ♿ (partly accessible)
(ground floor accessible) toilets for disabled
shop ⊗

Powerscourt House & Gardens

Powerscourt Estate
☎ 01 2046000 📄 01 2046900
web: www.powerscourt.ie
dir: Entrance 600mtrs out of Enniskerry village

In the foothills of the Wicklow Mountains, these
gardens were begun by Richard Wingfield in
the 1740s, and are a blend of formal plantings,
sweeping terraces, statuary and ornamental
lakes together with secret hollows, rambling
walks and walled gardens. The gardens cover
19 hectares and contain more than two hundred
varieties of trees and shrubs. The grounds
contain Powerscourt Waterfall, Ireland's highest,
6km from the main estate.

Times Open all year: Gardens & House daily
9.30-5.30 (Gardens close at dusk in winter),
closed 25-26 Dec. Waterfall open daily, Mar-
Apr & Sep-Oct 9.30-5.30; May-Aug 9.30-7;
Nov-Feb 10.30-4 (closed 2 weeks before Xmas).
Ballroom & Garden rooms open every Sun & Mon
9.30-1.30 (May-Sep) Fees House & Gardens €8
(ch under 13 €5 ch under 5 free, concessions
€7). Waterfall €5 (ch under 13 €3.50 ch under 2
free, concessions €4.50). Facilities 🅿 Ⓟ ⬚
🍽 licensed ♿ (partly accessible) (some areas
in gardens are flat and suitable for wheelchair
users) toilets for disabled shop ⊗